Violent Extremism Online

This book explores the interface between terrorism and the Internet, and presents contemporary approaches to understanding violent extremism online.

The volume focuses on four issues in particular: terrorist propaganda on the Internet, radicalisation and the Internet, counter campaigns and approaches to disrupting Internet radicalisation, and approaches to researching and understanding the role of the Internet in radicalisation. The book brings together expertise from a wide range of disciplines and geographical regions including Europe, the USA, Canada and Australia. These contributions explore the various roles played by the Internet in radicalisation, the reasons why terroristic propaganda may or may not influence others to engage in violence, the role of political conflict in online radicalisation, and the future of research in terrorism and the Internet. By covering this broad range of topics, the volume will make an important and timely addition to the current collections on a growing and international subject.

This book will be of much interest to students and researchers of cybersecurity, Internet politics, terrorism studies, media and communications studies, and International Relations.

Anne Aly is Professor and Director of the Countering Online Violent Extremism Research Program at Edith Cowan University, Australia.

Stuart Macdonald is Professor in Law at Swansea University, UK.

Lee Jarvis is Reader in International Security at the University of East Anglia, UK.

Thomas Chen is Professor in Cyber Security at City University London, UK.

Media, War and Security

Series Editors: Andrew Hoskins, *University of Glasgow* and
Oliver Boyd-Barrett, *Bowling Green State University*

This series interrogates and illuminates the mutually shaping relationship between war and media as transformative of contemporary society, politics and culture.

Global Terrorism and New Media
The Post Al-Qaeda Generation
Philip Seib and Dana M Janabek

Radicalisation and the Media
Legitimising Violence in the New Media
Akil N Awan, Andrew Hoskins and Ben O'Loughlin

Hollywood and the CIA
Cinema, Defense and Subversion
Oliver Boyd-Barrett, David Herrera and Jim Baumann

Violence and War in Culture and the Media
Athina Karatzogianni

Military Media Management
Negotiating the 'Front' Line in Mediatized War
Sarah Maltby

Icons of War and Terror
Media Images in an Age of International Risk
Edited by John Tulloch and R Warwick Blood

Memory, Conflict and New Media
Web Wars in Post-Socialist States
Edited by Julie Fedor, Ellen Rutten and Vera Zvereva

Violent Extremism Online
New Perspectives on Terrorism and the Internet
Edited by Anne Aly, Thomas Chen, Lee Jarvis and Stuart Macdonald

Violent Extremism Online

New perspectives on terrorism and the Internet

Edited by
Anne Aly, Stuart Macdonald,
Lee Jarvis and Thomas Chen

Routledge
Taylor & Francis Group
LONDON AND NEW YORK

First published 2016
by Routledge
2 Park Square, Milton Park, Abingdon, Oxon OX14 4RN

and by Routledge
711 Third Avenue, New York, NY 10017

First issued in paperback 2017

Routledge is an imprint of the Taylor & Francis Group, an informa business

© 2016 selection and editorial material, Anne Aly, Stuart Macdonald, Lee Jarvis and Thomas Chen; individual chapters, the contributors

The right of the editors to be identified as the authors of the editorial material, and of the authors for their individual chapters, has been asserted in accordance with Sections 77 and 78 of the Copyright, Designs and Patents Act 1988.

All rights reserved. No part of this book may be reprinted or reproduced or utilised in any form or by any electronic, mechanical, or other means, now known or hereafter invented, including photocopying and recording, or in any information storage or retrieval system, without permission in writing from the publishers.

Trademark notice: Product or corporate names may be trademarks or registered trademarks, and are used only for identification and explanation without intent to infringe.

British Library Cataloguing-in-Publication Data
A catalogue record for this book is available from the British Library

Library of Congress Cataloging-in-Publication Data
Names: Aly, Anne, 1967– editor.
Title: Violent extremism online : new perspectives on terrorism and the Internet / edited by Anne Aly, Stuart Macdonald, Lee Jarvis and Thomas Chen.
Description: Abingdon, Oxon ; New York, NY : Routledge, 2016. | Includes bibliographical references and index.
Identifiers: LCCN 2016003339 | ISBN 9781138912298 (hardback) | ISBN 9781315692029 (ebook)
Subjects: LCSH: Internet and terrorism | Extremist Web sites. | Terrorists—Recruiting.
Classification: LCC HV6431 .V567 2016 | DDC 363.3250285/4678—dc23
LC record available at https://lccn.loc.gov/2016003339

ISBN 13: 978-1-138-49855-6 (pbk)
ISBN 13: 978-1-138-91229-8 (hbk)

Typeset in Times New Roman
by Florence Production Ltd, Stoodleigh, Devon, UK

**Dedicated to the memory
of Mahmoud Fawzi Aly
(1932–2015)**

Contents

List of illustrations		ix
Notes on contributors		xi
Acknowledgements		xv
	Introduction Anne Aly, Thomas Chen, Lee Jarvis and Stuart Macdonald	1
1	"Electronic Jihad": the Internet as al-Qaeda's catalyst for global terror Martin Rudner	8
2	The call to Jihad: charismatic preachers and the Internet Angela Gendron	25
3	Why do terrorists migrate to social media? Gabriel Weimann	45
4	#Westgate: a case study – How al-Shabaab used Twitter during an ongoing attack David Mair	65
5	Violent extremism online and the criminal trial Keiran Hardy	87
6	Brothers, believers, brave mujahideen: focusing attention on the audience of violent jihadist preachers Anne Aly	106
7	Determining the role of the Internet in violent extremism and terrorism: six suggestions for progressing research Maura Conway	123

8 Grasping at thin air: countering terrorist narratives online   149
   Sarah Logan

9 Narratives and counter-narratives of Islamist extremism   167
   Halim Rane

   Index   187

Illustrations

Figures

4.1	Intended readership of tweets	72
4.2	Overarching tweet function	78
4.3	Tweet objective	80
4.4	Tweet objective by threat content	81

Tables

4.1	Number of tweets collected from each account during each phase of data collection	61
4.2	Tweets involving external links	73
4.3	Tweets involving direct contact with other Twitter users	75
6.1	Profile of online engagement with radicalising narratives	119

Notes on contributors

Anne Aly is Professor at Edith Cowan University and Adjunct Professor at Curtin University in Perth, Australia. She is the Director of the Global Issues Practice Centre and Founding Chair of PaVE, a not-for-profit civil society organisation to counter violent extremism in Australia and the region. Anne founded and led the Countering online Violent Extremism Research (CoVER) Program at Curtin University, and is the author of over fifty texts on radicalisation, violent extremism and terrorism. She is the author of *Terrorism and Global Security: Historical and Contemporary Perspectives* (Palgrave Macmillan, 2011).

Thomas Chen is a Professor in Cyber Security at City University London, and former Professor in Networks at Swansea University, UK. He is the co-editor (with Lee Jarvis and Stuart Macdonald) of *Cyberterrorism: Understanding, Assessment and Response* (Springer, 2014) and *Terrorism Online: Politics, Law and Technology* (Routledge, 2015). He has carried out research projects sponsored by various agencies (EPSRC, US National Science Foundation, US Department of Homeland Security) and companies (Nortel, Sprint, Alcatel). He has served as editor-in-chief of three IEEE publications.

Maura Conway is Associate Professor of International Security in the School of Law and Government at Dublin City University (DCU) in Dublin, Ireland, and Coordinator of VOX-Pol, a €5 million EU-funded project on violent online political extremism (voxpol.eu). Dr Conway's principal research interests are in the area of terrorism and the Internet, including academic and media discourses on cyberterrorism, the functioning and effectiveness of violent political extremist online content, and violent online radicalisation. She is the author of over forty articles and chapters in her specialist area(s). Her research has appeared in, among others, *Current History*, *Media, War and Conflict*, *Parliamentary Affairs* and *Social Science Computer Review*. She has presented her findings before the United Nations in New York, the Commission of the European Union in Brussels, the Royal United Services Institute (RUSI) in London, and elsewhere.

Angela Gendron was appointed Senior Fellow at the Canadian Centre of Intelligence and Security Studies, The Norman Paterson School of International

Affairs, Carleton University, Ottawa, Canada, following a former professional career as a British crown servant specialising in intelligence and security issues. Her time is divided between research, teaching and training on topics ranging from the ethics of intelligence collection and unmanned aerial systems, to privacy issues and cybersecurity. She has published on a wide range of topics in leading international journals and institution reports – including the *International Journal of Intelligence and CounterIntelligence*, the *Canadian Foreign Policy Journal*, the Royal United Services Institute, and the Caspian Strategic Institute – and co-authored with Martin Rudner an Occasional Paper published by the Canadian Security Intelligence Service, titled *Assessing Cyber Threats to Canadian Infrastructure* (2012). Besides teaching at Carleton University and on Master's courses at Brunel and Buckingham Universities in the UK, she has delivered training courses in Canada, the UK, USA, Turkey, Romania, Sweden and Trinidad and Tobago.

Keiran Hardy is a Lecturer in Criminology and Criminal Justice at Griffith University. He completed his PhD in law at the University of New South Wales (UNSW) on an ARC Laureate Fellowship: 'Anti-Terror Laws and the Democratic Challenge'. Following this, he worked as a Research Fellow at UNSW, initially on the Laureate Fellowship and subsequently on a project into data sharing and privacy for the Australian Centre for Cyber Security (UNSW Canberra). Keiran's research focuses on counterterrorism laws, cyberterrorism, counter-radicalisation and counter-insurgency.

Lee Jarvis is a Reader in International Security at the University of East Anglia. He has (co-)authored or edited nine books on the politics of security, terrorism and counterterrorism, including *Security: A Critical Introduction* (with Jack Holland, 2015), *Anti-terrorism, Citizenship and Security* (with Michael Lister, 2015) and *Counter-Radicalisation: Critical Perspectives* (with Christopher Baker-Beall and Charlotte Heath-Kelly, 2015). Lee's work has been published in journals including *Security Dialogue*, *Millennium*, *Political Studies* and *Terrorism and Political Violence*, and he is currently an editor of *Critical Studies on Terrorism*. Lee convenes UEA's *Critical Global Politics* research group, and is the co-director of *The Cyberterrorism Project*: a multidisciplinary global research network.

Sarah Logan is the inaugural Digital Politics Research Fellow in the Coral Bell School of Asia Pacific Affairs at the Australian National University. Her PhD thesis, completed in the Department of International Relations at the Australian National University, examined counter-extremism policy in the context of the theory of political community and included an extensive study of online counter-extremism policy in the USA and the UK. Dr Logan has been a visiting scholar at Columbia University, the London School of Economics and the University of Aberystwyth. Prior to joining the academy, Dr Logan worked as an intelligence analyst at Australia's leading foreign intelligence analysis agency, the Office of National Assessments, where she focused on issues including terrorism.

Notes on contributors xiii

Stuart Macdonald is a Professor of Law and Deputy Director of the Centre for Criminal Justice and Criminology at Swansea University, UK. He is the author of *Text, Cases and Materials on Criminal Law* (Pearson, 2015) and co-editor (with Lee Jarvis and Thomas Chen) of *Cyberterrorism: Understanding, Assessment and Response* (Springer, 2014) and *Terrorism Online: Politics, Law and Technology* (Routledge, 2015). He has published in a number of leading international journals, including *Modern Law Review*, *Sydney Law Review*, *Cornell Journal of Law and Public Policy* and *Georgetown Journal of International Affairs*. Dr Macdonald is the co-director of Swansea University's EPSRC-funded £7.6m CHERISH Digital Economy research centre, with specific responsibility for the Centre's cybersecurity strand. He has held visiting positions at Columbia Law School (2007), University of Sydney (2011) and Université de Grenoble (2015).

David Mair is an ESRC-funded PhD Candidate at Swansea University and a member of the Cyberterrorism Project. His research focuses on terrorists' use of social media platforms for the purpose of conducting psychological warfare. To date, he has examined Twitter content during threatened and ongoing terrorist incidents. David has experience of working within law enforcement as a special constable in Strathclyde Police and of conducting research for government as an ESRC intern within the Cyber Crime Research Team of the Home Office's Office for Security and Counter-Terrorism. David holds a Masters with Distinction in Intelligence and Security Informatics from the University of Abertay Dundee and a Bachelor of Science (Honours) in Psychology from Glasgow Caledonian University.

Halim Rane is Associate Professor of Islam-West Relations in the School of Humanities at Griffith University, Australia. He formerly worked for the Australian Government Department of Immigration and continues to be engaged with issues concerning migration, settlement and integration through his teaching and research. Rane's research is interdisciplinary, encompassing Islamic studies, sociology, international relations and media studies. He is the author of numerous articles and books on Islamic and Muslim issues including *Media Framing of the Muslim World: Conflicts, Crises and Contexts*; *Making Australian Foreign Policy on Israel-Palestine: Media Coverage, Public Opinion and Interest Groups*; *Islam and Contemporary Civilisation: Evolving Ideas, Transforming Relations*; and *Reconstructing Jihad amid Competing International Norms*.

Martin Rudner is a Distinguished Research Professor Emeritus at Carleton University, Ottawa. Prior to his retirement in July 2007, he served as a Professor at The Norman Paterson School of International Affairs and was Founding Director of the Canadian Centre of Intelligence and Security Studies at Carleton. Professor Rudner is author of over 100 books and scholarly articles dealing with Southeast Asia, international affairs, and security and intelligence studies. Recent publications include 'Protecting Canada's Critical National Infrastructure from Terrorism', *International Journal* (2009); 'Cyber-Threats to Critical

National Infrastructure: An Intelligence Challenge', *International Journal of Intelligence and CounterIntelligence* (2013); 'Al-Qaeda's 20-Year Strategic Plan: The Current Phase of Global Terror', *Studies in Conflict and Terrorism* (2013); 'Intelligence-led Air Transport Security: Pre-Screening for Watch-lists, No-Fly Lists to Forestall Terrorist Threats', *International Journal of Intelligence and CounterIntelligence* (2015); and the co-authored [with Angela Gendron] monograph *Assessing Cyber Threats to Canadian Infrastructure* (Ottawa, 2012). He has been a commentator and analyst on international security affairs for Canadian and international electronic and print media.

Gabriel Weimann is a Full Professor of Communication at the Department of Communication at Haifa University, Israel, and is currently at NYU Shanghai, China. His research interests include the study of media effects, political campaigns, persuasion and influence, modern terrorism and the mass media, and online terrorism. He has published nine books including *The Theater of Terror* (New York: Longman, 1994); *Terror on the Internet* (Washington, DC: USIP Press, 2006); *Freedom and Terror* (London: Routledge, 2011); and *Terrorism in Cyberspace: The Next Generation* (New York: Columbia University Press, 2015). His papers and research reports, more than 180 publications, have been published in scientific journals and books. He has received numerous grants and awards from international foundations and has been a Visiting Professor at various universities including University of Pennsylvania, Stanford University, Hofstra University, American University DC, University of Maryland, Lehigh University (USA), University of Mainz (Germany), Carleton University (Canada) and the National University of Singapore.

Acknowledgements

This edited collection emerged out of a symposium hosted by Swansea University in June 2014 on Terrorists' Use of the Internet. The conference was organised by the *Cyberterrorism Project*: an international, multidisciplinary research network that brings together researchers and other stakeholders with an interest in this area. In our time directing the project, we have benefited enormously from the inspiration and perspiration of a large number of talented interns, researcher associates and students, and it is appropriate that we acknowledge them here. In particular, we would like to thank the US Office of Naval Research Global, Swansea University and Curtin University for providing financial support for the symposium, and Verity Cannell, Julia Carroll, Kirstie Dunseath, Louise Edinton, Simon Lavis, David Mair, Lella Nouri, Guy Szablewski and Andrew Whiting for assisting with the hosting and promotion of the event. Further information on the Cyberterrorism Project, and individual team members, can be found on the Cyberterrorism Project website www.cyberterrorism-project.org/team/

We also gratefully acknowledge the support of our current and former colleagues at City University London, Curtin University, Swansea University and the University of East Anglia, for the time, expertise and experience that many have generously shared with us. We are grateful, too, for all the support we have received for this project from those at Routledge including Andrew Humphrys, Annabelle Harris and Hannah Ferguson. The book also benefited from the comments and suggestions of a number of anonymous referees, for which we would also like to express our gratitude here. Versions of chapters one, two, four, six and seven also appear in a special issue of *Studies in Conflict and Terrorism* 40 (1) and are reproduced here with permission of Taylor and Francis.

Finally, as always, we reserve our greatest thanks for our family and friends for their continuing support, advice and encouragement. We hope you know how grateful we are!

Introduction

Anne Aly, Tom Chen, Lee Jarvis and Stuart Macdonald

The ubiquity of the Internet in the everyday lives of individuals, governments and corporations has made it one of the most studied subjects of our time. Within a broad interest on the Internet and its social, political and economic significance, a developing strand of research has turned attention to the ways in which the Internet has become an integral part of the strategy of terrorism.[1] In particular, the considerable increase in cases of violent extremist actors who have been influenced by online preachers and Internet propaganda has focused the attention of governments, law enforcement and academia on the perceived role of the Internet in what has been termed 'radicalisation' towards violent extremism.[2]

When terrorism first took to the world stage during the era of airline hijackings and hostage takings, the focus was squarely on communicating with an international audience. Terrorism was projected into the daily lives and viewing habits of everyday people with little or no other connection to the events screened across their televisions. In today's connected world, communications have never been faster, more convenient or more prolific. On 11 September 2001, the largest terrorist attack in modern history was witnessed by millions of viewers in real time. More recently, news of the coordinated attacks in Paris on 13 November 2015 spread quickly through online channels and social media. Also, one of the suicide terrorists, Bilal Hadfi, had been openly advocating attacks on Facebook before the Paris attacks. While terrorists have always relied on communication technologies to connect not only with each other but also to a broader public of sympathisers, perceived enemies and potential recruits, online communications have undoubtedly changed the way these communications occur. Terrorist and violent extremist groups have taken full advantage of the Internet as a medium to communicate with mass audiences both collectively and individually.

Terrorists and counterterrorism practitioners alike are operating in relatively new terrain characterised by a media environment that is both complex and chaotic. In this environment, initiators of terroristic and counter-terroristic narratives alike no longer have control of their messages. Violent jihadist narratives have a regenerative capacity allowing them to become personalised, re-constructed and propagated by disparate individuals around the world. Likewise, the 'war on terror' narrative that was intended to frame the legitimacy of the US and allied forces interventions in Afghanistan and Iraq became co-opted by al-Qaeda and the global violent jihadi movement and reframed as a 'war on Islam'.

According to some media scholars, part of the reason for this chaos is the emergence of a new media ecology. While a difficult and sometimes contentious term, media ecology offers a useful concept for advancing the idea that developments in media technologies are part of an ever transforming 'ecology' that fundamentally impacts human society. McLuhan's view of media ecology placed emphasis on the role of communication in all forms of media. Accordingly, the focus is not on what is being communicated – the words, symbols or messages embedded in a communication act – but the form of media chosen to communicate those messages and the consequences of those choices on the message itself and how it is received (Levinson 2000).

Technological developments in communication therefore impact the interrelationships between sender, message and receiver. The contemporary 'new media ecology' is characterised by digital technologies that emerge and transform the ways in which events are documented and broadcast (Hoskins and O'Loughlin 2010). Unlike the surreal images of aircraft crashing into the Twin Towers against the backdrop of the Manhattan skyline, the images that defined the London 2005 public transport bombings came from the camera phones of commuters. News sources in London were inundated with mobile phone images sent in by the public. The low-resolution, gritty images enhanced the immediacy of the coverage and narrowed the divide between the public and the media – what Hoskins (2006) refers to as the 'granular intimacy of the visual exposure' to the London bombings. The black-and-white images of the four bombers caught boarding the underground on closed-circuit television complemented the grainy mobile phone visuals. How the resonant images of the London bombings were captured and the ways in which they were disseminated through both 'traditional' and 'new' forms of media define today's media ecology as one where the binary of 'old' and 'new' is no longer relevant.

The case of Australian foreign fighter Jake Bilardi attests to this. Born and raised in the suburbs of Melbourne, Bilardi's fascination with violent extremist groups developed at a young age, not through the Internet but through watching documentaries and news reports about conflicts in the Middle East. By his own account, Bilardi formed much of his opinion about the Taliban by watching the morning news program earlier, then turning to the Internet in search of information and news that supported his opinions:

> in the media, the reports every morning when I sat on the couch eating breakfast and watching the news before school had to include a story on the Taliban's brutality or fears of al-Qaeda operatives hiding in Europe. It was Channel 7's program 'Sunrise' that I turned on most mornings, watching discussions such as, 'Another attack in America, should we be suspicious about the Muslims in Australia?' Still, as an Atheist of only 13-years-of-age I couldn't believe everything I was seeing and hearing, my views of the Muslims were very positive and when it came to organisations such as the

Taliban, my views almost six years ago would be considered by the Australian government as extreme and myself an Islamic extremist, although I was still an Atheist, a little confusing I know. I saw the Taliban as simply a group of proud men seeking to protect their land and their people from an invading force, while I did not necessarily agree with their ideology, their actions were in my opinion completely justified. I saw the foreign troops burning villages, raping local women and girls, rounding up innocent young men as suspected terrorists and sending them overseas for torture, gunning down women, children and the elderly in the streets and indiscriminately firing missiles from their jets. Who was I to believe was the terrorist?

(Bilardi 2015)

This collection explores the interface between terrorism and the Internet within a complex media environment in which tweets during a shopping mall siege and Facebook statuses have become as much a part of terrorist communications as television news broadcasts. The collection emerges from the Terrorists' Use of the Internet Symposium hosted by Swansea University on 5–6 June 2014 as part of the ongoing Cyberterrorism Project (www.cyberterrorism-project.org), an international, multidisciplinary research network that was established by academics working across a number of fields. The project has four primary objectives:

1 to further understanding among the scientific community by engaging in original research on the concept, threat and possible responses to cyberterrorism;
2 to facilitate global networking activities around this research theme;
3 to engage with policymakers, opinion formers, citizens and other stakeholders at all stages of the research process, from data collection to dissemination;
4 to do the above within a multidisciplinary and pluralist context that draws on expertise from the physical and social sciences.

The symposium hosted forty-three delegates, including researchers from a number of UK universities, as well as institutions in the Republic of Ireland, France, the Netherlands, Norway, Turkey, Canada and Australia. Other attendees included representatives from the Home Office, South Wales Police and the Scottish Organised Crime and Counterterrorism Police Unit. Papers presented explored different forms of online terrorist activity, evaluated legislative and policy responses to these activities, and spoke to the opportunities that the Internet provides for intelligence and enforcement agencies. These opportunities include not only surveillance and intelligence activities, but also the construction and promotion of counter-narratives and other strategic communications.

The chapters that follow cover four main themes:

- terrorist propaganda on the Internet;
- Internet radicalisation;
- counter campaigns and approaches to disrupting Internet radicalisation;

- approaches to researching and understanding the role of the Internet in radicalisation.

Together, these four themes can be loosely grouped into two broad foci: (i) the phenomenon of online radicalisation through explorations of terrorists' use of the Internet, and (ii) responses to this phenomenon through explorations of the policy and research agendas dealing with the growing influence of the Internet in violent extremism. As such, the text covers issues ranging along the gamut of how terrorists use the Internet to how governments are responding to the increasing risk posed by exposure to online terroristic content.

Despite the focus on terrorism and the Internet within various disciplines, there are numerous outstanding questions about this relationship. These include questions about the role of the Internet in radicalisation, the reasons why terroristic propaganda does or does not influence violent extremists, the role of political conflict in online radicalisation and the future of research into terrorism and the Internet. This range of interests has never been previously covered by a single volume and so this book makes a unique and timely addition to the understanding of terrorism and the Internet.

In the opening chapter, Martin Rudner examines al-Qaeda's Electronic Jihad' as a strategy for mobilising support for the global violent jihadist movement. Rudner explores the attributes of this 'electronic jihad' in terms of strategy, operation and connectivity. Rudner's chapter highlights both the tactical and communicative functions that the Internet serves for terroristic communications, and consolidates the basis for examining online terrorist communications as an important, and indeed integral component of the ways in which modern terrorist organisations operate.

Angela Gendron's chapter – The call to Jihad: Charismatic leaders and the Internet – picks up on some of the themes in the first chapter. Gendron discusses online materials of charismatic preachers and propagandists as mobilisers for radicalisation. While there is still no clear understanding of the exact role that the Internet plays in the process of radicalisation, there is general agreement among researchers that the Internet provides opportunities for radicalisation. Central to this is the charismatic preacher who is able to exert influence by framing violent action as a religious requirement. Gendron's chapter poses some necessary questions about the role of such radicalising influences, and the importance of the Internet as a medium of influence. While much attention has tended to focus on the role of preachers in mosques, madrassas and other offline institutions, Gendron's chapter highlights how sermons delivered through the medium of the Internet can be as influential.

Gabriel Weimann's chapter continues the theme of terrorists' use of the Internet by examining the use of online social media by terrorists and their supporters with a particular focus on the leading platforms, namely Facebook, Twitter and YouTube. Weimann argues that these platforms act as a virtual firewall that maintains the anonymity of those who participate in the communication between creators of terrorist content and their intended audiences. Citing extensive research involving the monitoring of thousands of terrorist websites and online forums,

Weimann reveals a clear trend of terrorist 'migration' from older forms of Internet-based media to new social media. Weimann's chapter attests to the ever transforming nature of media ecology. Whereas researchers were once concerned with the migration from old to new media, it seems that, even within 'new' media, migrations are occurring in response to trends in global terrorism.

David Mair's case study of the Westgate shopping mall attack in Chapter 4 provides the book's most in-depth analysis of the use of media technologies in the context of a specific attack. Mair's chapter offers a detailed insight into how Twitter was mobilised during that attack as a communication platform between the attackers, and between the attackers and their audience. Mair presents his analysis of live tweets during the attack, identifying to whom the tweets were targeted at and the motivation behind them. His findings illuminate the ways in which a social media platform has become a primary form of communication for terrorists who no longer need to vie for attention from the international news media. Social media platforms like Twitter and Facebook have also become vital sources of information for a range of actors, from law enforcement to journalists to indirect audiences, all 'following' events as they unfold in real time. Mair's chapter reminds us that new media is indeed changing the ways in which events are recorded, disseminated and interpreted.

The fifth chapter by Keiran Hardy takes a different approach, examining the use of the Internet in two prominent Australian terrorism trials. Hardy's chapter raises some significant questions about the assumptions of the role of the Internet in radicalisation, asking: Should guilt be determined on the assumption that the viewing or consumption of terroristic content on the Internet leads to radicalisation? Hardy explores this by examining how the presentation of online material as evidence influenced the prosecution of individuals in terrorism trials. His chapter makes an important and timely contribution to the debate about the role of the Internet in radicalisation, by touching not only on how terrorists use the Internet but also the nexus between 'online' and 'offline' behaviours.

Anne Aly's chapter titled 'Brothers, believers, brave mujahideen' draws attention to a deficit in terrorism studies caused by the field's primary concern with the *messages* contained in terroristic online content. This focus has meant that the ways in which those messages are constructed, the mediums used to construct them and the contexts in which they are interpreted, are all often ignored. Drawing on a long tradition of media studies, Aly offers an alternative approach to the study of terrorism and the Internet – one that places the audience at the centre of research, and that takes into account the diverse ways in which a single message can be interpreted by even homogenous groups of individuals. Aly provides an example of this approach in practice and presents the findings of a recent research project that looked at how users respond to different messages online.

Chapter 7 presents Maura Conway's contribution to the debate on the role of the Internet in radicalisation. Conway starts with the question 'Is it possible for persons to be radicalised online?' In light of the content presented in previous chapters – particularly Hardy's examination of online content and activity as evidence in terror trials – the question has both theoretical and practical significance. To answer her question, Conway picks up on an ongoing debate in scholarly circles around the role of the Internet. She confirms that some scholars insist that the Internet is significant while others dismiss its role as minimal. Not surprisingly, this debate has been ongoing in other areas of research unconnected to terrorist violence. The role of violent Internet games in promoting violence, for example, has been and continues to be a subject of contestation. Conway's chapter both takes stock of these debates and pushes them forward by identifying major strands of current research, the theory and evidence underlying these, and fruitful future research trajectories.

Sarah Logan's chapter 'Grasping at thin air: Online counterterrorism in the US and the UK' turns the focus from research to policy and the implications for states attempting to grapple with the issue of terrorism online. Logan argues that states need to navigate the practicalities of policing the Internet and curtailing citizens' access to information while also attempting to address the seemingly exponential growth in terroristic content online. The conundrum facing liberal states that have a democratic obligation to their citizens is borne out in the development of policy approaches to terrorism on the Internet. Logan's chapter speaks to the powerful influence that media and communications have on human society – not just in the messages that are transmitted but in the ways in which individuals and governments respond to messages and, significantly, their mediums.

The final chapter in this collection is provided by Halim Rane. Rane explores narratives about the Israel–Palestine conflict as they are used by violent jihadist extremists. In doing so, he looks at the role of social media and Internet-based communications in the development and manifestation of global Muslim identities. Rane concurs with other authors in this collection that the Internet has become a critical tool for terrorists, and uses this as the starting point for examining the master narratives of violent jihadist extremists derived from Islamic doctrine and texts. Rane also looks at how these historical narratives are applied to the modern context of the Israel–Palestine conflict. He concludes by offering a series of alternative narratives that challenge the basis of online terroristic narratives.

Together the nine chapters in this book therefore present a comprehensive overview of the direction of research into the phenomenon of terrorism on the Internet. While there exists an important body of literature in this field of inquiry, much of it has been fragmented along disciplinary boundaries (as a result of the technical nature of much of the literature) and jurisdictional boundaries. This text is intended to address some of these shortcomings. Presenting chapters by some of the world's leading researchers in the field, the text does not approach the phenomenon from a singular angle or disciplinary lens. Rather the combination of chapters cuts across disciplines and themes, and draws attention to the relationship between 'new' media and human society – from the everyday lives of individuals to the policy goals of states.

The text is primarily aimed at academics and students (undergraduate and postgraduate) who are working in the fields of terrorism, radicalisation, the Internet and political violence, communication studies, international security, criminology and cybersecurity. Though these fields are diverse, the text is equally relevant to those working in the technology-focused space of cybersecurity as it is to students of communication and human society. The text covers topics that are widely taught in several disciplines and includes contributions from several regions. Its interdisciplinary focus makes it useful to students and academics in both the humanities and sciences.

A secondary, but equally important, audience for the text comprises policymakers and practitioners working in countering violent extremism, intelligence, cybersecurity and surveillance. The text will also hold particular interest for members of the general public interested in the reality of an increasingly digitalised world where a tweet or a Facebook status has replaced the news headline as the most common source of news and information.

Notes

1 The meaning and utility of the term 'terrorism' remain, of course, much debated and contested. For reasons of space and focus, we do not explore these debates in this introduction. Useful contemporary introductions – from rather different starting points, include: Jackson *et al.* (2011), Schmid (2011) and Wilkinson and Bryan (2012).
2 The concept of 'radicalisation' is also a heavily contested one. For a critical overview of its genealogy, implications and functions, see Kundnani (2015).

References

Bilardi, J (2015) *From the Eyes of the Muhajir*, no longer available on the internet.
Hoskins, A (2006) 'Temporality, Proximity and Security: Terror in a Media-Drenched Age', *International Relations*, vol. 20, pp. 453–68.
Hoskins, A. and O'Loughlin, B (2010) *War and Media: The Emergence of Diffused War*, Cambridge: Polity Press.
Jackson, R., Jarvis, L., Gunning, J. and Smyth, M (2011) *Terrorism: A Critical Introduction*, Basingstoke: Palgrave.
Kundnani, A (2015) 'Radicalisation: The Journey of a Concept', in C. Baker-Beall, C. Heath-Kelly and L. Jarvis (eds) *Counter-Radicalisation: Critical Perspectives*. Abingdon: Routledge, pp. 14–35.
Levinson, P (2000) McLuhan and Media Ecology. Media Ecology Association, available at www.media-ecology.org/publications/MEA_proceedings/v1/McLuhan_and_media_ecology.html
Schmid, A (2011) 'The Definition of Terrorism', in A. Schmid (ed.) *The Routledge Handbook of Terrorism Research*. Abingdon: Routledge, pp. 39–98.
Wilkinson, P. and Bryan, D (2012) 'Is Terrorism Still a Useful Analytical Term or Should It Be Abandoned?', in R. Jackson and S.J. Sinclair (eds) *Contemporary Debates on Terrorism*. Abingdon: Routledge, pp. 11–25.

1 "Electronic Jihad"

The Internet as al-Qaeda's catalyst for global terror

Martin Rudner

Introduction

Al-Qaeda has deemed the Internet "a great medium for spreading the call of Jihad and following the news of the mujahideen (Islamic warriors)" (al-Alwaki 2009). Hence, the al-Qaeda (2015) operational manual titled *Military Studies in the Jihad Against the Tyrants* describes one of its primary missions as "spreading rumors and writing statements that instigate people against the enemy." Subsequently, al-Qaeda's Twenty-Year Strategic Plan (2001–2020) outlined a seven-stage jihadist struggle for global supremacy, culminating in a Definitive Victory for a renewed Islamic caliphate by the year 2020.[1] Already at the second stage of this Strategy, spanning the years 2003–2006, the Internet had emerged as a key instrument in al-Qaeda's effort to mobilize jihadist empathy among Muslims worldwide (Springer et al. 2009, p. 76). Radical Islamist leaders underlined their encouragement for what they defined as "Electronic Jihad," insisting that "any attempt to 'spite the enemy' and endorse religion is legitimate" (Atayf 2012). By the current fifth stage of the Strategy, covering the years 2013–2016, Electronic Jihad has come to play an expanded role in pursuit of the declared objective of mobilizing Muslim support for the "Declaration of the Caliphate." Indeed, the Internet has come to serve as a choice means of communications outreach on the part of al-Qaeda and its regional affiliates, for its pronounced, digitalized multiplier effects on jihadist consciousness-raising, recruitment, training, fund-raising, and operational activities (Weimann 2012; Gendron and Rudner 2012; Rudner 2013b).

The methodological approach utilized in this study of al-Qaeda's and its jihadist associates' use of the Internet for the promotion of global terror is empirically focused, and may be described as a "descriptive analysis." This essentially empirical approach highlights al-Qaeda's self-proclaimed doctrine, strategy, tactics, and goals as it has evolved in utilizing Internet technology in pursuit of its own declared objectives. These descriptive elements are then accompanied by a detailed analysis of the actual activities that ensured, including incitement for jihad, recruitment, training, fund-raising, and terror operations. Alas, in the author's opinion, there exists no relevant theoretical framework, in the academic sense of the term, which can explain terrorist motivations and behavioristics in their use of the Internet, and from which one can draw simple "conclusions." In the absence of appropriate theoretical applications, the empirical methodology to be used here describes, analyzes, and explains actual practices.

The study commences with an overview of the al-Qaeda conceptualization of its so-called Electronic Jihad. It reviews the formulation of this strategy and its perceived role as in the promotion of jihadist aims. This is followed by an examination of the operative elements of Electronic Jihad, including the provision of online library resources, serving as virtual platforms for radical preachers, and facilitating forums for extremist discourse. Consideration is furthermore given to the actual impact of these Internet-based polemics on shaping attitudes, beliefs, and behaviors on the part of Muslim communities worldwide. The study then proceeds to scrutinize how Internet connectivity has actually been deployed by al-Qaeda and its associates for terrorist-related purposes. Detailed attention is paid to their utilization of the Internet for such purposes as inciting prospective cadres to action, recruiting jihadist operatives and fighters, providing virtual training in tactical methods and manufacture of explosives, terrorism financing, and for operational planning and preparations for specific terror attacks. Reference is also made to cyberterrorism, but this will be addressed in lesser detail here since it has been dealt with fully elsewhere, including by the present author (Gendron and Rudner 2012; Rudner 2013b;).

The thrust of the present study thus emphasizes the actionable intentions of al-Qaeda and its partners in availing themselves of the Internet as a catalyst for militant jihadism. By describing and analyzing the doctrines, strategies, tactics, and objectives of al-Qaeda and its jihadist partners, the threat arising from jihadi terrorist use of the Internet could be contextualized. Understanding adversarial intentions should help to facilitate further research and analysis relating to the impact of Electronic Jihad on targeted individuals and communities, and furthermore on ways and means of counteracting its harmful effects in the interests of public safety and national security.

The strategy of Electronic Jihad

To capitalize on the intrinsic capabilities of the Internet, prominent al-Qaeda stalwarts like the late, notorious preacher Anwar al-Awlaki urged followers to become "Internet mujahideen" by setting up dedicated websites to cover specific areas of jihad, such as news about jihadist activities and operations or jihadist literature, what he termed "WWW Jihad" (al-Alwaki 2009). Jihadist websites have come to play a prominent part in propagandizing on behalf of militant Islam, mobilizing prospective adherents, and inciting terrorist actions. Thus, a 2009 judgment by a Canadian court found that an extremist website posted by the Global Islamic Media Front purveyed messaging characteristic of militant jihadism, which was tantamount to a terrorist threat, by way of:

- publicizing and expounding upon the speeches of al-Qaeda leaders;
- inciting people to carry out violent jihad;

- urging people to support jihadist groups like al-Qaeda and its affiliates and al-Shabaab in Somalia;
- disseminating al-Qaeda textual propaganda;
- glorifying jihadist "martyrs";
- providing advice on computer security, and instructions about hacking into computer networks;
- engaging in psychological warfare by threatening targeted societies and communities;
- delivering military training to carry out violent jihad, including tactics for urban and gang warfare, concealing explosives, executing ambushes, arrests, and explosions;
- webcasting news reports from jihadist battlefronts;
- publishing online magazines like *Sawt al-Jihad* (Voice of Jihad) and *Inspire*;
- translating its propaganda material into various languages to reach out to a wide audience especially in the West.

Accordingly, the Court held that jihadist websites like the Global Islamic Media Front contribute directly or indirectly to actual terrorist activities.[2]

The Internet and other related digital and electronic technologies like YouTube and Twitter offer certain unique advantages for radical preachers, jihadist proponents, and militant operatives, as compared to other traditional media. A key feature of the Internet is its digitalization of information, which enables the material to be infinitely copied without loss of fidelity and be disseminated endlessly. The scope and reach of these Internet discussion forums create, in effect, a near-global digital *ummah* (Muslim realm), linking up potential jihadist fellow travelers from various communities across the Asia, the Middle East, Western Europe, and the Americas. The emergence of what some have called a "digitalized ummah" contributes to a homogenization of political attitudes and religious sentiments shaped by a relentless flow of identical messages and images (verbal and graphic) across cyberspace (Kaya 2010). These cyberspace communities, unbounded by territory or civic loyalty, can spawn a virtual radicalism among prospective recruits and neophytes, thereby fostering a jihadist counterculture that challenges the traditional authority of established religious scholars in Muslim communities as well as in the diaspora.

Proponents of Electronic Jihad seek to exploit the strategic capabilities of the Internet and related technologies for promoting the spread of radical Islamist principles and fomenting jihadist militancy among Muslim communities, especially in the Western diaspora. In that regard, al-Qaeda and proxy jihadist websites seem to have had a both direct and more diffuse impact on actual terrorist operations. The direct impact relates to their influence in indoctrinating and inspiring terrorist operatives to mount attacks on specific targets. In addition, these websites can and do have a more diffuse effect by way of motivating jihadist recruitment and training efforts. At a broader community level, these and similar Internet domains may play their part in inciting wider Muslim identification with and support for the militant jihadist cause (Lennings et al. 2010).

Operative elements of Electronic Jihad

The Centre for Social Cohesion, a British research institution, has identified three core Internet-based functions performed by jihadist websites, chatrooms, and social media (Brandon 2008):

> *Online Libraries*: Jihadist websites perform a key role as repositories of archival writings by preeminent figures in the jihadi pantheon like Abdullah Azzam, founder of al-Qaeda, and jihadist e-magazines like al-Qaeda's *Inspire*;
>
> *Platform for Extremist Preachers*: Jihadist websites offer posting of sermons and tracts by prominent radical Islamist preachers and expositors of jihadism like Anwar al-Awlaki, which can be readily accessed through the Internet;
>
> *Forums for Radical Discourse*: Jihadist websites usually host newsgroups, chatrooms, discussion forums, and newsgroups which serve to facilitate e-conversations among like-minded followers, and represent networking hubs for addressing key issues, planning and coordinating activities, and promoting group dynamics.
>
> (Brandon 2008, Chapter 5; Simon Wiesenthal Center 2010)[3]

Jihadists and other Islamist extremists make extensive use of the Internet and social media for the dissemination of propaganda, as well as for the recruitment and training of operatives (Brandon 2008; Europol 2009, pp. 13–14, 20). The Internet and social media, for their part, offer radical preachers, strategists, and enthusiasts especially advantageous capabilities for reaching out and influencing, inciting, and motivating jihadist activism at a global level (Taylor and Ramsay 2010, p. 106). Arguably the preeminent Jihadist preacher on the Internet to date was the late Anwar al-Awlaki, an American-born and later a high-profile spokesman for al-Qaeda in the Arabian Peninsula, where he was assassinated by a U.S. drone strike in 2011 (Koplowitz 2013). Anwar al-Awlaki utilized the Internet to purvey al-Qaeda's militant Islamist doctrine to a targeted audience of educated, English-speaking Muslim youth (including converts), in particular, with a view to fomenting a jihadist struggle "from within" the democratic societies of Europe and North America, a homegrown "Western Jihad" (al-Awlaki 2010). Indeed, his Internet-based guide on "44 Ways to Support Jihad" insisted that "Jihad today is obligatory on every capable Muslim" (al-Alwaki 2009; Moon 2010).

Preliminary inquiries into the recruitment of "homegrown" terrorists in Western societies suggest the particular importance of "religious teaching" as a precursor and trend-setter, more so than, for example, "strategy" documents (Lia 2007, pp. 226–227; Springer et al. 2009, pp. 132–133, 143–146). An assessment by the British Security Service (MI5) discerned that the Internet had come to serve as a more pronounced instrument for the promotion of Islamist radicalization, especially among youth, than more conventional meeting spaces (Andrew 2009, pp. 827–828; U.K. House of Commons 2012).

Jihadist messaging across the Internet, and through other digital formats, may be assessed according to the extent to which they instigate, promote, or enable activities that directly or indirectly facilitate terrorist acts. The actual thrust of Electronic Jihadi messaging may be rated, in ascending order of severity, in terms of their impact on:

- subverting Muslim communities in Western democracies while deceiving and distracting their governments from reacting to the threat at hand (Phares 2005, p. 263);
- cultivating supportive attitudes toward acts of terrorism;
- offering theological justification to acts of political violence and terror;
- providing technical instructions and operational guidelines for terrorist acts;
- promoting direct involvement in preparatory activities that expedite terrorist operations;
- encouraging personal engagement in committing acts of terrorism (Taylor and Ramsay 2010, p.100).

For proponents of Electronic Jihad, probably the most pertinent attribute of the Internet is its potential to affect the mindset and behavior of followers in various ways that help to transform hitherto placid individuals into jihadist militants (Taylor and Ramsay 2010, p. 107). It is indicated that jihadist terrorists are increasingly utilizing Internet-based social media, such as Facebook and Twitter, for messaging and communications (Gertz 2013). Virtual interaction between militant elements through the Internet and social media has fostered widespread radicalization across countries and regions along with the emergence of new jihadist networks (The Netherlands General Intelligence and Security Service 2012). The World Wide Web remains overall a significant platform for promoting jihadist activism and for facilitating terrorism. For al-Qaeda, Electronic Jihad is tantamount to a virtual globalization of it calling.

Internet connectivity to terrorist activities

As will be addressed in greater detail below, the Internet has become a powerful catalyst for facilitating al-Qaeda-sponsored terrorist activities and operations. Al-Qaeda's Electronic Jihad has created a threat environment wherein terrorist activities can emanate from a large number of countries and elements within countries (Zelin 2013a). Other militant Islamist movements, like the Islamic State of Iraq and al-Sham (ISIS), once affiliated with al-Qaeda but now proclaiming itself as the Caliphate ("The Islamic State"), likewise make extensive use of the Internet to promote its jihadist agenda globally (Azman 2014). In a special report prepared for the United States Institute of Peace, Gabriel Weimann identified eight ways in which contemporary jihadist militants exploit the capabilities of the Internet, notably for psychological warfare, propaganda and publicity, data mining, fund-raising, recruitment and mobilization, group networking, sharing information, and for planning and coordination of actual attacks (Weimann 2004; Stalinsky and Sosnow 2014). An analysis of recent incidents attributable to al-Qaeda and its affiliated network points to their utilization of Internet connectivity to directly and significantly instigate specific terrorist activities having multiplier effects for global jihad, most notably inciting belligerence, jihadist recruitment, militant training, terrorism financing, terror operations, and cyber-warfare (Zelin 2013; Nuraniyah 2014).

Incitement

Terrorist groups like al-Qaeda and its jihadist affiliates and associates utilize the Internet to inspire and motivate cadres to action (Rudner 2013a; Gulsby and Desa 2014). Renowned terrorism expert Bruce Hoffman has pointed out that such Internet communications are typically constructed and contextualized to address particular objectives. Their purpose could be "didactic," designed to inform, attract, or indoctrinate new adherents; "disciplinarian," using blandishments or threats to ensure obedience; "promotional," in an effort to attract new converts or recruits to the ranks of fighters; "bombastic," aimed at intimidating local authorities and weakening public confidence in government; or what may be termed "auto-propaganda," serving to uphold the morale of the already committed (Hoffman 2006, p. 199). Jihadist websites highlight extremist preaching intended to indoctrinate the faithful and propagate a militant jihadism, while providing theological justification for terrorism and "martyrdom" operations (Roy 2004, pp. 234–257; Vidino 2005, Chapter 1; Europol 2009, p. 19; Weimann 2011). More recently, al-Qaeda, Islamic Jihad, and related jihadist groups have been utilizing the more accessible social media, such as You Tube, as distinct from websites, to broadcast their messaging to a wider global audience (Klausen et al. 2012; Berger and Strathearn 2013). Indeed, a 2015 analytical study by the Brookings Institution reported that some 46,000 Twitter accounts are held by Islamic State supporters globally (Berger and Morgan 2015).

Jihadist Internet forums denote the core of the global virtual jihadi movement and are crucial to the dissemination of radical Islamism (Weimann 2004; Bertram and Ellison 2014). An inquiry mounted by the U.K. House of Commons Select Committee on Home Affairs in 2012 found that the Internet played a more significant role in fostering violent Islamic extremism than prisons, universities, or places of worship, and "was now one of the few unregulated spaces where radicalisation (sic) is able to take place" (Travis 2012; U.K. House of Commons 2012). Virtual interaction between jihadists stimulates and enhances their propensities toward radicalization while cultivating the emergence of new, localized jihadist networks. Homegrown radicalization, facilitated in good measure by these digital technologies, was so deeply dispersed such that al-Qaeda's own stalwart preacher, the late Anwar al-Awlaki, was able to boast that "Jihad is becoming as American as apple pie and as British as afternoon tea" (al-Awlaki 2010). Homegrown Western Jihadism, he warned, "is here to stay."

An Internet-based discourse may seem especially appealing to younger prospects, for whom access to more conventional meeting places (and the radicalizing influences therein) may be restricted. In July 2014, a British court convicted an Islamist activist youth for disseminating militant jihadist and terrorist material through the Internet, despite his participating in the government's "Prevent" program (Whitehead 2014). Chat rooms, message boards, and forums provide virtual opportunities for extremists to establish contacts and radicalize each other (Andrew 2009, pp. 827–828). It is noteworthy that Electronic Jihad not just aims at Western, Muslim diaspora targets, but also seeks to attract and mobilize Muslim youth within the Muslim world itself, in places like Saudi Arabia, for the jihadist endeavor, through these same digital technologies (al-Shehri 2014). It is something of a paradox that al-Qaeda websites directed at Saudi Arabia reportedly even deployed female activists to enhance their attractiveness to prospective youth targets, notwithstanding traditional Islamist strictures against feminine immodesty (Saudi Gazette 2014). Overall, the reach of al-Qaeda's Internet discussion groups creates, in effect, a near-global digital ummah unbounded by civic loyalty, linking up jihadi fellow travelers from various communities across the Asia, the Middle East, Western Europe, and North America.

The Internet has been noticeably instrumental for al-Qaeda in its ongoing efforts to foster locally homegrown terrorist activities directed against British, European, and North American targets (Musawi 2010; Kleinmann 2012; The Netherlands General Intelligence and Security Service 2012). As a notorious example, the December 2014 issue of its Web-based, English-language magazine *Inspire* propagated the "Lone Jihadist Campaign" to persuade and instruct individuals to attack specific economic and civil aviation targets as part of the al-Qaeda terror campaign against the West (Al-Qaeda in the Arabian Peninsula 2014, pp. 64–108).

Recruitment

Cyber-forums on the Internet have served as influential catalysts for the actual recruitment of jihadist operatives (The Netherlands General Intelligence and Security Service 2012). Recruitment efforts by al-Qaeda, its affiliated networks, and locally homegrown cells utilize the preachings by radical to promote enlistment, legitimize their militant cause, and justify violent acts. Prior to the 9/11 attacks, formal recruitment to al-Qaeda usually occurred in its training camps then operating in Afghanistan. Later, as a consequence of their expulsion from Afghanistan and the "Global War on Terror," al-Qaeda recruitment metamorphosed into a more loosely structured, distributed, and interactive procedure. Henceforward, prospective new members were galvanized by jihadist propaganda, through the Internet typically—and prepped for enlistment by local talent-spotters and recruiters (Gendron 2006; Rudner 2013a).

The Internet has vastly expanded the geographic and demographic catchment areas, as well as the missions for prospective recruits (Gulsby and Desa 2014). Up to just a few years ago, al-Qaeda was actually advertising on its prominent Web forum, Shumukh al-Islam, seeking jihadis to carry out suicide attacks (Kjuka 2013). More usually, its Internet sites and affiliated preachers endeavored to induce self-enlistment into locally homegrown cells with a view to galvanizing diaspora youth against their country of residence (Musawi 2010; Kleinmann

2012; The Netherlands General Intelligence and Security Service 2012). Over the years, Internet-linked homegrown recruits have perpetrated terror attacks on a multiplicity of jurisdictions, among them Canada (Ilardi 2013), Britain (Ilyas 2013), Germany (Sydow 2012), and Australia (Harris-Hogan 2012). Communications through the Internet also facilitated the phenomenon of so-called lone-wolf terrorism (Sageman 2009). As a notorious example, the Spring 2013 issue of its Web-based, English-language magazine *Inspire* propagated "individual jihad" to persuade even lone militants to attack "important targets" as part of the al-Qaeda terror campaign against the West (Al-Qaeda in the Arabian Peninsula 2013, p. 24).

Moreover, Internet-based recruitment performs an enabling role in the dispatch of foreign would-be combatants to embark on jihadist campaigns abroad. Thus, al-Shabaab had put in place a sophisticated social media and Internet presence in order to recruit Somali expatriates, most notably from Canada and the United States, for jihad in Somalia (Ungerleider 2013). Contemporary Syrian jihadists, both the al-Qaeda-linked al-Nusra Front and the so-called ISIS, utilize Internet communications for their respective recruitment efforts of foreign fighters from Europe, North America, Australia, and elsewhere across the Muslim world (Zelin 2013b; Zelin et al. 2013). British Muslim youth seem to be especially prone to recruitment through the Internet or social media to fight in jihadist campaigns abroad (Nelson 2014). Governments are concerned that these traveling jihadists could eventually return to their erstwhile homelands as potentially dangerous militants.

Training

The training delivered by al-Qaeda is intended to prepare recruits as activists and operatives (Lia 2008; Rudner 2013a, p. 964). The range of aptitudes and skills sought by militant jihadist groups like al-Qaeda span a wide spectrum of competencies, from flying aircraft to computer technology, to biological and chemical sciences, to finance; from the preparation of explosives and explosive devices to reconnaissance, sabotage, assassination; from urban insurgency to actual combat. Whereas, early on, the main emphasis used to be placed on real-life instruction in proper training camps in Pakistan, Syria, Iraq, or Yemen, or in some other safe havens, at least for the seemingly most competent recruits, some preliminary training and indoctrination did take place over the Internet (Europol 2009, p. 21). As security controls over prospective jihadist travel tightened, al-Qaeda and its partners have tended to purvey more of their training via the Internet, especially apropos European cadres (Nesser 2008).

Jihadist websites purvey operational indoctrination coupled with mission-specific instructions pertaining to weaponry, explosives, and tactics. Al-Qaeda's English-language e-magazine *Inspire* has exemplified this Internet-based blending of radicalization, indoctrination, and operational training. Its inaugural issue in summer 2010 highlighted "Open Source Jihad" with instructions on "How to Make a Bomb in the Kitchen of Your Mom." In addition, directives were provided on "How to Use Asrar al-Mujahideen: Sending and Receiving Encrypted Messages by Terrorist." Clearly the aim was to equip individual followers with inspiration and directions to engage in what Marc Sageman has described as "Leaderless Jihad" (Sageman 2011). This strategy was deliberately intended by al-Qaeda to enable Muslim followers to "train at home" and thus constitute "America's worst nightmare" (Al-Qaeda in the Arabian Peninsula 2010).

Follow-up issues of *Inspire* provided "Technical Details" about explosives used in al-Qaeda's "Operation Hemorrhage," a plot to bomb cargo aircraft (Issue 3, November 2010); about "Destroying Buildings" and "Training with the AK [Russian automatic rifle]" (Issue 4, Winter 2010); and about "Individual Terrorism Jihad" (Issue 5, Spring 2011). Featuring the theme "Targeting Dar al-Harb [i.e., countries not under Islamic rule] Populations," the eighth issue of *Inspire* (Fall 2011) reiterated al-Qaeda's encouragement for lone-wolf terrorism by detailing how to use small handguns and build remote-controlled detonators for explosives. *Inspire* Issue 9 (2012) recounted "The Convoy of Martyrs" emphasizing individual actions in gathering intelligence, preparing and ultimately executing attacks, with specific reference to committing acts of arson in forests and cities. *Inspire* Issue 11 in Spring 2013 offered instruction on how to torch cars and cause traffic accidents. The most recent issue 13, posted online on December 24, 2014, provided detailed instructions on preparing homemade undetectable bombs apropos a "lone jihadist campaign targeting specific economic and civil aviation targets" (Al-Qaeda in the Arabian Peninsula 2014, pp. 64–108).

Terrorism financing

Al-Qaeda, its affiliates, and related jihadist terror groups engage in systematic fundraising and money-laundering to finance their widespread system of networks and cells, and their various activities (International Monetary Fund 2003; Rudner 2006; Europol 2009, p. 13; Rudner 2013a, pp. 964–965). Militant Islamist organizations typically raise funds by soliciting private donations, by diverting revenues from quasi-legitimate Muslim charities, religious institutions, or sympathetic ethnocultural organizations (Levitt 2004). Probably the largest single source of revenue is the diversion to militant organizations of the charitable contributions (*Zakat*), which Islam enjoins the faithful to donate, as one of five principle pillars of faith, to Muslim causes. According to the Norwegian Defence Research Establishment report on *Jihad in Europe*, mosques in Germany, France, the UK, and elsewhere were "hijacked" by radical elements to be used for fund-raising, recruitment, incitement, and propaganda, and even for preparing terrorist assaults (Nesser 2004; Vidino 2005, pp. 89–94; Barrett and Mendick 2014). Similarly, Wahhabi or Salafi charities in Middle Eastern domains like Saudi Arabia are known to channel funds raised privately to jihadist networks in neighboring countries (Moniquet 2013).

Since terrorism financing is outlawed in many jurisdictions, terror organizations have become adept at money laundering. Transfers of funds to support terrorist activities may be channeled surreptitiously through financial institutions or through informal money exchangers or *hawalas* (Europol 2009, p. 13), through trade-based transactions in high-value merchandise like gemstones or—in the Middle East—honey, or through trustworthy couriers (Bardoloi 2004; Masciandaro 2004).

However, in recent years, the Internet and social media have emerged to become an increasingly important mechanism for al-Qaeda fund-raising and financial transfers in support of terrorist activities (Seymour 2008; Jacobson 2010; Freeman 2011; Freeman and Ruehsen 2013). Funds diverted or channeled through charities may be remitted to jihadist or front organizations, most readily by electronic means. Also, Islamist activities are known to use Twitter and other social media to mobilize crowdfunding from sympathetic Muslims so as to provide financial backing for jihadist militias operating in Iraq, Syria, and elsewhere (Warrick 2013). Al-Qaeda-sponsored websites are also used to fund-raise for the cause by the sale of inspirational tracts, advocacy literature, audio cassettes, videos and CDs, and other iconic paraphernalia to sympathizers (Friedman 2005).

Terror operations

The Internet has been deployed furthermore by al-Qaeda to marshal tactical guidance for terror assaults on designated targets. The twelfth issue of al-Qaeda in the Arabian Peninsula's e-magazine *Inspire*, in Spring 2014, for example, published detailed instructions for the construction and deployment of car bombs to attack specific targets in cities in Britain, France, and the United States (Crilly 2014). Issue 13 of *Inspire*, posted online on December 24, 2014, promulgated a "Lone Jihad Campaign" against Western economic interests and civil aviation in particular, by way of providing detailed instructions on preparing homemade undetectable bombs, on breaching airport security, and on the actual placement of bombs aboard the aircraft, and targeting specific American, British, and European airlines (Al-Qaeda in the Arabian Peninsula 2014).

Alas, there has been a marked lack of empirical research in the academic domain, at least, on actual terrorist operations (Jarvis et al. 2014; Biglan 2015). Yet there is evidence available that Internet communications have been utilized by al-Qaeda operatives at the individual and cell levels to plot and control specific terror operations. Thus, the perpetrators of the terror attacks on Paris in January 2015 reportedly obtained operational instructions from al-Qaeda leadership via the Internet (Aboudi 2015). Similarly, the Spanish terror cell that perpetrated the March 2004 attacks on Madrid commuter trains reportedly derived tactical directions from the Global Islamic Information Forum website (The Netherlands National Coordinator for Counterterrorism 2007, p. 87). Indeed, the Global Islamic Media Front had emerged as an important source of violent radicalization according to evidence collected in various Western jurisdictions (Soriano 2012). In yet other instances, the Internet had reportedly been utilized to convey tactical instructions to the Dutch Hofstad terror cell and to German al-Tawhid (Zarqawi group) plotters (Tucker 2010; Sageman 2011), whose planned assaults were—fortunately—thwarted. Even at the individual level, an American convert to radical Islamism, the so-called Jihad Jane, had evidently utilized the Internet "obsessively" to plot terror attacks (Lamb 2010).

Cyberterrorism

Cyberterrorism denotes the use of Internet technology to conduct disruptive or destructive operations in the digital domain so as to create and exploit fear through violence or the threat of violence at the behest of a militant belief system (Brickey 2012; Rudner 2013b). Disruptive cyber hacking involves the defacing or taking down of targeted Internet services, and gaining illicit access to and disclosure of sensitive or private information. Critical infrastructures represent a prominent target for disruptive cyberterrorism, most notably government websites and industry online services. However, the aspect of cyberterrorism that actually aims to impair industrial control systems or otherwise damage digitalized production processes lies outside the purview of the present study (Gendron and Rudner 2012).

Conclusion

Reportedly, al-Qaeda has accessed the Internet in order to map vulnerabilities in targeted countries and industries (Varner 2007). It is noteworthy that al-Qaeda recruitment seems to have produced a very strong contingent of university graduates in computer science and information technology among its ranks. A University of Oxford study of Islamic radicals indicates that computer engineers are highly overrepresented among members of militant jihadist groups in jurisdictions across the world (Gambetta and Hertog 2007, pp. 8, 12). Al-Qaeda leader Dr. Ayman al-Zawahiri issued a video pronouncement in February 2011, urging his jihadist cadres to innovate and find new ways and means of attacking high value infrastructure targets:

> If we are not able to produce weapons equal to the weapons of the Crusader West, we can sabotage their complex economic and industrial systems and drain their powers . . . Therefore, the mujahideen (Islamic warriors) must invent new ways, ways that never dawned on the minds of the West.
>
> (Agence France Presse 2011)

Notes

1 This strategic plan was initially made public by journalist Fouad Hussain, an al-Qaeda sympathizer, and has since been widely disseminated on jihadist websites (Hussein 2005; quoted in Musharbash 2005; Rudner 2013a; Springer 2009, pp. 76–79).
2 Court of Québec, District of Montreal, Criminal and Penal Division: H.M. The Queen v Said Namouh, No. 500-73-002831-077 and 500-73-002965-081, October 1, 2009. The individual concerned, Said Namouh, was convicted of terrorism offences under Canada's Anti-Terrorism Act.
3 Cited in Fox News, "Terrorists Targeting Children Via Facebook, Twitter," March 16, 2010.

References

Aboudi, S. (2015), "Al Qaeda Claims French Attack, Derides Paris rally," *Reuters*, January 14, 2015, available at www.reuters.com/article/2015/01/14/us-france-shooting-aqap-idUSKBN0KN0VO20150114 (Accessed September 25, 2015).

Agence France Presse (2011), "Al-Qaeda Calls for New Attacks on West," February 25, 2011, available at www.mysinchew.com/node/53796 (Accessed September 25, 2015).

al-Alwaki, A. (2009), "44 Ways to Support Jihad" [Online], available at www.anwar-alawlaki.com and www.nefafoundation.org/miscellaneous/FeaturedDocs/nefaal-Awlaki 44wayssupportjihad.pdf (Accessed September 25, 2015).

al-Awlaki, A. (2010), "Western Jihad is Here to Stay" [Online], *NEFA Foundation*, March 19, 2010, available at www.nefafoundation.org/miscellaneous/nefa_awlaki0310.pdf (Accessed September 25, 2015).

Al-Qaeda in the Arabian Peninsula (2010), *Inspire*, issue 2.

Al-Qaeda in the Arabian Peninsula (2013), *Inspire*, issue 10.

Al-Qaeda in the Arabian Peninsula (2014), *Inspire*, issue 13.

Al-Qaeda (2015), "Military Studies in the Jihad Against the Tyrants: General Introduction: Missions Required of the Military Organization" [Online], available at www.justice.gov/sites/default/files/ag/legacy/2002/10/08/manualpart1_1.pdf (Accessed September 25, 2015).

al-Shehri, A. (2014), "Al-Qaeda Uses Twitter to Mobilize Saudi Youth," *Al-Monitor*, April 9, 2014, available at www.al-monitor.com/pulse/security/2014/04/al-qaeda-twitter-mobilize-saudi-youth.html (Accessed September 25, 2015).

Andrew, C. (2009), *The Defence of the Realm: The Authorized History of MI5*, Toronto: Viking Canada.

Atayf, M. (2012), "Scholars Speak out in Favour of "Electronic Jihad" Against the Enemy" [Online], available at http://english.alarabiya.net/articles/2012/01/29/191307.html (Accessed September 25, 2015).

Azman, N.A.B. (2014), "Strategic Communication: ISIL's Race to Dominate the Web," *Counter Terrorist Trends and Analysis*, vol. 4, no. 6, pp. 9–13.

Bardoloi, S. (2004), "Money Not Always Honey!" *Information Management*, January 20, available at www.information-management.com/specialreports/20040120/7996-1.html (Accessed September 25, 2015).

Berger, J.M. and Morgan, J. (2015), "The ISIS Twitter Census: Defining and Describing the Population of ISIS Supporters on Twitter," *The Brookings Institution Analysis Paper No. 20*, available at www.brookings.edu/~/media/research/files/papers/2015/03/isis-twitter-census-berger-morgan/isis_twitter_census_berger_morgan.pdf (Accessed September 25, 2015).

Barrett, D. and Mendick, R. (2014) "Mainstream charities have donated thousands to Islamic group fronted by terror suspect," *Sunday Telegraph*, March 2, 2014, available at www.telegraph.co.uk/news/uknews/terrorism-in-the-uk/10670120/Mainstream-charities-have-donated-thousands-to-lslamic-group-fronted-by-terror-suspect.html (Accessed September 25, 2015).

Berger, J.M. and Strathearn, B. (2013), *Who Matters On-Line: Measuring Influence, Evaluating Content, and Countering Violent Extremism in Online Social Networks*, London, International Centre for the Study of Radicalization and Political Violence.

Bertram, S. and Ellison, K. (2014), "Sub Saharan Terrorist Groups' Use of the Internet," *Journal of Terrorism Research*, vol. 5, no. 1, pp. 5–26.

Biglan, A. (2015), "Where Terrorism Research Goes Wrong," *New York Times*, March 7, 2015, available at www.nytimes.com/2015/03/08/opinion/sunday/where-terrorism-research-went-wrong.html (Accessed September 25, 2015).

Brandon, J. (2008), *Virtual Caliphate: Islamic Extremists and their Websites*, London, Centre for Social Cohesion, available at www.civitas.org.uk/pdf/VirtualCaliphate.pdf (Accessed September 25, 2015).

Brickey, J. (2012), "Defining Cyberterrorism: Capturing a Broad Range of Activities in Cyberspace" [Online], *CTC Sentinel*, vol. 5, no. 8, available at www.ctc.usma.edu/posts/defining-cyberterrorism-capturing-a-broad-range-of-activities-in-cyberspace (Accessed September 25, 2015).

Crilly, R. (2014), "Al-Qaeda Urges Followers to Bomb the Savoy," *Daily Telegraph*, March 19, 2014, available at www.telegraph.co.uk/news/worldnews/al-qaeda/10704708/Al-Qaeda-urges-followers-to-bomb-the-Savoy.html (Accessed September 25, 2015).

Europol (2009), "EU Terrorism Situation and Trend Report 2009" [Online], available at www.europol.europa.eu/content/publication/te-sat-2009-eu-terrorism-situation-trend-report-1471 (Accessed September 25, 2015).

Freeman, M. (2011), "The Sources of Terrorist Financing: Theory and Typology," *Studies in Conflict and Terrorism*, vol. 34, no. 6, pp. 461–475.

Freeman, M. and Ruehsen, M. (2013), "Terrorism Financing Methods: An Overview" [Online], *Perspectives on Terrorism*, vol. 7, no. 4, available at www.terrorismanalysts.com/pt/index.php/pot/article/view/279/html (Accessed September 25, 2015).

Friedman, T. (2005), "Giving the Hatemongers No Place to Hide," *New York Times*, July 22, 2005, available at www.nytimes.com/2005/07/22/opinion/giving-the-hatemongers-no-place-to-hide.html (Accessed September 25, 2015).

Gambetta, D. and Hertog, S. (2007), "Engineers of Jihad," *Department of Sociology, University of Oxford, Sociology Working Paper 2007–10*, available at www.sociology.ox.ac.uk/materials/papers/2007–10.pdf (Accessed September 25, 2015).

Gendron, A. (2006), "Militant Jihadism: Radicalization, Conversion, Recruitment," *Integrated Threat Assessment Centre (ITAC)*, Government of Canada, Trends in Terrorism Series, Vol. 4, available at www.itac.gc.ca/pblctns/pdf/2006-4-eng.pdf (Accessed September 25, 2015).

Gendron, A. and Rudner, M. (2012), *Assessing Cyber Threats to Canadian Infrastructure*, Ottawa, Canadian Security Intelligence Service (CSIS): Occasional Paper – Priority Issue 1, p. 25.

Gertz, B. (2013), "Islamist Terrorists Shifting from Web to Social Media" [Online], October 23, 2013, available at http://freebeacon.com/islamist-terrorists-shifting-from-web-to-social-media/

Gulsby, K. and Desa, A. (2014), "The New Al-Qaeda: Decentralization and Recruitment," *The Security and Intelligence Studies Journal*, vol 1, no 2.

Harris-Hogan, S. (2012), "Australian Neo-Jihadist Terrorism: Mapping the Network and Cell Analysis Using Wiretap Evidence," *Studies in Conflict and Terrorism*, vol. 35, no. 4, pp. 298–314.

Hoffman, B. (2006), *Inside Terrorism, Revised and Expanded Edition*, New York: Columbia University Press.

Hussein, F. (2005) *Al-Zarqawi–al-Qaeda's Second Generation, in Arabic*.

Ilardi, GJ. (2013), "Interviews with Canadian Radicals," *Studies in Conflict and Terrorism*, vol. 36, no. 9, pp. 713–738.

Ilyas, M. (2013), "Islamist groups in the UK and recruitment," *Journal of Terrorism Research*, vol. 4, no. 2, pp. 37–48.

International Monetary Fund (2003), *Suppressing the Financing of Terrorism: A Handbook for Legislative Drafting* [Online], available at www.imf.org/external/pubs/nft/2003/SFTH/pdf/SFTH.pdf (Accessed September 25, 2015).

Jacobson, M. (2010), "Terrorist Financing and the Internet," *Studies in Conflict and Terrorism*, vol. 33, no. 4, pp. 353–363.

Jarvis, L., Macdonald, S. and Nouri, L. (2014), "The Cyberterrorism Threat: Findings from a Survey of Researchers," *Studies in Conflict and Terrorism*, vol. 37, no. 1, pp. 68–90.

Kaya, A. (2010), "Individualization and Institutionalization of Islam in Europe in the Age of Securitization," *Insight Turkey*, vol. 12, no. 1, p. 53.

Kjuka, D. (2013), "Digital Jihad: Inside Al-Qaeda's Social Networks," *The Atlantic*, March 6, 2013, available at www.theatlantic.com/international/archive/2013/03/digital-jihad-inside-al-qaedas-social-networks/273761/ (Accessed September 25, 2015).

Klausen, J., Barbieri, E.T., Reichlin-Melnick, A. and Zelin, A. (2012), "The YouTube Jihadists: A Social Network Analysis of Al-Muhajiroun's Propaganda Campaign," *Perspectives on Terrorism*, vol. 5, no. 1.

Kleinmann, S. (2012), "Radicalization of Homegrown Sunni Militants in the United States: Comparing Converts and Non-Converts," *Studies in Conflict and Terrorism*, vol. 35, no. 4, pp. 278–297.

Koplowitz, H. (2013), "US Formally Admits Killing Anwar Al-Awlaki, 3 Other Citizens, In Drone Strikes," *International Business Times*, May 23, available at www.ibtimes.com/us-formally-admits-killing-anwar-al-awlaki-3-other-citizens-drone-strikes-full-text-1275805 (Accessed September 25, 2015).

Lamb, C. (2010), "Jihad Janes spread fear in suburban America," *The Sunday Times*, March 14, 2010, available at www.thesundaytimes.co.uk/sto/news/world_news/Americas/article25673.ece (Accessed September 25, 2015).

Lennings, C., Amon, K., Brummert, H. and Lennings, N. (2010), "Grooming for Terror: The Internet and Young People," *Psychiatry, Psychology and Law*, vol. 17, no. 3, available at www.tandfonline.com/doi/full/10.1080/13218710903566979#.U7_0JECGcSU (Accessed September 25, 2015).

Levitt, M. (2004), "Charitable Organizations and Terrorist Financing: A War on Terror Status Check" [Online], *The Washington Institute*, March 19, 2004, available at www.washingtoninstitute.org/policy-analysis/view/charitable-organizations-and-terrorist-financing-a-war-on-terror-status-che (Accessed September 25, 2015).

Lia, B. (2007), *Architect of Global Jihad: The Life of Al-Qaida Strategist Abu Musa'ab al-Suri*, Oxford: Oxford University Press.

Lia, B. (2008), "Doctrines for Jihadi Terrorist Training," *Terrorism and Political Violence*, vol. 20, no. 4, pp. 518–542.

Masciandaro, D. (2004), *Global Financial Crime: Terrorism, Money Laundering and Offshore Centres*, Burlington, VT: Ashgate.

Moniquet, C. (2013), The Involvement of Salafism/Wahhabism in the Support and Supply of Arms to Rebel Groups Around the World, European Parliament Directorate for External Policies, available at https://docs.google.com/viewer?a=v&pid=sites&srcid=ZGVmYXVsdGRvbWFpbnxoYWlkZXJub3Rlc3xneDo3NDEwMDI3NjViZTNjODZm (Accessed September 25, 2015).

Moon, D. (2010), "Anwar al-Al-Awlaki: Translator of jihad," *Asia Times* [Hong Kong], January 7, 2010.

Musawi, M.A. (2010), *Cheering for Osama. How Jihadists Use Internet Discussion Forums*, Quilliam Foundation, available at www.quilliamfoundation.org/wp/wp-content/uploads/publications/free/cheering-for-osama-how-jihadists-use-the-internet-forums.pdf (Accessed September 25, 2015).

Musharbash, Y. (2005), "The Future of Terrorism: What al-Qaida Really Wants," *Der Spiegel*, August 12, 2005, available at www.spiegel.de/international/the-future-of-terrorism-what-al-qaida-really-wants-a-369448.html (Accessed September 25, 2015).

Nelson, F. (2014), "Terrorism in the UK: Social Media is Now the Biggest Jihadi Training Camp of Them All," *Daily Telegraph*, April 25, 2014, available at www.telegraph.co.uk/news/uknews/terrorism-in-the-uk/10786205/Terrorism-in-the-UK-Social-media-is-now-the-biggest-jihadi-training-camp-of-them-all.html (Accessed September 25, 2015).

Nesser, P. (2004), "Jihad in Europe: A Survey of the motivations for Sunni Islamist terrorism in post-millennium," Norwegian Institute for Defence Research, Report FFI/RAPPORT-2004/01/1146, available at www.ffi.no/no/Rapporter/04-01146.pdf (Accessed September 25, 2015).

Nesser, P. (2008), "How did Europe's Global Jihadis Obtain Training for their Militant Causes?," *Terrorism and Political Violence*, vol. 20, no. 2, pp. 234–256.

Nuraniyah, N. (2014), "Online Extremism: Challenges and Counter-Measures," RSIS Commentary No. 218/2014, S. Rajaratnam School of International Studies, Nanyang Technological University, Singapore, available at www.rsis.edu.sg/rsis-publication/cens/co14218-online-extremism-challenges-and-counter-measures/#.VgaEOc5nKt8 (Accessed September 25, 2015).

Phares, W. (2005), *Future Jihad: Terrorist Strategies Against the West*, New York: Palgrave Macmillan.

Roy, O. (2004), *Globalised Islam: The Search for a New Ummah*, London, Hurst & Co.

Rudner, M. (2006), "Using Financial Intelligence Against the Funding of Terrorism," *International Journal of Intelligence and Counter Intelligence*, vol. 19, no. 1, pp. 32–58.

Rudner, M. (2013a), "Al Qaeda's Twenty-Year Strategic Plan: The Current Phase of Global Terror," *Studies in Conflict and Terrorism*, vol. 36, no. 12, pp. 953–980.

Rudner, M. (2013b), "Cyber-Threats to Critical National Infrastructure: An Intelligence Challenge," *International Journal of Intelligence and Counter Intelligence*, vol. 26, no. 3, pp. 455–458.

Sageman, M. (2009), "Confronting al-Qaeda: Understanding the Threat in Afghanistan and Beyond," *Testimony to the Senate Foreign Relations Committee*, October 7, 2009, available at www.fpri.org/articles/2009/10/confronting-al-qaeda-understanding-threat-afghanistan-and-beyond (Accessed September 25, 2015).

Sageman, M. (2011), *Leaderless Jihad. Terror Networks in the Twenty-first Century*, Philadelphia: University of Pennsylvania Press.

Saudi, G. (2014), Al-Qaeda women use websites to entice youth, March 20, 2014, available at http://english.alarabiya.net/en/News/middle-east/2014/03/20/Al-Qaeda-women-use-websites-to-entice-youth.html (Accessed September 25, 2015).

Seymour, B. (2008), "Global Money Laundering," *Journal of Applied Security Research*, vol. 3, no. 3, pp. 373–387.

Simon Wiesenthal Center (2010), *Digital Terrorism and Hate Report 2010*.

Soriano, M.R.T. (2012), "Between the Pen and the Sword: The Global Islamic Media Front in the West," *Terrorism and Political Violence*, vol. 24, no. 5, pp. 769–786.

Springer, D., Regens, J. and Edger, D. (2009), *Islamic Radicalism and Global Jihad*, Washington, DC: Georgetown University Press.

Stalinsky, S. and Sosnow, R. (2014), *From Al-Qaeda to The Islamic State (ISIS), Jihadi Groups Engage in Cyber Jihad: Beginning With 1980s Promotion Of Use Of 'Electronic Technologies' Up to Today's Embrace of Social Media to Attract a New Jihadi Generation*, Middle East Media Research Institute (MEMRI) Jihad *and* Terrorism Studies Project, available at www.memri.org/report/en/0/0/0/0/0/0/8250.htm (Accessed September 25, 2015).

Sydow, C. (2012), "'Leaderless Jihad': German Islamists Target Youth on the Internet," *Spieel Online International*, November 1, 2012, available at www.spiegel.de/inter

national/germany/german-jihadists-target-youth-on-the-internet-study-finds-a-864797.html (Accessed September 25, 2015).

Taylor, M. and Ramsay, G. (2010), *Violent Radical Content and the Relationship between Ideology and Behaviour, in Countering Violent Extremist Narratives*, The Hague, National Coordinator for Counterterrorism.

The Netherlands General Intelligence and Security Service (2012), "Jihadism on the Web, a Breeding ground for Jihad in the Modern Age" [Online], available at www.aivd.nl/english/publications-press/@2873/jihadism-web/ (Accessed September 25, 2015).

The Netherlands National Coordinator for Counterterrorism (NCTb) (2007), "Jihadis and the Internet" [Online], available at www.investigativeproject.org/documents/testimony/226.pdf (Accessed September 25, 2015).

Travis, A. (2012), "Internet biggest breeding ground for violent extremism, ministers warn," *The Guardian*, February 6, 2012, available at www.theguardian.com/uk/2012/feb/06/internet-violent-extremism-breeding-ground (Accessed September 25, 2015).

Tucker, D. (2010), "Jihad Dramatically Transformed? Sageman on Jihad and the Internet," *Homeland Security Affairs*, vol. 6, no. 1, p. 4.

U.K. House of Commons (2012), "Home Affairs Committee: Roots of Violent Radicalization," February 6, 2012, available at www.publications.parliament.uk/pa/cm201012/cmselect/cmhaff/1446/1446.pdf (Accessed September 25, 2015).

Ungerleider, N. (2013), "How Al-Shabaab Uses The Internet To Recruit Americans," *Fast Company*, September 26, 2013, available at www.fastcompany.com/3018339/how-al-shabaab-uses-the-internet-to-recruit-americans (Accessed September 25, 2015).

Varner, J. (2007), "Is there a Terrorist Threat to our Critical Infrastructure," *Frontline Security*, available at http://inhomelandsecurity.com/is_there_a_terrorist_threat_to/ (Accessed September 25, 2015).

Vidino, L. (2005), *Al Qaeda in Europe: The New Battleground of International Jihad*, New York, Prometheus Books.

Weimann, G. (2004), "www.Terror.Net. How Modern Terrorism Uses the Internet," *United States Institute of Peace Special Report 116*, available at www.usip.org/sites/default/files/sr116.pdf (Accessed September 25, 2015).

Weimann, G. (2011), "Cyber-Fatwas and Terrorism," *Studies in Conflict and Terrorism*, vol. 34, no. 10, pp. 765–781.

Weimann, G. (2012), "Press release: 'Friend' Request from Al-Qaeda," [Online], available at http://newmedia-eng.haifa.ac.il/?p=5680 (Accessed September 25, 2015).

Whitehead, T. (2014), "Self Styled 'Father of Terrorism' Facing Jail," *Daily Telegraph*, July 5, 2014, available at www.telegraph.co.uk/news/uknews/terrorism-in-the-uk/10947387/Self-styled-father-of-terrorism-facing-jail.html (Accessed September 25, 2015).

Warrick, J. (2013), "Private Donations Give Edge to Islamists in Syria, Officials Say," *Washington Post*, September 22, 2013, available at www.washingtonpost.com/world/national-security/private-donations-give-edge-to-islamists-in-syria-officials-say/2013/09/21/a6c783d2-2207-11e3-a358-1144dee636dd_story.html (Accessed September 25, 2015).

Zelin, A. (2013a), "The State of Global Jihad Online: A Qualitative, Quantitative, and Cross-Lingual Analysis," *New America Foundation* [Online], available at www.washingtoninstitute.org/uploads/Documents/opeds/Zelin20130201-NewAmericaFoundation.pdf (Accessed September 25, 2015).

Zelin, A. (2013b), "Foreign Jihadists in Syria: Tracking Recruitment Networks," *Washington Institute for Near East Policy*, December 19, 2013 [Online], available at www.washingtoninstitute.org/policy-analysis/view/foreign-jihadists-in-syria-tracking-recruitment-networks (Accessed September 25, 2015).

Zelin, A., Neumann, P.R., Maher, S. and ICSR_Centre (2013), "Up to 11,000 Foreign Fighters in Syria; Steep Rise Among Western Europeans," *International Centre for the Study of Radicalisation*, December 17, 2013 [Online], available at http://icsr.info/2013/12/icsr-insight-11000-foreign-fighters-syria-steep-rise-among-western-europeans/ (Accessed September 25, 2015).

2 The call to Jihad
Charismatic preachers and the Internet

Angela Gendron

Introduction

The activities of charismatic preachers promote "violent radicalization"[1] by encouraging their followers in the diaspora to engage in violent extremism, whether as foreign fighters in insurgencies abroad or in acts of homegrown terrorism. Despite the various explanatory models that confront counterterrorism authorities in their attempts to understand the phenomenon, the inspirational role of these charismatic preachers in promoting violent extremism warrants further analysis and understanding. By examining the basis for the authority and influence of certain charismatic preachers, particularly the late Anwar al-Awlaki,[2] this chapter aims to prompt further empirical research into an aspect of radicalization that has been relatively neglected and that may offer opportunities for countering violent extremism.

The first section of the chapter provides a brief overview of existing research approaches to radicalization. The current wave of radical Salafi-Jihadist activities is then set within an historical continuum of resurgent militant Islam as a prelude to an examination of "charisma" in the current context and the prerequisite conditions for the exercise of charismatic power and authority to radicalize violent extremists. The remainder of the chapter develops and describes this process and the charismatic preachers' influence over susceptible individuals based on examples and evidence from recent investigations. In particular, it examines the role played by the Internet and considers whether and how the Internet has strengthened the "charismatic bond" between leaders and followers.

Radicalization: research approaches

The need to understand the radicalization phenomenon—that is, when, why, and how people living in a democracy become radicalized and susceptible to violent extremism—has been at the center of academic and public debate for some years. Dalgaard-Nielson (2010) provides a useful summary of the empirical, social movement, and social network theories, which are briefly referred to in this chapter. They focus on different levels of analysis and different aspects of the radicalization phenomenon, but are mutually complementary. Collectively these studies support the view that no single explanation or cause can explain the radicalization phenomenon. Rather, a range of psychological, social, and environmental factors in combination renders some individuals more susceptible to radicalization than others (Borum 2011). Not only do motivations differ, but the paths taken from radicalization to militancy are also varied (Stern 2004; Pantucci 2011; Feldman 2013). The contention here is that charismatic preachers can be highly influential in accelerating and guiding this process.

Research has not yet explained why it is that only a minority of individuals exposed to the same societal structural influences and opportunities turn to violence nor indeed why those with divergent formative experiences do so—Muslim converts, for example. Keppel (2004) suggests that indoctrination through radical preachers may make the difference. Support for the influence of a charismatic leader, spiritual advisor, or trusted peer as a "trigger" factor in initiating and driving the radicalization process can also be found in the work of Tomas Precht (2007: 50). A study by the Dutch National Coordinator for Counterterrorism (NCBt 2007: 75–76) refers to the "devastating effect" (on those disposed to listen) of the kind of preaching for which Sheikh Abdullah al-Faisal Omar Bakri Mohammed, Abu Hamza al-Masri, and Abu Qatada became notorious. Sheikh Anwar al-Awlaki was perhaps the most measured and persuasive of them all in terms of his ability to relate to young Muslims in the West.

In questioning how it is that such men have the power to persuade others to do what they otherwise would not, the term "charisma" comes to mind. However, as a recent study by Hofmann (2015) contends, the social scientific concept of charismatic authority is widely misused in terrorism studies and as a consequence research on the subject has been impeded. If we are to understand how religious ideological commitments are instilled [within terrorist groups], it is imperative that more attention be given to analyzing the role of charismatic leaders and forms of authority. Hofmann presents a theoretical framework for measuring the presence of charismatic authority in terrorist groups, based on Max Weber's work on legitimate domination. This chapter draws on this work as well as a study of charismatic authority in new religious movements (Hofmann and Dawson 2014).

Resurgent Islam: extreme radical Islamist movements in historical context

The current wave of radical Islamism is not new but yet another manifestation of a cyclical dynamic of crisis and resurgence which has characterized Islamist movements throughout history. Passive periods of dormancy have been punctuated by periodic religious resurgence and a call for a return to Islamic roots (Lewis 2002). This call has usually gathered momentum when two interrelated conditions were met: the appearance of a charismatic leader, and a society in deep turmoil— perhaps because traditional and legal forms of authority appear impotent in the face of fundamental societal change and the apparent absence of non-violent solutions. Leadership is always a central feature of religious and revolutionary movements but in Islam, which fuses the religious and political realms, the role of the charismatic preacher/leader has been indispensable as the fountainhead and propagator of the revivalist message (cf. Springer et al. 2009).

Now, as in the past, Salafi-Jihadist preachers respond to or capitalize on societal turmoil and crisis situations in both foreign and Muslim lands. In his book *What Went Wrong*, Bernard Lewis (2002) argues that Muslim majority countries have failed to keep pace with Western counterparts and, over recent centuries, have occupied the lower rungs of any indices of human development be it literacy, scientific research, or industrial diversification (see also UNDP 2002). It has been said that "Islamist ideologues strive to reconstruct the past, within a present crisis setting, in order to shape the future" (Dekmejian 1985). In explaining the failure of Islam to achieve prosperity and opportunity for Muslims in the modern world, extremist preachers interpret regional and world events as a conspiracy by the West to oppress the world Muslim *ummah* (Arabic: community). The following is an illustrative example:

> This is a war against Islam. It is a war against Muslims and Islam. Not only is it happening worldwide, but it is happening right here in America, that is claiming to be fighting this war for the sake of freedom while it's infringing on the freedom of its own citizens, just because they're Muslims.
> (al-Awlaki 2002)

In response to this perceived enmity, extremist preachers justify the necessity for violent jihad as a legitimate (defensive) response. Furthermore, selected Islamic texts and perverse interpretations are cited to support the claim that only by returning to a "pure" Islam will its power be restored so that it can resume its rightful place in the world and achieve victory over its (infidel) enemies.

Increasing numbers of young Muslims have been leaving Europe, the United States, Canada, Australia, and other Western democracies to join the jihad in foreign lands—an activity that has been described as engaging in "paramilitary tactics in confined theatres of war" (Hegghammer 2010/2011: 55)—notwithstanding considerable efforts by security authorities to stem the "tide." The opportunity to participate in the "defense" of Muslim lands has undoubtedly drawn volunteers who may otherwise have been doubtful about the religious legitimacy of a *global jihad* against the West. For others, however, religious obligation is less of a draw than the chance to participate in an adventure that bestows status and provides a challenging alternative to the boring predictability and disappointments of life in the diaspora. The demonstrable ability of radical Islamist movements to win new recruits, whether for al-Qaeda's global jihad or for Islamic State's traditional territorial jihad, has strengthened concerns in the West about the threat from homegrown terrorism—the likelihood being that at least some of the battle-hardened foreign fighters returning to host countries in the diaspora will have been socialized to continue jihad in the West.

In the past, a failure to communicate with and win the support of the wider Muslim community meant that periodic outbreaks of militant Islam were short-lived (Mus'ab al-Suri 2010: 17). Communicating with the wider Muslim community today is no longer the challenge it once was, given the advent of new information and communication technologies. The distant leadership and hierarchical structure of past Islamist movements have also given way to chain networks within which there are many levels of leadership and a mix of individual, small and disconnected cells as well as open front cooperative warfare. The "leaderless jihad" (Sageman 2008) as it has been called—largely self-radicalized and self-activated cells with minimal, if any, links to any terrorist network whose members come together through a "bottom-up" rather than "top-down" recruitment process (Malet 2015; Pere_in 2015)[3]—resembles the structure envisioned by al-Qaeda strategist Abu-Mus'ab al-Suri in his major work *The Call in Iraq and Syria to Global Islamic Resistance* (Lia 2015). The potential threat to the West posed by the "leaderless" model and the importance of charismatic preachers were demonstrated by the example of the "Toronto 18," a Canadian terrorist group, inspired by al-Qaeda, that planned a series of attacks in the Province of Ontario in 2006. Its members were radicalized in part by watching the sermons of Anwar al-Awlaki online (McCoy and Knight 2015).

Islamic State's propaganda draws extensively on the writings of al-Qaeda strategists and their global jihadist theory of guerrilla war, politics, and governance, but it has been more effective than al-Qaeda in its use of the Internet and social media to win recruits. Large numbers of volunteers have been attracted to fight in Iraq and Syria (Lia 2015) in defense of territorial gains and the newly established Caliphate. Many are seemingly drawn by an intense and brutal campaign, which is reminiscent of the methods employed by al-Qaeda's former leader in Iraq, Abu Mus'ab al-Zarqawi. Although al-Qaeda disputes the appointment of al-Baghdadi as Caliph and leader of the Muslim world, nevertheless, it was an event anticipated in Stage Five of al-Qaeda's Twenty Year Strategic Plan (Rudner 2013), and charismatic preachers associated with al-Qaeda have taken advantage of the struggle in Iraq and Syria (graphically recorded in the field on videos and cell phone images) to promote the Salafi-Jihadist worldview and justify violence against the perceived enemies of Islam, including "taqfir" Muslims.

Whether particular Salafi-Jihadist preachers are associated with Islamic State, al-Qaeda, or any other militant jihadist group makes little difference to the analysis in this chapter, since all justify violence to achieve the same end goal and share the same radicalization and recruitment techniques and strategies (Engel 2015a). Despite its *traditional, defensive jihad* against the "near enemy" in Muslim lands, in October 2014 Islamic State called for a *global jihad* against the so-called "far enemy," that is, the West. This was a call to jihad intended to unite jihadist factions by capitalizing on al-Qaeda's reach and influence:

> [Muslims] wherever you may be, hinder those who want to harm your brothers and state as much as you can. The best thing you can do is strive to your best and kill any disbeliever, whether he be French, American, or from any of their allies
>
> (Bakier 2014)

"Charismatic" power and authority[4]

"Charisma" was a topic much studied in the 1960s and 1970s (e.g., Tucker 1970; Conger and Kanungo 1988) as a force in politics and central to what constitutes both political and business leadership. Max Weber's (1946) work on legitimate domination (see also Eisenstadt 1968: 48) conceived three pure types of authority: traditional, rational-legal, and charismatic. The last of these was not conferred by tradition or position but accorded because others recognized that a particular individual was in some way so special that he had an "inner authority." Weber noted that "it is the recognition on the part of those subject to authority which is decisive for the validity of charisma" (Eisenstadt 1968: 48). Recent research has focused on this charismatic bond between leader and follower rather than the personal qualities or characteristics of individual charismatic leaders (Madsen and Snow 1991). Further, the difficulty in quantifying or qualifying "charisma" (Jordan 2009), as well as "charismatic authority" as defined by Weber, has prompted Hoffman (2015) to develop a theoretical framework for measuring the presence of charismatic authority in terrorist groups.

Charisma is associated with hero worship and demigod status; those who possess it are described as captivating and able to galvanize others into action. The one factor that emerges from the various studies from the 1960s through to the present (see Tucker 1970; Anderson 2013) is that the "charismatic" individual is someone who is gifted at reading other people and eliciting from them a particular response.

In defining charisma, or rather explaining the authority that charismatic figures exert, Weber refers to a certain quality that sets the charismatic leader apart from ordinary men: a quality that is perceived as having supernatural or superhuman elements or, at the least, exceptional powers not available to others. Weber's social-scientific concept of charismatic authority, which was developed within a Western sociological framework, needs to be adapted to the normative and cultural context of Islamic societies in which only a prophet can directly receive transcendental truths: For Muslims, the definitive and last of these was the Prophet Mohammad. Therefore, the charismatic authority of preachers in Islam is not transcendent in the strictly divine sense but derives from the *perception* of followers that preachers have the ability to *interpret* Allah's will. Anwar al-Awlaki, for example, was not one of the *ulema* (Arabic: learned scholars) but derived his charismatic authority by virtue of his avowed commitment to and study of Islam's texts and traditions, his exceptional body of specialist knowledge and oratorical talents, which convinced his followers (and perhaps himself) that he was divinely inspired.

The decentralization of sacred authority in Islam means that the *ulema (learned scholars)* do not have a monopoly on sacred authority. This allows for "ordinary" people to become "extraordinary" provided they are accepted as such by their followers. Charismatic types range from the "fire-brand" to the "scholastic," which points to the fact that each meet different needs and respond to their followers in different social situations. Charismatic authority is a relationship that crucially depends upon the recognition of the preacher's exceptional gifts by his followers.

The role of charismatic preachers

The role of Salafi-Jihadist preachers is to "awaken" potential activists to their particular worldview by broadcasting aims and interpreting Islamic texts in ways that make them accessible to target audiences, especially those in the West, who may have little knowledge of their faith and speak no Arabic, the language of the Qu'ran. In order to shift perceptions, values, and beliefs toward Salafi-Jihadism, they must identify and exploit the preexisting sentiments of potential recruits by taking advantage of their religious ignorance, personal grievances, and vulnerabilities. For example, they present Muslims worldwide as the oppressed victims of the West: Only by practicing a purer form of Islam and fulfilling the individual obligation of jihad, will Islam be restored to its former power in the world. Western civilization and its "immoral" ways and institutions must be rejected in order to identify with and fight on behalf of the Muslim (Open Source Center 2011). Such "victimization" narratives are common to all violent, extremist groups regardless of their ideological or social claims.

If preachers are to be persuasive and win adherents to this extreme interpretation of Islam, they must ground their message in traditional texts and the *hadith* in order to provide the necessary reassurance as to its morality and religious legitimacy. Jihad is presented as a simple solution to all social and personal problems, intrinsically beneficial in its own right, and providing a direct path to redemption and paradise for the fortunate few.

Overcoming the moral doubts of potential recruits about using violence to achieve a noble goal is a key challenge for preachers: Radicalized individuals who are to become jihadis must believe that violence against the enemy is justifiable and that it will achieve a higher moral condition for the group to which they belong, that is, the world Muslim *ummah*. Fighting for the good of others is a significant motivator for many volunteers who are assured that jihad is a religious duty, not an act of terrorism.

Teachers, spiritual guides, and ideologues such as Abu Muhammad al-Maqdisi, an al-Qaeda supporter, and Yusuf Qaradawi, the spiritual leader of the Muslim Brotherhood, have a faithful following but are not "front-line" preachers in the sense of being tasked to radicalize and recruit young Muslims using the rhetorical and manipulative techniques of the propagandist. Al-Maqdisi, a Salafist respected for his pronouncements on the legitimacy of certain actions in support of militant jihad, has not supported Islamic State's campaign in Iraq and Syria, and Qaradawi has declared the caliphate established by Islamic State to be legally void.

The principal means by which young Muslims in the diaspora are exposed to radical revisionist ideas is no longer through sermons delivered in the mosques, but via the Internet and other powerful information and communications technologies (Neumann 2013), which have played a major role in increasing the number of jihadi groups. It is still not entirely clear what role the Internet plays in the process of radicalization. Certain charismatic preachers have used these same technologies to access, and be accessible to, a worldwide audience, thus achieving international status. At the global level they convey to audiences worldwide, in an intelligible and digestible form, the political and religious doctrine of the organizations they serve. They act as "mediators" between the sometimes dense ideological pronouncements of the movement's leaders and particular target audiences, especially those in the West.

The decentralization of Islam associated with new information and communications technologies and organizational changes have further empowered rather than marginalized charismatic preachers. They can now influence and facilitate the radicalization of "self-recruiting" cells at every stage by posting their sermons, lectures, and other multimedia materials on social media and dedicated jihadist websites. This is the *content* that motivates, justifies, and drives the radicalization process. The Internet has provided preachers with new opportunities to expose potential recruits to their extreme interpretation of Salafi-Jihadism and in some respects help to counter the lack of unity and factionalism resulting from what is now a more decentralized Islam.

The Internet was a force multiplier for the late Anwar al-Awlaki who was adept at exploiting its potential for outreach. He remains an influential and enduring presence despite his death in a 2011 American drone strike in Yemen. A YouTube search on al-Awlaki in August 2015 produced 40,000 hits (New York Times Magazine 2015), and his fifty-three CD series on the life of the Prophet Muhammad was once a bestseller among English-speaking Muslims. His digital legacy is demonstrated by the popularity of the materials he posted online, which continue to be downloaded and remain influential in the radicalization process. Many of those who have been apprehended in the last few years and charged with terrorist offences in the West, as well as those who have volunteered to fight abroad, are known to have accessed Awlaki's online sermons (McCoy and Knight 2015).

Individuals who access this material or engage with preachers in interactive forums will be driven by different motivations that will determine which, if any, of the many possible paths they take from radicalization to militancy. The key role of the Salafi-Jihadist preacher possessed of the requisite knowledge, skills, and aptitude, is to identify those drivers and tailor the message accordingly in order to guide the individual (and through the individual the group, if he leads one) from passive radicalism to violent militancy. The preacher's online presence and participation on interactive sites enable him to identify, manipulate, and exploit the sentiments and needs of those who are susceptible and vulnerable. There is considerable pressure on individuals to conform to the group consensus. If the group has a charismatic leader, an individual's identity and morality will be subordinated to that of the group.

Preconditions or triggers for radicalization

Many researchers believe that a "trigger" or event of some kind may ignite or accelerate the radicalization process—for example, the death of a parent. Precht and Keppel postulated that the trigger could be the influence of a charismatic preacher or spiritual adviser but according to a study of new religious movements by Hofmann and Dawson (2014), charismatic authority alone is not sufficient to move an individual or group to commit acts of violence; apocalyptic or world-rejecting beliefs and social isolation must be present. The revivalist message is one of world rejection (the West and other non-believers) as presented by Salafi-Jihadist preachers who promote an ideology that is framed as an apocalyptic battle between the world of war (*dar al harb*) and the world of peace (*dar al Islam*) that justifies violence, (terrorism and guerrilla insurgency) as necessary to restore the purity and power of an Islam corrupted by the *jahiliya* (Arabic: state of ignorance), which prevails in the Muslim world and in the West. The message that a war is being waged on Islam is a narrative that is dictated by the reality of history as well as the particular interpretation of events and the worldview of past and present Islamist ideologues.

Social isolation factors too (Hofmann and Dawson 2014) are applicable: Salafi-Jihadist preachers urge their followers to distance themselves from those who do not accept their interpretation of the Qu'ran and encourage followers to adopt rules of dress and behavior that set them apart from family and friends. The resulting isolation makes individuals more vulnerable because, as social movement theorists emphasize, "people make decisions, especially important ones, in a social context by discussing them with trusted others" (Wiktorowicz 2005). Those who are trusted by radicalizing Muslims in a situation of increasing isolation are fellow cell members who are often related and well-known to each other: like-minded others whom they meet online on radical social media sites and the charismatic preachers who are grooming them online. Extreme beliefs are thereby affirmed and reinforced without the moderating influence of family and friends, of mainstream preachers, or society more broadly.

Paradoxically, the success of charismatic preachers is likely, in part, to be due to the deficiencies of those many mainstream preachers who come from countries such as Saudi Arabia and Yemen who have neither the necessary communication skills nor cultural understanding for building a rapport with their congregants in the Western diaspora. This opens the way for radical preachers like Anwar al-Awlaki who, apart from being proficient in Arabic, the language of Islamic texts, are able to express themselves in the vernacular of English-speaking audiences, to understand and empathize with young Muslims, and know what will resonate with them and what might render certain messages directly translated from the Arabic bizarre or anachronistic. This gives them instant credibility and access to Muslim youths for whom idiomatic speech is a cultural norm. Jihadist websites now have sections in Western languages that are designed to win recruits from Europe and North America for jihad in conflict areas (Europol 2010: 15).

Anwar al-Awlaki thrived on the celebrity status and media attention he received in Washington by virtue of being an excellent communicator. He became more radicalized and extreme as his "oratorical career progressed but he was a risk-taker who did not practice what he preached (Shane 2015).

Radicalization: demand and supply

A significant contributory factor regarding the accelerating pace of the radicalization process is the role the Internet plays as a catalyst and force multiplier.

On the demand side, susceptible individuals are looking for information and materials on Islam—perhaps because of a crisis of identity or a sense of injustice (e.g., von Knop and Weimann 2008; Aly 2009). This information gathering process, which is a critical first step along the path to radicalization, is facilitated by the Internet, which provides young Muslims with opportunities and the means by which young Muslims are exposed to radical revisionist ideas.

Trusted peer relationships and kinship are important to the radicalization and recruitment process, because they provide a secure physical environment in which to share and test ideas. The Internet too provides support in that it is a space in which individuals can easily and safely find like-minded others in the virtual world. However, a commonly held assumption that the Internet accelerates the process of radicalization or promotes self-radicalization without physical contact with others has been challenged by a RAND report (von Behr et al. 2013). The Internet provides opportunities for exposure but it may not be the main factor driving recruitment and radicalization.

On the supply side, the Internet is the principal means by which radical preachers disseminate the information and propaganda that shapes the beliefs of young Muslims who then go on to seek out and join "virtual communities" of like-minded others—described by Jerrold Post as "virtual communities of hatred." Jihadist propaganda justifies the organization's existence and activities to the broader Muslim support base, as well as documenting the "evidence" of the West's depravity to support its interpretation of world events and the necessity for jihad.

The demand side

A range of psychological, social, and environmental factors renders some individuals more vulnerable than others to the grooming techniques of preachers as indicated by empirical studies that seek to identify the different drivers, motivations, and paths leading to violent radicalization.

de Poot and Sonnenschein (2011), for instance, identified four typologies of activists and the roles they perform in radical groups. Of these, it is the idealists who tend to be the group leaders and, as such, critical to the "bottom-up" outreach and recruitment process (Dalgaard-Nielsen 2010). It is they who motivate and recruit others within their family and social networks. According to this study, idealists are predominantly driven by social, external factors, rather than personal vulnerabilities, needs, and experiences, and it is they who are the most likely to turn to religiously inspired ideology to explain and provide solutions to perceived injustices in the world. Their views are shaped not by personal experiences, but by television images, videos, audiotapes, websites, online sermons, or the stories of others. They are therefore prime targets for the manipulative attentions of preachers.

Khosrokhavar (2009: 233–235) also identified distinct personality types though he categorized them differently as "missionary, macho, upholder of justice, adventurer and existential man:" a typology that clearly indicates the various ways in which preachers might tailor their message to maximize its appeal. Islamic State's territorial jihad is likely to attract several of these identified types and is certainly being used by radical preachers to justify violence and recruit volunteers. Muslim youth have been attracted to fighting fronts on the Afghanistan-Pakistan border, Yemen, Somalia, Iraq, Libya, Nigeria, and Syria, which have seen an influx of volunteers from the West who have chosen to fight abroad rather than carry out attacks in their host countries as part of a global jihad.

We are not yet in a position to determine why societal or individual-level drivers lead to the radicalization of some individuals but not others, in part because of the lack of solid empirical data. The following four main contributory factors cited in a Quilliam Foundation Briefing paper (2010: 3) currently inform the UK Government's counter radicalization program "Channel":

a   exposure to an ideology that sanctions, legitimizes, or requires violence often by providing a compelling but fabricated narrative of contemporary politics and recent history;
b   exposure to people or groups who can directly and persuasively articulate that ideology and relate it to aspects of a person's own background and life history;
c   a crisis of identity that might be triggered by a range of personal issues and experiences including racism, discrimination, deprivation, criminality, family breakdown, or separation;
d   a range of perceived grievances, real or imagined, to which no effective non-violent response seems credible.

The supply side

The four "susceptibility" factors listed above are neither definitive nor uncontested, but they indicate the opportunities available to charismatic preachers who prey on the aspirations and needs of their targets by becoming that "trusted other," and providing carefully timed explanations and solutions during the radicalization and recruitment process.

Two separate tendencies together form contemporary radical Islam: the violent jihad and the radical *dawa* (meaning the "Call"; NCBt 2007). Radical Salafi-fundamentalist movements exist, which are outspokenly hostile to the values of Western democracy but which eschew violence: "The ideology of non-violent Islamists is broadly the same as that of violent Islamists; they disagree only on tactics."[5]

Salafism, a traditionalist variant of radical Islam, does not necessarily lead to religiously legitimated violence (Chrisafis 2013), but it does have the effect of reducing resistance to jihadism because it shares the same end goal even if, generally speaking, by non-violent means. Salafist "Callers to Islam" (*Du'aat*) come in many guises but the function of self-styled Imams, clerics, preachers, ideologues, and propagandists is to "call" as many Muslims (and non-Muslims) as possible to become active practitioners of the faith: to return non-practicing Muslims to avowal and persuade non-Muslims to convert.

Dawa, the proselytization of Islam by non-violent means, is generally accepted by many, if not all, Muslims as a commendable activity. Sheikh Yusuf al-Qaradawi's (2002: 242) aim is to bring about "a general Islamic awakening to awake minds, revive hearts and bring new life to people." He is interested in the broader mission of spreading the message of Islam—to reform first the individual, then the larger society, and eventually, the entire world through "the tongue, pen, and every contemporary legitimate medium, be it recorded, audio, or visual" (International Union of Muslim Scholars, 2014). However, Qaradawi's peaceful gradualism is under strain given the more tangible and immediate results of Islamic State's campaign, which has established a caliphate and implemented Islamic law. Disillusionment with the slow, gradual *dawa* Qaradawi advocates has led some Brotherhood factions to call for violence.

Salafi-Jihadist preachers who support militant Islam's senior leadership, however, propagate an extreme interpretation of Sunni Islam that is often in conflict with mainstream Islam. At a broader community level, extremist preachers play their part in inciting agitation against perceived "injustices" as a way to foster Muslim identification with and support for the militant jihadist cause. However, charismatic preachers have well-honed techniques for "awakening" young radicalized Muslims to Salafi-Jihadism and turning them into militant activists eager to demonstrate their commitment to the faith by undertaking jihad, whether global or traditional, at home or abroad.

To make their message accessible to the masses, they articulate it directly and persuasively in the language and idiom of their target audience, tailoring the message to meet particular sensitivities, needs, and circumstances in order to prime the beliefs and shape the perceptions of young Muslims to conform with those of militant jihadism. World events are interpreted in ways that justify the necessity for violence as in the case of Islamic State's insurgency in Iraq and Syria for which significant numbers of radicalized Muslims have been recruited by online preachers in the West prior to their departure (PET 2014: 3).

Preachers have used the concept of jihad (from the Arabic *Jihada* meaning to strive, struggle, or exert oneself) to give their political objectives a cloak of religiosity. The concept dates back to the earliest stages of Islam but because Islamic sources have defined the term broadly, it has always been open to interpretation to meet particular perceptions and needs.[6] A distinction is drawn by some scholars between the "greater jihad"—the spiritual struggle against one's own passions to strive in the path of Allah (*jihad sabil Allah)* and the "lesser jihad" of warfare. The greater jihad is a term little used by Muslims themselves (Peters 1996: 116; Firestone 1999: 139–140) and the veracity of the hadith supposedly referring to the Prophet Muhammed's injunction for Muslims to turn to the greater jihad or spiritual struggle following the success of his military campaign, was disputed by Ibn Tamiyah.[7]

Salafism claims that each individual in the community has a responsibility to wage jihad (*jihad al-ayn*) when Muslims are under direct or indirect attack (Picken 2015: 126). Armed jihad against the enemy under current circumstances (i.e., the

West's war on Islam) is an individual duty (*fard 'ayn*) for every Muslim because the ummah is under direct and indirect attack.[8]

Despite being a defensive response, it has been used by a number of Salafi-jihadist preachers, leaders, and ideologues to justify violence to reclaim former Muslim territory even those that now have very small minority Muslim populations (e.g., Burma and the Philippines). Osama bin Laden justified his attacks on the West as a defensive response to America's "war on terrorism" in Afghanistan though the 9/11 attacks were as much a means to awaken Muslims in the diaspora to the coming battle between *dar al-harb and dar al-Islam*. Homegrown terrorism is justified as an offensive defense of Islam: an attack on the corrupting influence of the West that is held responsible for the decline in the purity and power of Islam.

Anwar al-Awlaki, a "preeminent "translator of jihad" and importer of al-Qaeda's jihadist ideology, was instrumental in "awakening" Muslim youth in the diaspora to al-Qaeda's interpretation of Islam and the necessity for a global Islamic jihad. He was able to translate and interpret original texts in ways that made them accessible to those with a limited religious education or knowledge of Arabic because of his fluency in English and a cultural knowledge of the West derived from having spent his formative years in the USA and returning for higher education.

> Arabic is the international language of jihad. Most of the jihad literature is available only in Arabic and publishers are not willing to take the risk of translating it. The only ones who are spending the money and time translating jihad literature are the Western intelligence services . . . and too bad, they would not be willing to share it with you
>
> (al-Awlaki 2009)[9]

His "charismatic authority" derived from his exceptional religious knowledge as a writer on original Islamic texts, his talent as a motivational speaker and effective communicator, and his "people" skills in terms of his ability to relate to other people, to understand and identify with their needs, and imbue them with a sense of self-worth. He also had the status of a jihadist: one who had spent time in prison and had studied the works of Yusuf al'Uyayree, a preeminent al-Qaeda ideologue, during his incarceration. In his most influential audio lecture "Constants on the Path of Jihad," (Berger 2011), which has been described as a classic of radicalization in the West, Awlaki reinterprets al'Uyayree's jihadist text. He traveled extensively both in the Middle East and the West and was an inspirational speaker much in demand who remains influential to this day.

The importance of information and communications technologies

The Centre for Social Cohesion, a British research institution, has identified three core Internet-based functions performed by jihadist Websites, chatrooms, and social media (Brandon 2008):

- **Online Libraries**: Jihadist websites perform a key role as repositories of lectures by keynote figures in the jihadi pantheon like Abdullah Azzam or Yusuf al'Uyayree; videos prepared by al-Qaeda and other militant groups; and *Nasheeds*, traditional Arabic songs glorifying Islamic violence;[10] much of this material is made available online in English translations from the original Arabic sources.
- **Venue for Preachers**: Jihadist websites offer postings of sermons and tracts by prominent radical Islamist preachers and expositors of jihadism, like Anwar al-Awlaki, Abu Mohammas al-Maqdisi, or Abu Bashir al-Tartusi, which can be readily accessed through the Internet.
- **Forums for Discourse**: Jihadist websites usually host chat rooms, discussion forums, and newsgroups, which facilitate e-conversations among like-minded followers and serve as organizational hubs for planning and coordinating activities addressing key issues; social networking and media sites like Facebook, Muslim, YouTube, MySpace, Twitter, or Flicker create and support online communities that enable jihadists and fellow activists to share information, reinforce bonding, and stimulate group dynamics.[11]

The Internet is also a conveyor belt for endlessly repeated extreme messages and conspiracy theories that go largely unchallenged and thereby acquire a certain veneer of "truth" and acceptability because of constant repetition.

The emergence of what some have called a "digitized ummah" contributes to a homogenization of political attitudes and religious sentiments shaped by a relentless flow of identical messages and images (verbal and graphic) across cyberspace (Kaya 2010: 53). These cyberspace communities, unbounded by territory or civic loyalty, can spawn a virtual radicalism in the Muslim diaspora. Internet-based propaganda and incitement can thereby foster a youth subculture of jihadism that challenges the traditional authority of established religious scholars in Muslim communities.

The Internet as a virtual knowledge bank

The Internet has become, in effect, a virtual "knowledge bank" of jihad and a vital resource for preachers and followers alike. Online libraries and discussion forums are the backbone of this "virtual knowledge bank," which contains radical materials posted on dedicated jihadist websites, blogs, and other social media. These can be easily accessed (with a degree of anonymity), by young Muslims in search of information and answers to their questions about Islam. The materials that constitute the "knowledge bank" cover a wide range of topics and are supplied both by radical preachers and the "Internet mujahideen"—an initiative originally encouraged by al-Awlaki. These resources inspire and support the activities and exchanges that take place on social media and are especially useful to the small, self-directed, and probably self-financed cells typical of the "leaderless" model of jihad. By supplying these materials that serve to form and validate beliefs, radical preachers are able to exercise a pernicious and pervasive influence in the radicalization and recruitment process (Weimann 2004, 2011).

Because the authors of this content are recognized by the movement's leaders and followers as having exceptional knowledge and skills, their articulation of religious and political principles, interpretations of original Islamic texts, and admonitions regarding the practice of Salafi-jihadism is accepted as definitive and their perspective on world events a lens for aspiring jihadists. While it is not yet possible to draw any firm conclusions apropos the actual "consumers" of electronic preaching and materials, preliminary research findings point to the particular importance of materials on "religious teaching" rather than "strategy" documents (cf. Brynjar 2007: 226–227; see also Springer et al. 2008, pp. 132–133 and 143–146) as a precursor and trendsetter for radicalization.

Using the Internet and social media to advance the Salafi-Jihadism

Given the frequency with which young people now interact in the virtual world, Anwar al-Awlaki's (2009) statement that "the internet has become a great medium for spreading the call of Jihad and following the news of the mujahideen" is hardly surprising. In order to connect with potential recruits, preachers must have an online presence by participating in Internet forums: These have become powerful magnets and havens for prospective jihadist recruits and neophytes.

The validity and meaning of numbers are difficult to assess, but in *less than two full years* of operation the English-language portal for one such forum, Ansar al-Mujahideen, rapidly amassed nearly 15,000 discussion threads involving some 60,000 individual message posts (Kohlmann 2010: 2). Forum participants dedicate countless hours of their own personal time to translating and redistributing jihadist propaganda and instructional materials, and establishing new online sanctuaries for jihadist activists. The scope and reach of these Internet discussion fora create, in effect, a near-global virtual ummah, linking up jihadi fellow travelers from various communities across Asia, the Middle East, Western Europe, and North America.

As the first web-based militant movement, the Internet gave al-Qaeda, and now Islamic State, a global cyber reach, which was hitherto unattainable. Al-Qaeda's "Electronic Jihad" enabled it to promote the spread of Islamist principles and its political and religious doctrine in support of militant jihadism more widely, attract a continued flow of fighters to the cause, and establish a virtual community of supporters and sympathizers. Islamic State has been even more aggressive in using the Internet and social media sites to communicate its message to Muslims in the West and elsewhere to join its territorial jihad in Iraq and Syria. Its propaganda campaign includes battlefield footage of foreign fighters in action as well as the tweets of jihadists themselves to friends back home who urge others to join them by sending pictures and videos, on YouTube, Instagram, and Twitter, that glorify the fighting: Joining the jihad is presented as more exciting than leading a life of boredom or engaging in petty crime back home.

Anwar al-Awlaki was particularly adept at exploiting new technologies to reach young Muslims in Western democracies. His lecture series "Constants on the Path of Jihad" and his Internet guide "44 Ways to Support Jihad" are among the most frequently downloaded and circulated jihadist materials on the Internet. YouTube features an "Anwar Awlaki Lectures Channel" that "friends" can join. Islamic State propagandists not only tweet in multiple languages but closely monitor and respond to tweets on jihadist sites (Berger and Strathearn 2013; Carter et al. 2014).

Al-Awlaki's participation in social networking sites enabled him to stay directly in touch with followers and track the trigger issues of the day, which he could then exploit for purposes of radicalization and recruitment by giving an Islamic perspective. Jihadist preachers maximize their influence by providing "an after-sales service." This enables them to identify the committed from the merely curious and facilitate their transition to militant activism. It also allows preachers to keep a finger on the pulse, that is, the prevailing "mood" of the community and the events or "triggers" that are causing anger among young Muslims. Those Muslims in the West who enlisted in homegrown jihadist groups from the 1990s onward were prompted to do so by the so-called "big events" that enraged Islamic opinion: for example, the Algerian insurrection, the war in Bosnia, the struggle over Afghanistan, and the invasion of Iraq. These actions enabled jihadists to appropriate religious doctrines that enjoined a militant response to perceived threats to Islam.

Outsourcing propaganda production

Before 9/11, al-Qaeda had one website that published only in the Arabic language. Today, over 4,000 overtly jihadi websites help sustain al-Qaeda's global presence as an ideological movement, and as many again are hosted by radical Islamist groups that support al-Qaeda explicitly (Atwan 2007: 122) or, like Islamic State, share common goals but differ over strategy. A jihadist statement posted on azzam.com in 2002 proclaimed: "The more web sites, the better it is for us. We must make the Internet our tool."

The online English-language jihadist magazine *Inspire*, produced by al-Qaeda in the Arabian Peninsula (AQAP), seems to be focused on broadening al-Qaeda's reach inside the USA (Gulf News 2010). Islamic State produced its first official jihadist magazine called *Dabiq* in 2014, when the Caliphate was established under the leadership of Abu Bakr al-Baghdadi (Caliph Ibrahim). It too is a glossy publication, published in English and aggressively action-oriented to appeal to aspiring young warriors. Both magazines have provided a platform for charismatic preachers to extol the necessity for jihad as a defense against the enemies of Islam.

Radicalization and recruitment techniques

Islamic State's tactics in approaching, grooming, and recruiting young Muslims follow the guidelines set out in al-Qaeda's manual *A Course in the Art of Recruiting* (Engel 2015a). Recruiters seek out high school and college students, those living in isolated areas away from the big cities, and prefer the non-religious over the religious because they consider those ignorant of the tenets of Islam to be more susceptible to guidance and indoctrination. A gradual introduction to Islam is advised during which a relationship/friendship is to be established with the potential recruit long before jihad is mentioned.

Internet-based propaganda and incitement can foster a youth subculture of jihadism that challenges the traditional authority of established mainstream Salafist preachers in the diaspora.[12] Some young Muslims gravitate instead toward online charismatic preachers who offer an alternative interpretation of Islam that is more appealing and seems more relevant to the world in which they live. These young people often feel distant from their religious roots, are grappling with issues of identity, social deprivation and status, and reject both the authority of their parents and these mainstream Imams, many of whom are unfamiliar with the language, culture, and complexities of Muslim youth living as minorities in secular societies in the West.

Charismatic preachers exploit these feelings of alienation for recruitment purposes: They empathize with target individuals about their personal problems and anxieties and offer them understanding and concern; they stand ready to provide information and religious guidance to those seeking an identity through a better knowledge of their faith; and they have *the* solution to offer for all personal and societal ills—the practice of a purer form of Islam and the duty of jihad. These and other classic indoctrination techniques are commonly used by preachers in the West.

While violence as a means to an end rather than an end in itself holds true of most terrorist groups, the doctrine of jihad to which al-Qaeda and other militants subscribe (following in the footsteps of Ibn Taimiyyah) emphasizes the inherent value of the militant act itself regardless of the outcome. As a profession of faith, Anwar al-Awlaki claimed for it a redemptive quality worthy in its own right: "Practicing Jihad is always a victory—it is intrinsically beneficial and therefore will never entail loss even if there is a physical defeat."[13] Once recruits accept this, they are then encouraged by jihadist preachers to demonstrate their new-found commitment by joining the jihad.

The sustainability of militant jihadism ultimately depends upon its ability to appeal to an expanding pool of both active supporters and passive sympathizers. In this respect, Islamic State's aggressive propaganda campaign has been responsible for the large number of foreign fighters departing for Iraq and Syria (Engel 2015b). Their path has been facilitated by Internet propaganda and training, as well as practical information about how to reach the fighting fronts, but the declaration of a Caliphate in Syria and the perceived success of jihadis in capturing and holding territory has generated a new momentum.

In sum, the following combination of factors have been significant: the success of radical preachers in inculcating an individual obligation to participate in jihad; a widespread decision by Muslim youth to obey the newly declared leader (*Kalifah*) who traditionally has the authority to call Muslims to jihad in defense of Islam and the Muslim *ummah* as well as the restoration of jihadist divine law; and the prospect of adventure that is associated with participating in world-changing events and carries with it the status that attaches to joining the jihad.

Conclusion

It is important to recognize the "charismatic bond" between leaders and followers in the radicalization and recruitment process. The Internet has strengthened that bond insofar as it has enabled charismatic preachers to achieve a global reach; social media sites provide them with access to and information about target audiences and individuals which they can then exploit; and the materials they post on dedicated jihadist sites give them an enduring and pervasive presence within radical virtual communities. Cyber technologies and interactive sites have been used by charismatic preachers to inspire and develop trusted relationships with individuals and motivate their movement along a path from passive activism to militant jihadism. Counterterrorism strategy should focus on undermining the credibility and appeal of both the message and the messenger so as to break the charismatic bond.

Notes

1 A definition used by the Vox-Pol Network of Excellence that refers to those who employ physical violence against other individuals and groups to forward their political objectives.
2 This chapter draws on research contained in an unpublished commissioned study by Angela Gendron and Martin Rudner on Anwar al-Awlaki.
3 The "leaderless jihad" theory is contested insofar as it questions the evolution of al-Qaeda and its current ability to pose a threat to the West. See Bruce, H. (2013) "Al Qaeda's Uncertain Future," *Studies in Conflict and Terrorism* vol 36, no 8.
4 "Charis," from the Greek for gift or grace (of God)—an exceptional talent or quality.
5 Vikram Dodd, "List sent to terror chief aligns peaceful Muslim groups with terrorist ideology," *The Guardian* (UK) August 6, 2010, report on a Secret briefing document authored by the Quilliam Foundation and sent to the Office for Security and Counter-Terrorism. Quillam was founded by former Islamist Hizb ut-Tahrir members who are now partnering the UK government in its counter- radicalization program called "PREVENT."
6 Encyclopedia of Islam: "The duty of Jihad exists as long as the universal domination of Islam has not been attained"; Ibn Khaldun Muslim historian and philosopher (d. 1406), "In the Muslim community, holy war [jihad] is a religious duty because of the universalism of the Muslim mission and the *obligation* to convert everybody to Islam either by persuasion or force."
7 Taqiy Din Ibn Tamiyya (1263–1388) developed many aspects of jihad during his time. His views are still influential with Salafists, Jihadists, and the Muslim Brotherhood.
8 Op cit. Muslim FFI-rapport 2010/00960
9 The NEFA Foundation released a transcript of this document on February 5, 2009. Accessible at www.nefafoundation.org/miscellaneous/FeaturedDocs/nefaal-Awlaki44 wayssupportjihad.pdf
10 Brandon, Virtual Caliphate, Chapter 4.
11 Brandon, Virtual Caliphate, Chapter 5; "Digital Terrorism and Hate," Simon Wiesenthal Center for Tolerance, 2010; cited in Fox News, "Terrorists Targeting Children Via Facebook, Twitter," March 16, 2010.
12 Radicalisation in a Broader Perspective, NCBt. Op.cit.
13 Constants on the Path to Jihad, op.cit.

References

al-Awlaki, A. (2002) Sermon delivered on March 22, 2002 at the Dar al-Hijrah Mosque in Falls Church, Washington, DC.

al-Awlaki, A. (2009) "44 Ways to Support Jihad," No. 19, posted on January 5, 2009. Available at www.anwar-alawlaki.com

al-Qaradawi, Y. (2002) *Ibn al-Qarya wa-l-Kuttab: Malamih Sira wa-Masira*, vol.1, Cairo, Dar al-Shorouq. Translated by Gavi Barnhard.

Aly, A. (2009) "The Terrorists" Audience: A Model of Internet Radicalisation," *Journal of Australian Professional Intelligence Officers*, vol 17, no 1, pp. 3–19.

Anderson, K. (2013) "Bring out their Best Side and They'll See and Support Yours" *Forbes Magazine*. Available at www.forbes.com/sites/kareanderson/2013/04/29bring-out-their-best-side-and-theyll-see-and-support-yours/ (Accessed September 14, 2015).

Atwan, AB. (2007) *The Secret History of Al-Qa'ida*, London, Abacus.

Bakier, A. (2014) "IS Spokesman Issues Appeal to End the Inter-Jihadist Rivalry," *Terrorism Monitor*, vol 12, no 19. October 10, 2014.

Berger, JM and Strathearn, L. (2013) "Who Matters Online: Measuring Influence, Evaluating Content and Countering Violent Extremism in Online Social Network." Developments in Radicalisation and Political Violence, London: ICSR.

Berger, JM. (2011) "The Enduring Appeal of Al-Awlaki's 'Constants on the Path of Jihad,'" *Combating Terrorism Center at West Point*, October 31, 2011. Available at www.ctc.usma.edu/posts/the-enduring-appeal-pf-awlaqi%E2%80%99s-%E280%/90%Constants-on-the-path-of-jihad%E2%80%9D (Accessed September 17, 2015).

Borum, R. (2011) "Radicalization into Violent Extremism I: A Review of Social Science Theories," *Journal of Strategic Security*, vol 4, no 4, pp. 7–36.

Brandon, J. (2008) *Virtual Caliphate: Islamic Extremists and their Websites*, London: Centre for Social Cohesion.

Carter, JA, Maher, S, and Neumann, PR. (2014), "Greenbirds: Measuring Importance and Influence in Syrian Foreign Fighter Networks" *Developments in Radicalisation and Political Violence*, London: ICSR.

Chrisafis, A. (2013) "Violent Tide of Salafism Threatens Arab Spring," *Gulf News* [Dubai, UAE], February 15, 2013. Available at http://gulfnews.com/news/region/tunisia/violent-tide-of-salafism-threatens-arab-spring-1.1146808

Conger, JA and Kanungo, RN. (1988) *Charismatic Leadership: The Elusive Factor in Organizational Effectiveness*, San Francisco CA, Jossey-Bass.

Dalgaard-Nielsen, A. (2010) "Violent Radicalization in Europe: What We Know and What We Do Not Know," *Studies in Conflict and Terrorism*, vol 33, no 9, pp. 797–814.

de Poot, CJ and Sonnenschein, A. (2011) *Jihadi terrorism in the Netherlands*, Wetenschappelijk Onderzoek-en Documentatiecentrum, Ministeri van Veiligheid en Justice.

Dekmejian, RH. (1985) *Islam in Revolution: Fundamentalism in the Arab World*. Syracuse, NY: Syracuse University Press.

Eisenstadt, SN. (1968) *On Charisma and Institution Building*, Chicago IL: The University of Chicago Press.

Engel, P. (2015a) "Here's the Manual that Al Qaeda and now ISIS Use to Brainwash People Online," *Business Insider [USA]*. Available at: www.businessinsider.in/Heres-the-manual-that-al-Qaeda-and-now-ISIS-use-to-brainwash-people-online/articleshow/47915154.cms

Engel, P. (2015b) "ISIS Has Mastered a Crucial Recruiting Tactic no Terrorist Group Has Ever Conquered," *Business Insider [USA]*, May 9, 2015. Available at: www.businessinsider.com/isis-is-revolutionizing-international-terrorism-2015-5

Europol Te-Sat (2010), *EU Terrorism Situation and Trend Report*, Brussels.
Feldman, M. (2013) "Comparative Lone Wolf Terrorism: Toward a Heuristic Definition," *Democracy and Security*, vol 9, no 3, pp. 270–286.
Firestone, R. (1999) *The Origins of the Holy War in Islam*, New York, NY: Oxford University Press.
Gulf News. (2010) "Al-Qaida launches first English Language Propaganda Magazine" [Manama, Bahrain], July 1, 2010.
Hegghammer, T. (2010/2011) "The Rise of Muslim Foreign Fighters: Islam and the Globalization of Jihad," *International Security*, vol 35, no 3, pp. 53–94.
Hofmann, D. (2015) "Quantifying and Qualifying Charisma: A Theoretical Framework for Measuring the Presence of Charismatic Authority in Terrorist Groups," *Studies in Conflict and Terrorism*, vol 38, no 9, pp. 710–733.
Hofmann, D and Lorne LD. (2014) "The Neglected Role of Charismatic Authority in the Study of Terrorist Groups and Radicalization," *Studies in Conflict and Terrorism*, vol 37, no 4, pp. 348–368.
International Union of Muslim Scholars (2014) official website.
Jordan, J. (2009) "When Heads Roll: Assessing the Effectiveness of Leadership Decapitation," *Security Studies*, vol 18, pp. 719–755.
Kaya, A. (2010) "Individualization and Institutionalization of Islam in Europe in the Age of Securitisation," *Insight Turkey*, vol 12, no 1, pp. 47–63.
Keppel, G. (2004) *The War for Muslim Minds*, Cambridge, MA: The Belknap Press of Harvard University Press.
Khosrokhavar, F. (2009) *Inside Jihadism: Understanding Jihadi Movements*, London, Worldwide Paradigm Publishers.
Kohlmann, E. (2010) "A Beacon for Extremists: The Ansar al-Mujahideen Web Forum," *CTC Sentinel*, Vol. 3, Issue 2 (February).
Lewis, B. (2002) *What Went Wrong?: The Clash Between Islam and Modernity in the Middle East*, Oxford: Oxford University Press.
Lia, B. (2007) *Architect of Global Jihad: The Life of Al-Qaida Strategist Abu Musa'ab al-Suri*, London, Hurst & Co.
Lia, B. (2015) "Understanding Jihadi Proto-States," *Perspectives on Terrorism*, vol 9, no 4. Available online at: www.terrorismanalysts.com/pt/index.php/pot/article/view/441.
McCoy, J and Knight, A. (2015) "Homegrown Terrorism in Canada," *Studies in Conflict and Terrorism*, vol 38, no 4, pp. 253–274.
Madsen, D., and Snow, P. (1991) *The Charismatic Bond: Political Behaviour in Time of Crisis*, Cambridge: Harvard University Press.
Malet, D. (2015) "Foreign Fighter Mobilization and Persistence in a Global Context," *Terrorism and Political Violence*, vol 27, no 3, pp. 2–15.
Mus'ab al-Suri, A. (2010) "The Open Fronts and the Individual Initiative," *Inspire Magazine*, Issue 2, An extract from his book *Global Islamic Resistance Call*, Chapter 8, Section 4.
NCBt. (2007) *Radicalisation in a Broader Perspective*.
Neumann, P. (2013) "Options and Strategies for Countering Online Radicalization in the United States," *Studies in Conflict and Terrorism*, vol 36, no 6, pp. 431–459.
New York Times Magazine. (2015) "The Lessons of Anwar al-Awlaki," August 30, 2015.
Open Source Center (2011) *Master Narratives, Al-Qaeda Master Narratives and Affiliate Case Studies: Al-Qaeda in the Arabian Peninsula and Al-Qaeda in the Islamic Maghreb*, Special Report (Open Source Center, Monitor 360).

Pantucci, R. (2011) *A typology of lone wolves: Preliminary analysis of lone Islamist terrorists*, International Centre for the Study of Radicalisation and Political Violence, King's College, London: ICSR.

Perešin, A. (2015) "Fatal Attraction: Western Muslims and ISIS," *Perspectives on Terrorism*, vol 9, no 3. Available at www.terrorismanalysts.com/pt/index.php/pot/article/view/427

PET. (2014) "Developments in the Threat from Foreign Fighters from Denmark in Syria," *Centre for Terrorism Analysis*, June, 2014.

Peters, R. (1996) *Jihad in Classical and Medieval Islam*, Princeton, NJ: Marweiner.

Picken, G. (2015) "The "Greater" Jihad in Classical Islam," in E. Kendall & E. Stein (Eds.) *Twenty-first Century Jihad: Law, Society and Military Action*, London: I.B. Tauris.

Precht, T. (2007) *Home Grown Terrorism and Islamist Radicalization in Europe: From Conversion to Terrorism*. Danish Ministry of Justice.

Quilliam Foundation. (2010) Briefing Paper, "Radicalisation on British University Campuses: A case Study."

Rudner, M. (2013) "Al Qaeda's Twenty-Year Plan," *Studies in Conflict and Terrorism*, vol 36, no 12, pp. 953–980.

Sageman, M. (2008) *Leaderless Jihad: Terrorism Networks in the Twenty-First Century*, Pennsylvania, University of Pennsylvania Press.

Shane, S. (2015) "The Lessons of Anwar al-Awlaki," *New York Times Magazine* [USA] August 30, 2015.

Springer, DR, Regens, JL, and Edger, DN. (2009) *Islamic Radicalism and Global Jihad*, Washington, DC: Georgetown University Press.

Stern, J. (2004) *Terror in the Name of God: Why Religious Militants Kill*, New York, NY: Harper Perennial.

Tucker, R. (1970) "The Theory of Charismatic Leadership," in D.A. Rustow, (Ed) *Philosophers and Kings: Studies in Leadership*, New York, NY: George Braziller.

United Nations Development Program. (2002) *Arab Human Development Report 2002. Creating Opportunities for Future Generations*, New York, NY: UNDP Regional Bureau for Arab States.

von Behr, I, Reding, R, Edwards, C, and Gribbon, L. (2013) *Radicalisation in the Digital Era: The Use of the Internet in 15 cases of Extremism and Terrorism*, Brussels: RAND.

von Knop, K and Weimann, G. (2008) "Applying the Notion of Noise to Countering Online-Terrorism," *Studies in Conflict and Terrorism*, vol 31, pp. 883–902.

Weber, M. (1946) *Essays in Sociology*, New York, NY: Oxford Press.

Weber, M. (n.d) "Charisma and Institution Building," p. 48.

Weimann, G. (2004) "*www.Terror.Net. How Modern Terrorism Uses the Internet.*" United States Institute of Peace Special Report 116 (March, 2004).

Weimann, G. (2011) "Cyber-Fatwas and Terrorism," *Studies in Conflict and Terrorism*, vol 34, no 10.

Wiktorowicz, Q. (2005) *Radical Islam Rising: Muslim Extremism in the West*, Lanham, MD: Rowman and Littlefield.

3 Why do terrorists migrate to social media?

Gabriel Weimann

Introduction

On October 17, 2014, three teenage girls from Denver, Colorado—two sisters and their friend—boarded a flight to Frankfurt, Germany, planning to continue from there to Syria (Daily Mail 2014). The minor girls, whose identities therefore cannot be disclosed, reportedly lied to their parents, stole money, and planned to sever all ties with their families, friends, and the Western world in general. Instead, they planned to start a new life by joining the Islamic State, also known as the Islamic State of Iraq and Syria or Islamic State of Iraq and al-Sham (ISIS) or Islamic State of Iraq and the Levant (ISIL). The abrupt journey of the three girls from American teenagers to jihadi recruits, as shocking as it may appear, is far from unique. The online radicalization and recruitment process they underwent follows the pattern shared by several hundreds of Westerners. The girls followed online jihadists from around the world, including the UK, Australia, Germany, France, Canada, the Netherlands, and Syria.

On the evening of March 1, 2011, Arid Uka, an Albanian Muslim living in Germany, was online looking at YouTube videos. Like many before him, he watched a jihadist video that presented the gruesome rape of a Muslim woman by U.S. soldiers—a clip edited and posted on YouTube for jihadi propaganda purposes. Within hours of watching the video, Arid Uka boarded a bus at Frankfurt Airport, where he killed two U.S. servicemen and wounded two others with a handgun. After he was arrested, investigators reviewed the history of Arid Uka's Internet activity. It showed—most obviously in his Facebook profile—a growing interest in jihadist content, subsequent online-guided self-radicalization, and ultimately his viewing of the aforementioned video, which led him to take action in an alleged war in defense of Muslims. Arid Uka was not a member of a terrorist organization, nor had he visited any of the infamous training camps for terrorists. His entire radicalization, from early attraction to jihadi preaching to the final deadly mission, was accomplished online, using social media platforms (Jost and Weimann 2015).

Arid Uka and the teenage girls from Denver are just two of many cases of the new trend of terrorists being engaged through the newest online platforms, commonly known as the "social media." As cyberterrorism expert Evan Kohlmann had argued already in 2006:

> Today, 90 percent of terrorist activity on the Internet takes place using social networking tools. . . . These forums act as a virtual firewall to help safeguard the identities of those who participate, and they offer subscribers a chance to make direct contact with terrorist representatives, to ask questions, and even to contribute and help out the cyberjihad
>
> (cited in Noguchi 2006)

The growing attraction of social media for modern terrorists relies on the combined impact of several trends: the expansion of online social media and its advantages for terrorists, the virtual interactivity that terrorist propaganda and recruitment are using especially with the targeting of specific audiences ("narrowcasting"), and the emergence of the "lone wolf" terrorist whose virtual pack is found in the terrorists' social media.

The rise of social media

Social media depends on communication technologies such as mobile- and web-based networks to create highly interactive platforms through which individuals and communities share, co-create, discuss, and modify user-generated content. Social media differentiates from traditional/conventional media in many aspects such as interactivity, reach, frequency, usability, immediacy, and permanence (Morgan, Jones, and Hodges 2012). It is comparatively inexpensive and easily accessible. It enables anyone to upload, download, or access information in an easy, user-friendly, and fast way. Traditional media such as radio, television, or the press is characterized as "one-to-many" communication, where the audience might be virtually limitless, but a small cohort of established institutions selectively disseminates information. Social media platforms, by contrast, allow information consumers to also act as communicators, yielding a vast expansion in the number of information transmitters present in the media landscape. This process has resulted in lowering the barriers to enter communication markets by letting in small, diffused sets of communicators and groups who can easily share news, pictures, and videos online with others. Popular social media tools and platforms include the following:

- Blogs: A platform for casual dialogue and discussions on a specific topic or opinion.
- Facebook: The world's largest social network, with more than 1.35 billion users as of June 2014. Users create a personal profile, add other users as friends, and exchange messages, including status updates. Brands create pages and Facebook users can "like" brand pages.
- Twitter: A social networking/microblogging platform that allows groups and individuals to stay connected through the exchange of short status messages, with a 140-character limit.
- YouTube and Vimeo: Video hosting and watching websites.

- Flickr: An image and video hosting website and online community. Photos posted to Flickr can be shared on Facebook, Twitter, and other social networking sites.
- Instagram: A free photo and video sharing app that allows users to apply digital filters, frames, and special effects to their photos and then share them on a variety of social networking sites.
- LinkedIn Groups: A place where groups of professionals with similar areas of interest can share and participate in conversations happening in their fields.

The growing use of social media is impressive. In the USA, according to the Pew Internet Project (2014), 74 percent of American online adults use social networking sites, 71 percent of online adults use Facebook, 17 percent use Instagram, 21 percent use Pinterest, 22 percent use LinkedIn, and 19 percent use Twitter (Pew Research Center 2014). The growing ubiquity of cell phones, especially the rise of smartphones, has made social networking just a finger tap away. Forty percent of cell phone owners use a social networking site on their phone, and 28 percent do so on a typical day. The total time spent on social media in the USA increased by 37 percent to 121 billion minutes in July 2012 compared to 88 billion minutes in July 2011. In 2013, *eMarket* research found that the average American user spends 23 hours a week e-mailing, texting, and using social media and other forms of online communication (eMarket 2013).

These trends are global: As of 2014, more than approximately 1.8 billion Internet users have accessed social networks, of which only 170 million were located in the USA (Statista Report 2014). Since 2004, the global growth of social media has been near exponential. Back in 2004, Facebook only had about 1 million users. In 2014, Facebook had more than 1.35 billion active users. Twitter saw a steep growth from 2010 to 2014 (reaching 284 million active users in 2014) with 500 million tweets sent every day.

The global spread of the cellular phone with online access to social media has made these platforms so widely accessed and used, even in some—though not all—of the poorest places in the world. There were 1.75 billion users of these mobile phones in the world and most of them used at least one social networking channel. For example, 78 percent of active Twitter users are on mobile phones. These trends were noticed also by Internet-savvy terrorists who quickly learned how to harness the new social media for their purposes. Thus, for example, ISIS introduced its Arabic-language Twitter application called "The Dawn of Glad Tidings": an official ISIS application, advertised as a way to keep up on the latest news about the jihadi group. Hundreds of users have signed up for the application on the web or on their Android phones through the Google Play store. When downloading the application, ISIS asks for a fair amount of personal data. The application first went into wide use in April 2014, but its posting activity has ramped up during the group's offensive in Iraq. Its thunderclap nature helped it reach an all-time high of almost 40,000 tweets in one day (Berger 2014).

The growing appeal of social media for terrorists

Terrorists' use of online platforms is not new. After the events of 9/11 and the antiterrorism campaign that followed, a large number of terrorist groups moved to cyberspace, establishing thousands of websites that promoted their messages and activities (Weimann 2004, 2006a, 2015). Many terrorist sites were targeted by intelligence and law enforcement agencies, counterterrorism services, and activists, who monitored the sites, attacked some of them, and forced their operators to seek new online alternatives. The turn to social media followed. The main motivation to use Facebook and other social media was properly outlined by the terrorists themselves in a jihadi online forum calling for "Facebook Invasion." While the identity of the writer is unknown, the password-protected forum, al-Faloja, is a very popular and effective jihadi platform. The posting noted:

> This [Facebook] is a great idea, and better than the forums. Instead of waiting for people to [come to you so you can] inform them, you go to them and teach them! . . . [I] mean, if you have a group of 5,000 people, with the press of a button you [can] send them a standardized message. I entreat you, by God, to begin registering for Facebook as soon as you [finish] reading this post. Familiarize yourselves with it. This post is a seed and a beginning, to be followed by serious efforts to optimize our Facebook usage. Let's start distributing Islamic jihadi publications, posts, articles, and pictures. Let's anticipate a reward from the Lord of the Heavens, dedicate our purpose to God, and help our colleagues
>
> (cited in Department of Homeland Security 2010)

Terrorists have good reasons to use social media. First, these channels are by far the most popular with their intended audience, which allows terrorist organizations to be part of the mainstream. Second, social media channels are user-friendly, reliable, and free. Finally, social networking allows terrorists to reach out to their target audiences and virtually "knock on their doors"—in contrast to older models of websites in which terrorists had to wait for visitors to come to them. Furthermore, the new forms of social media have technical advantages for terrorists: sharing, uploading, or downloading files and videos no longer requires fast computers, or any computer for that matter; it no longer requires sharing sites or savvy members capable of uploading such videos. Rather, smartphones and social media accounts are all that are needed to instantly share material in real time with tens of thousands of jihadists. There are, of course, some disadvan-tages and risks involved: Terrorists may be identified online, their intentions may be revealed, and their content may be removed by social media companies. However, as we will explore, terrorists have learned how to respond to these risks and apply sophisticated countermeasures to avoid identification or removal of material.

Terrorists' shift to social media

Increasingly, terrorist groups and their sympathizers are shifting their online presence from websites, chat rooms, and forums to social platforms. This shift was acknowledged by Adam Gadahn, who headed al-Qaeda's media wing al-Sahab. In a March 1, 2013 interview with *Inspire*, al-Qaeda's online magazine, he noted the importance of American social media companies:

> This is your day, so rise to the challenge and become a part of history in the making ... we must make every effort to reach out to Muslims both through new media like Facebook and Twitter ... and we should fully acquaint ourselves with both the people to whom we are reaching out, as well as the methodology and cause to which we are inviting them, so that we are able to hone our methods, refine our techniques, and spread our message in an intelligent and educated fashion accessible to all sectors, sections, levels and factions of the ummah
>
> (cited in MEMRI 2013)

In a similar vein, Umar Patek, who masterminded the October 2002 bombing in Bali that left 202 dead, warned on June 7, 2012, during his trial: ". . . For those who do not know how to commit jihad, they should understand that there are several ways of committing jihad." He added: "This is not the Stone Age . . . This is the Internet era, there is Facebook, Twitter and others" (cited in MEMRI 2012a).

Indeed, all terrorist groups have added social media such as Facebook, Twitter, YouTube, Instagram, and others to their online platforms. Abdul Sattar Maiwandi, a Taliban commander and administrator of the Taliban's official website, said in an interview published on February 18, 2011, by *al-Somood*, the Taliban's Arabic-language magazine: ". . . We are also active on Facebook and Twitter, where we publish the news every day and reach thousands of people" (cited in MEMRI 2011). Terrorists encourage their audiences, followers, and operatives to join social media and use them: On January 27, 2012, the jihadi website *Kavkaz Center*, the influential media outlet of the Chechen fighters, particularly the Islamic Emirate of the Caucasus (IEC), posted an announcement that urged its followers to

> [c]reate accounts on Twitter, Facebook and share the information . . . Modern technologies make it possible for anyone who genuinely cares about the Mujahideen not to stand aside [but to] render them real help, becoming a participant in the fight of truth against the lie
>
> (cited in MEMRI 2012b)

Other terrorist groups have emerged on these new media, expanding their online presence to newer online platforms as they develop—Ask.fm, Kik, Friendica, and, most recently, VK.com, Diaspora, JustPaste.it, and SoundCloud. They are also utilizing smartphone apps that are available on Google Play and Apple's App Store.

Several groups fighting in Iraq and Syria have turned to social media for propaganda, psychological warfare, and weapons tutorials. Abu Mohammed al-Golani, the head of an al-Qaeda branch operating in Syria called al-Nusra Front, uses Facebook and other social media extensively. In August 2013, al-Golani vowed unrestrained rocket attacks on Alawite communities, alongside attacks on President Bashar Assad's government in revenge for an alleged chemical strike—a message that was posted on Facebook and Twitter, as well as on a militant website that often broadcasts the views of al-Qaeda and similar extremist groups. Al-Nusra Front has its own Facebook page, which contains press releases, photographs, and videos from the fighting in Syria; eulogies for the organization's *shaheeds* (martyrs for Islam); and news on the fighting on the ground. The most recent trend in the Syrian conflict on Facebook, and often also on the Flickr photo-sharing site, is posting eulogies for killed ("martyred") jihadis. These eulogies present the fighters as role models for Muslims and immortalize them—an appealing prospect for radical Muslims who feel marginalized in their respective societies.

Recently, the Sunni terrorist group ISIS, which is on a rampage in northern Syria and Iraq, launched a multi-platform online campaign, covering the entire range of social media. ISIS is using social media to seduce, radicalize, and recruit. In 2014, ISIS opened numerous social media accounts for distributing its videos, audios, and images via various channels and in many languages, thereby avoiding online censorship. As part of these intensive propaganda efforts, it has launched al-Hayat Media, a new media branch specifically targeting Western and non-Arabic speaking audiences. Launched in May 2014, this new media branch follows ISIS's general media strategy of distributing online videos, "news" reports, articles, and translated jihadi materials. Its main Twitter account is in German, but it also publishes materials in English and French, as well as other languages. For instance, it posted a speech by ISIS spokesman Abu Muhammad al-'Adnani translated into seven languages (English, Turkish, Dutch, French, German, Indonesian, and Russian). Following the aggressive ISIS offensive in Iraq in June 2014, Twitter closed down many official ISIS and pro-ISIS accounts, including the main accounts of al-Hayat Media, in German, English and French, but these were soon replaced by new Twitter accounts. The recruitment of hundreds of fighters from European and North American countries, as revealed recently in their active presence in Syria and Iraq, indicates the success of ISIS's online campaign.

On Twitter, ISIS is very active and dynamic. For example, under the hashtag #AllEyesOnIsis, ISIS tried to appeal to Muslim youth, scare ISIS's enemies on the ground, and intimidate the rest of the world. A Twitter campaign entitled "One Billion Muslims to Support the ISIS" was launched on June 13, 2014. From the six re-tweets and four favorites from the initial post, the campaign has grown to encompass content shared hundreds of times an hour. On Twitter, the hashtag has been shared over 9,500 times since it was first introduced. Besides Twitter, the campaign includes video contributions hosted on YouTube along with activity on the Facebook social networking site. Among the Facebook activity devoted to the campaign, a Facebook "causes" page using the hashtag had gathered hundreds of "likes" since being established on June 16, 2014.

A growing number of al-Qaeda affiliates and other designated terrorist organizations, as well as online operatives, followers, and supporters, have been active on Facebook; while some of their accounts have been shut down, they often return with new accounts, using similar names and addresses. Some leading pages are those of the al-Qaeda offshoot ISIS's media company al-Furqan, al-Qaeda in the Islamic Maghreb (AQIM), and Jihad Umma, which reports from jihadi websites. Other organizations on Facebook include the Taliban, Hamas, Hezbollah, Palestinian Islamic Jihad (PIJ), and many more. The move to online platforms and social media is not only acknowledged and encouraged, it is also rewarded. Such online jihadists are awarded a remarkable status in the conclusion to a comprehensive paper on "Electronic Jihad," published on January 4, 2012, on leading jihadist forums al-Fida and Shumukh al-Islam:

> [...] any Muslim who intends to do jihad against the enemy electronically, is considered in one way or another a mujaheed, as long as he meets the conditions of jihad such as the sincere intention and the goal of serving Islam and defending it, even if he is far away from the battlefield. He is thus participating in jihad indirectly as long as the current contexts require such jihadi participation that has effective impact on the enemy.
> (cited in SITE 2012)

The terrorist migration to social media integrates with three other new trends in terrorist communications: "narrowcasting," "virtual interactivity," and the "Lone Wolves." Let us examine how these trends are interrelated.

"Narrowcasting" on social media

An emerging trend in online terrorism is "narrowcasting," a concept based on the postmodern idea that mass audiences do not exist. Narrowcasting refers to the dissemination of information (usually via Internet, radio, or television) to a narrow audience, not to the broader public at large. Also called "niche marketing" or "target marketing," narrowcasting involves aiming media messages at specific segments of the public, defined by characteristics such as values, preferences, demographic attributes, or location. Sophisticated persuasion is more likely to succeed when the medium, the stimuli, the appeals, and the graphics are tailored to specific receivers. Terrorists have learned about this new concept and now apply it in their cyber campaigns. Instead of "one-website-for-all," Internet-savvy terrorists target specific subpopulations, including children, women, "lone wolves," overseas communities, or diasporas (Weimann 2015). The al-Qassam brigades have specifically designated websites based on whether the website is being viewed in English or Arabic (thus highlighting human rights focus versus mujahideen focus).

The unmistakable growth in the participation of women and youth in suicide terrorism with the evident growth in persuasive online messages targeting these groups may provide alarming signals of the success of the narrowcasting tactic.

Just as marketing companies can view members' information to find potential customers and select products to promote to them, terrorist groups can view people's profiles to decide whom to target and how to approach each individual. Social media allows terrorists to use this targeting strategy of narrowcasting more effectively. On social media, messages are tailored to match the profile of a particular social group or social category. These methods enable terrorists to target youth especially; counterterrorism expert Anthony Bergin says that terrorists view these youth-dominated websites as recruitment tools "in the same way a pedophile might look at those sites to potentially groom would-be victims" (cited in Advertiser 2008). Many social media users join interest groups, and these groups enable terrorists to target users whom they might be able to manipulate. These users often accept people as "friends" on a social media site whether or not they know them, thereby giving strangers access to personal information and photos. Some people even communicate with these strangers and establish virtual friendships. Terrorists can therefore apply the narrowcasting strategy used on the broader Internet to specific and more personal social networking. They can tailor their name, accompanying default image, and information on a group message board to fit the profile of a particular social group. Interest groups also provide terrorists with a list of predisposed recruits or sympathizers. In the same way that marketing groups can view a member's information to decide which products to target on their webpages, terrorist groups can view people's profiles to decide who they are going to target and how they should configure the message.

The use of narrowcasting combined with social media platforms is evident in the case of recruiting foreigners to fight for ISIS in Syria and Iraq. While in the past, jihadi groups published most of their materials on traditional media outlets, such as websites, chat rooms, and forums, ISIS has pioneered the use of social media as the main means for recruitment of foreigners, especially from North America and Europe (e.g., the Diaspora.com network allows them to reach a variety of new members).[1] Very often, ISIS uses foreign fighters recruited from a certain Western country to appeal to potential recruits from their homeland. For example, in a video posted on December 20, 2014, on the pro-ISIS jihadi forum Alplatformmedia.com, a masked and armed ISIS fighter calls on Muslims in that country to either make "hijra" (immigrate) to the Caliphate (i.e., the parts of Syria and Iraq controlled by ISIS) or to "blow up France" and kill unbelievers by any means: with a gun, a rock, or a knife. The fighter speaks in French with a North African accent, and his statements are subtitled in Arabic.

On October 15, 2014, ISIS, via its al-Hayat Media, released a video featuring several foreign fighters, including a British national named Abu Abdullah, a French national named Abdul Wadoud, and a German national named Abu Dauoud. The 9-minute 14-second video, entitled "Wait. We Too Are Waiting," shows the three men sitting in Dabiq, a town in Aleppo, Syria, and delivering speeches in their native tongues. Abu Abdullah boasts that the IS will kill every single soldier sent against it, and declared: "We will chop off the heads of the Americans, chop off the heads of the French, chop off the heads of whoever you may bring." Also, remarking on the presence of foreign fighters, he states: "Know this, that it is not just one American, it is not just one European that is here. Know that we are many and we are many in numbers and we will take your lives, [Allah willing, Allah permitting]." On December 9, 2014, ISIS released a German chant promoting both ISIS and allegiance to its leader Abu Bakr al-Baghdadi. The English-subtitled video was distributed on Twitter and jihadi social media, stating: "Mujahidin from all over the whole world are here / Nothing will stop us / We are fighting for the cause of Allah / Our State is victorious!" Footage shows fighters pledging allegiance to Baghdadi. Both Abdul Wadoud and Abu Dauoud gave similar messages. Additionally, Abu Dauoud urged German Muslims to come join the ISIS in the battlefield, and Abdul Wadoud addressed French President Francois Hollande: "We shall take revenge for every drop of blood spilt as a result of your actions. Because the Muslims who have arrived from France (to the Islamic State)." The success of these recruitment efforts is impressive: According to a Soufan Group report, more than 12,000 foreign fighters, 3,000 of them from Western countries, have joined the war in Syria within three years (Barrett 2014). Social media outlets have been a powerful tool for luring these people into these groups. Many of the recruits may have had personal motives to join ISIS but social media platforms provided the initial contact, the appeals, the directions, and final instructions.

Virtual interactivity on social media

Online media is a two-way communication: it allows users to interact with the communicators, to ask questions and get answers, to become communicators themselves, and to become an active and interactive audience. This advantage is important for online terrorists who use the two-way platforms to communicate, seduce, radicalize, and instruct followers and future operatives. Social media provides more opportunities for interactive communication, and Internet-savvy terrorists are well aware of this and even acknowledge it openly. As mentioned previously in this chapter, in December 2008, jihadists called for a "Facebook Invasion." Noting the prevalent use of Facebook among global users, a jihadist post suggested that it would be useful to strengthen jihadist use of Facebook and thus reach a wider audience. Moreover, the post noted that this Facebook invasion will "move from an elite society ([on] jihadi forums and websites) to mainstream Muslims, [encourage] their participation, and interact with them, advance media operations and encourage creativity, innovation, flexibility, and change."[2]

The interactive nature of these online platforms allows for dynamic exchanges of questions and answers. For example, in June 2012, Sanda Ould Bouamama, the spokesman for the Ansaruddin Movement in northern Mali, gave forum members a ten-day period to ask questions about Ansaruddin and the situation in Azawad, an unrecognized state in northern Mali. Later, he released his answers. The sixty-four-page document containing questions and answers was posted on the Ansar al-Mujahideen forum on August 5, 2012. The questions and answers are divided into five groups, the first of which concerns Ansaruddin's origins and objectives. Here, Bouamama apologized for the group's lack of media presence and said that Ansaruddin is now focusing on "clarifying its call." He stated: "As it is clear so far, people don't know anything about us other than what the media publishes that seeks to maim the new jihadi Islamic baby."

Similarly, the Harakat al-Shabaab al-Mujahideen group in Somalia released in August 2012 the first part of answers from its spokesman, Ali Mahmoud Ragi, to questions posed by members of the jihadist forum community. The questions and answers came in an online video produced by the group's media arm, al-Kata'ib Foundation, and posted on jihadist forums and social media. In January 2012, the Global Islamic Media Front (GIMF), which has distributed al-Shabaab's propaganda on jihadist forums for the past five years, announced the commencement of an open interview with Ragi and invited jihadists and non-jihadists alike to present questions during a two-week period. The first part features thirty Q&As regarding al-Shabaab's military strategy in cities it once controlled, its relationship with local tribes and opposing groups, and its refusal to negotiate with the Somali government.

Open debates are also possible on interactive terrorist platforms (Weimann 2006b, 2009). Thus, for example, Omar Hammami (aka Abu Mansour al-Amriki) presented online his criticism of the Harakat al-Shabaab al-Mujahideen group and its leader, Mukhtar Abu al-Zubeir. Hammami was an American citizen who became a member and leader in the Somali Islamist militant group al-Shabaab. In November 2012, the FBI added Hammami to its Most Wanted Terrorists list. He posted his criticism in a set of questions and answers: Hammami's answers were presented as answers to the open interview held between him and jihadist forums members. He said that he brought the conflict public in order to reach al-Qaeda leader Ayman al-Zawahiri and have him intervene, after he failed to find a way to communicate with him in secret and "losing patience." Omar Hammami was killed on September 12, 2013, in an ambush by al-Shabaab militants.

ISIS is also using interactive social media in its outreach to English-speaking recruits. In its 3rd issue of the online magazine *Dabiq*, ISIS included email addresses for contacting it, stating: "The Dabiq team would like to hear back from its readers, and for this reason, we are providing email addresses to submit your opinions, suggestions, and questions." It also included a public encryption key "for those of you who would like to use Asrar Al-Mujahideen" encryption software for secure communication. The use of encryption was suggested online by numerous postings of terrorist groups including the famous al-Qaeda magazine *Inspire*: its 10th issue includes a "How to Communicate with Us" section, providing the readers with Asrar El Moujahedeen 2.0 encryption coding. There are numerous social media platforms used by ISIS for online interactions; these include Skype, Twitter, Facebook, and the mobile messaging application WhatsApp. Texas-based WhatsApp, which in February 2014 was bought by Facebook, is now used widely by interactive jihadis; for example, a senior member of the leading jihadi forum *Shumoukh al-Islam* suggested that online jihadis not only use it to publish jihadi material, but also to actively interact online.

A recent example is the Ask.fm platform. Latvia-based Ask.fm is a social media website in which interactions take the form of questions and answers. It states on its website that it "allows for anonymous content which ask.fm does not monitor."

The Middle East Research Institute (MEMRI) has published a number of reports about jihadists in Syria using Ask.fm to answer questions from readers wanting to know about joining the jihad there.

For example, a British jihadi using the alias of Abu Abdullah al-Britani, and is believed to have traveled via Turkey to Syria to join ISIS and to be fighting close to the Syria–Iraq border, was active on Twitter. He was originally named @Al_Brittani, and—after this account was suspended—as @AlBrittani. However, Abu Abdullah was also active on Ask.fm, where he answered questions about jihad, about traveling to Syria, about weapons, fighting, and so on. On Ask.fm, he confirmed that his old Twitter account was suspended, and discussed the importance of social media to ISIS. He told users not to worry about getting a foreign mobile phone SIM card because they will not get any signal, but he added, "There r internet cafes and houses of dawlah with internet so just make sure inhave [sic] a smart phone to connect to wifi."

Lone wolves and their virtual packs

The shift to social media merges with another noted trend in recent terrorism: the emergence of lone wolf attacks, committed by individual terrorists who are not members of any terrorist organization. Before 9/11, the largest terror threat came from men who went to terrorist camps and to jihadi mosques where radical Imams preached jihad. Today, the real threat comes from the single individual, the "Lone Wolf," living next door, being radicalized on the Internet, and plotting strikes in the dark (EUROPOL 2012). Lone wolf terrorism is the fastest growing kind of terrorism. Recent studies reveal an increased number of countries targeted by lone wolf terrorists, an increased number of fatalities and injuries caused by lone wolves, higher prevalence and success rates for lone wolf attackers than for other types of terrorism, and increased targeting of military personnel. The United States is the most targeted country, accounting for 63 percent of all global lone wolf attacks between 1990 and 2013, followed by the United Kingdom, Germany, and other Western countries (Teich 2013). Acts of lone wolf terrorism have been reported in France, Spain, Italy, Canada, Australia, the Netherlands, Russia, Denmark, Portugal, Poland, and Sweden.

However, it should be noted that the metaphor of the lone wolf is misleading in terrorism as in nature. Wolves never hunt alone—they hunt in packs. Lone wolf terrorists are not completely out of contact. They are recruited, radicalized, taught, trained, and directed by others. They connect, communicate, and share information, know-how, and guidance exclusively online, through the "Deep Web." The Deep Web (also known as the Undernet, Invisible Web, and Hidden Web) consists of data that is impossible to locate with a simple Google search. Some of it is hidden on purpose but most of it is just hard for current search engine technology to find and read. Since the deep web is larger than the surface web, the analogy of an iceberg has frequently been used to represent the division between surface web (only the tip of the iceberg) and the Deep Web. An aspiring terrorist can find online everything from instructions on how to build a homemade bomb to maps and diagrams of potential targets. In addition, social media provides easy venues for cultivating extremism in a way that was previously possible only through in-person gatherings. Indeed, all recent lone wolf attacks involved individuals who were radicalized, recruited, trained, and even launched on social media platforms (Weimann 2012, 2014).

Online social networking platforms have become a powerful apparatus for terrorists to attract potential members and followers. Because of the increasing popularity of these virtual communities all over the world, especially among the young, jihadist terrorist groups use them to target youths for propaganda, recruitment, and incitement. The Internet has been the meeting ground for all lone wolf cases of recent years, and it appears to be very effective as indicated by the growing number of lone attackers who were radicalized and trained online, where lone wolves can access radicalizing material, instruction manuals, and videos. It also gives them direct access to a community of like-minded individuals around the world with whom they can connect, who in some cases provide them further instigation and direction for carrying out terrorist activities.

Dzhokhar and Tamerlan Tsarnaev, who were the attackers in the bombings at the Boston Marathon on April 15, 2013 (which left three dead), and in the shooting that resulted in the death of an MIT police officer on April 18, were motivated by extremist Islamic beliefs, according to FBI interrogators. They were active on social networks. On Facebook, Tamerlan posted links to videos of fighters in the Syrian civil war and to Islamic web pages with titles like "Salamworld, my religion is Islam" and "There is no God but Allah, let that ring out in our hearts." He also had links to pages calling for independence for Chechnya, the region of Russia that lost its bid for secession after two wars in the 1990s. Tamerlan's YouTube screen name was "muazseyfullah," which combines the names of two prominent militant leaders in Russia's North Caucasus where Chechnya is found. "Seyfullah," the second part, also translates as "sword of Allah." Though not connected to any known terrorist groups, Dzhokhar and his brother were radicalized and taught to build explosive weapons by *Inspire*, an English-language online magazine published by al-Qaeda affiliates.

Al-Qaeda's *Inspire*, launched and promoted on social media, became an important tool for recruiting, informing, and motivating these lone jihadists. Each edition of the magazine has a special section, called "Open Source Jihad," which is intended to equip aspiring jihadist attackers with the tools they need to conduct attacks without traveling to jihadist training camps. It helps terrorist sympathizers in the West carry out attacks by including, among other pieces of advice, bomb-making recipes. Since its foundation, *Inspire* has advocated the concept that jihadists living in the West should conduct attacks there, rather than travel to places like Pakistan, Somalia, or Yemen, since such travel might bring them to the attention of the authorities. Indeed, *Inspire* views attacking in the West as "striking at the heart of the unbelievers."

The recruitment of lone wolf terrorists relies on online platforms and requires a gradual transition through numerous phases. The first step is the "net," which views the whole population as primed for recruitment, and exposes it to an online message, video, taped lecture, etc. The target audience is viewed as homogeneous enough and receptive enough to be approached with a single undifferentiated pitch, to which some members will respond positively, others negatively. For this "netting" stage, all online platforms may be used, from Facebook pages to personal mail, from YouTube video clips to Twitter or official websites. Second is the "funnel." The potential recruits who start at one end of the process, after some culling along the way, are transformed into dedicated members when they emerge at the other end. When a recruiter believes a target individual is ripe for recruitment yet requires a significant transformation in identity and motivation, he or she uses an incremental, or phased, approach that capitalizes on a wealth of techniques well studied in cognitive, social, and clinical psychology. This stage relies on a social bonding (though a virtual one), based on the target's alienation, social frustration, solitude, and personal pessimism. It involves online exchanges and further exposure to religious, political, or ideological material. Next is the "infection" stage, in which selected target members who are dissatisfied with their social status or have a grudge against their political or religious system are directed to self-radicalization. The lone wolves in training, following only online sources, gradually advance in commitment and extremism. The final stage, "activation," launches the lone wolf. This includes practical instructions through online manuals on using explosives, weapons, poisons, and chemicals; directions regarding the selection of target, location, and timing; and the final send-off.

Numerous groups and individuals are launching lone wolf campaigns on social media. For example, in December 2014, a Chechen fighter in ISIS appeared in a video and called upon Muslims in America, Chechnya, and Europe to mount lone wolf attacks at home if they are unable to physically travel to and join the group in Iraq and Syria. The featured Chechen fighter, Abdul Halim al-Shishani, first promoted the role of Chechens in the jihad in Iraq and Syria, then answered questions from an off-camera interview. His statements included the call "you will rise among the enemies of Allah and will attack them in the heart of their lands." To Muslims in the West, Abdul Halim echoed the words of ISIS spokesman Abu Muhammad al-'Adnani, inciting them to kill the enemy wherever they are found. He added:

> Fight and kill the Americans, kill the Europeans, and burn their houses, and burn their cars. Do what you can. You must do and you must expend efforts if you wish to be of the surviving group and of the supported group and so that Allah does not bring someone other than you.

Similarly, a French-speaking ISIS fighter called upon Muslims in France to take Toulouse shooter Mohamed Merah as their example and carry out lone wolf attacks in France. The call was made in a video entitled "To You, O People of Mine, a Message." It was distributed on Twitter and jihadi forums on December 19, 2014. The fighter questioned Muslims in France what they have presented to defend their oppressed brethren, and told them that if they are unable to immigrate to the jihadi battlefield, they should mount attacks at home. He stated:

> Ignite France! Blow up the heads of those disbelievers! Just as they permit themselves to hit our sisters and make lawful what Allah forbade, and just as they prevented our sisters from wearing the niqab, blow up their heads by all means! By stones or anything! The matter does not require the availability of a pistol, for you have stones and knives and all that you need.

In the 13th issue of *Inspire*, posted online in January 2015, a representative of the magazine interviewed the "AQ Chef," the author of the "Open Source Jihad" articles. In an answer to the question "What is the idea of lone Jihad?" the AQ Chef answered:

> My view is that a lone Mujahid is he who has the two aforementioned characteristics: To be independent of a group and an organization in both the administration and military, and to act alone. This mode of Jihad is unpredictable to the Western intelligence. This is whom they call a "lone wolf." It is hard to uncover, because none knows him but Allah. He has no relationship with any group or any individuals. This is what we call to, and hereby assert . . . I believe, if done oftentimes, lone Jihad has great importance surpassing other Jihadi activities. In my opinion, this type of Jihadi method can be one of the crucial reasons of ending the aggressive war on Muslims. I am not exaggerating. I am very well aware of what I say. Lone Jihad against the West, especially when intensified, will create a state of terror, anxiety, public resentment and complaint against the governments and policies that brought about lone Jihad.

The impact of lone wolf online campaigns is significant and clear. As demonstrated by several studies, in all the recent cases of lone wolf attacks, virtual tracks to online communities were found, mostly on social media platforms (Weimann 2012, 2014). For example, in January 2015, U.S. officials arrested an Ohio man in connection with a plan to attack the U.S. Capitol building in Washington, D.C. Christopher Lee Cornell—also known as Raheel Mahrus Ubaydah—was arrested by the FBI for the attempted killing of a U.S. government officer and for possession of a firearm in furtherance of attempted crime of violence. From the summer of 2014 through this month, Cornell, 20, established and used Twitter accounts under the alias Raheel Mahrus Ubaydah. He posted videos, statements, and other content expressing support for ISIS, according to the criminal complaint. On Aug. 29, 2014, Cornell allegedly told an FBI informant via an instant messaging platform that he wanted to commit violent jihad: "I believe we should meet up and make our own group in alliance with the Islamic State here and plan operations ourselves."

Finally, social media is used to glorify lone wolf attackers and use these "martyrs" for their online recruitment. After the deadly assault by gunmen on the offices of the French satirical newspaper Charlie Hebdo in Paris on January 7, 2015, jihadists redistributed a November 2014 video from ISIS inciting for lone wolf attacks in France. The ISIS's al-Hayat Media Center released the video "What

Are You Waiting for" on Twitter and jihadi forums on November 19, featuring three French fighters urging Muslims among their fellow countrymen to travel to Iraq or Syria to join the group, and told those unable to do so to carry out lone wolf attacks in France. One of these fighters, Abu Maryam al-Faranci, stated:

> And if you are sincere to Allah in your worship and in your creed and are unable to make *Hijra* [immigrate], then operate within France. Terrorize them and do not allow them to sleep due to fear and horror. There are weapons and cars available and targets ready to be hit. Even poison is available, so poison the water and food of at least one of the enemies of Allah. Kill them and spit in their faces and run over them with your cars. Do whatever you are able to do in order to humiliate them, for they deserve only this.

Counterterrorism on social media

The terrorist migration to new online resources challenges the counterterrorism agencies as well as the academics who research terrorism. The meteoric rise of social media has let radical groups and terrorists freely disseminate ideas through multiple modalities, including websites, blogs, social networking websites, forums, and video sharing services. Counterterrorism is certainly lingering behind terrorists' manipulative use of the new channels. Despite the growth of Internet research in recent years, it has not yet provided efficient strategies or fruitful countermeasure devices or tactics. William McCants of the Center for Naval Analysis asserted during his December 2011 testimony before the U.S. House of Representatives Homeland Security Subcommittee on Counterterrorism and Intelligence:

> There is little research to go on, which is striking given how data-rich the Internet is. In hard numbers, how widely distributed was Zawahiri's last message? Did it resonate more in one U.S. city than another? Who were its main distributors on Facebook and YouTube? How are they connected with one another? This sort of baseline quantitative research barely exists at the moment
>
> (McCants 2011)

The security community has to adjust counterterrorism strategies to the new arenas, applying new types of online warfare, intelligence gathering, and training for cyber warriors. The National Security Agency, the Department of Defense, the CIA, the FBI, the Defense Intelligence Agency, other U.S. and foreign intelligence agencies, and some private contractors are already fighting back. They are monitoring suspicious websites and social media, cyberattacking others, and planting bogus information. The virtual war between terrorists and counterterrorism forces and agencies is vital, dynamic, and ferocious. Researchers around the world from disciplines such as psychology, security, communications, and computer sciences are coming together to develop tools and techniques to respond to terrorism's online activity. Recognizing the online threat, the White House's counter-radicalization strategy, published in August 2011, acknowledged "the important role the Internet and social networking sites play in advancing violent extremist narratives." In April 2013, the Bipartisan Policy Center's Homeland Security Project released the Countering Online Radicalization in America report, which identifies shortcomings in U.S. online counter-radicalization strategy and recommends improvements (Homeland Security Project 2012).

Most of the terrorist online platforms are on sites provided in Western, democratic, liberal countries. Almost all of the new social media platforms, from Facebook and Twitter to Instagram and YouTube, are managed and owned by Western companies, mostly American. According to studies conducted by MEMRI, 76 percent of the terrorist websites are hosted in the United States, with only 8 percent of sites hosted in the Middle East. This raises the question of what can be done about it, especially since most Internet service providers, web hosting companies, file sharing sites, and social networking sites have terms of service agreements that prohibit certain content. Many such companies reserve the right to remove items that support, promote, or encourage violence or crime.[3] However, such self-censorship has not been very effective: the companies are not eager to become censors, do not have the manpower to search huge amounts of online postings, are not equipped with the expertise required to translate and understand many of the postings, and are removing or blocking content only in the case of "flagging"—when the users complain about the content as violating the terms of use. However, Internet users currently do not have enough easy ways of reporting terrorist use of social media. In addition, Internet users are not used to reporting what they believe is illegal. As a consequence, some terrorists' use of the Internet is currently not brought to the attention of Internet companies and competent authorities. Moreover, even in the case of removal, terrorists quickly re-post the contents, videos, and photos, using new identities and new "addresses." Terrorists even teach others how to use social media in a "safe mode": ISIS, for example, released in October 2014 an online manual instructing its readers how to avoid revealing location and other data when using Twitter. In March 2015, ISIS published two English-language e-books, advising potential recruits how to evade detection. Similar guidance was posted by al-Qaeda and other groups.

Self-policing requires exposure: first, to expose the extremist content and to inform the social media companies and the public at large of their content, and second, to bring legal measures against companies that continue to host extremist postings. Such implementations would require establishing a database—governmental or nongovernmental—that would regularly publish information about terrorist sites, forums, platforms, and social media, and provide it to the social media companies upon request. The service providers should also explain to their users how these flagging systems work and otherwise stimulate its use. This practice is primarily meant for social media or websites that provide user-generated content, but it could be considered to make the technology more widely available where this is technologically possible.[4]

The challenge of countermeasures has spawned an interdisciplinary research topic—intelligence and security informatics, also known as cognitive security—for studying the development and use of advanced information technologies and systems for national, international, and societal security-related applications. In her February 2014 Los Angeles Times op-ed article on "Future Terrorists," Wilson Center President Jane Harman argued that "we need to employ the best tools we know of to counter radicalizing messages and to build bridges to the vulnerable. . . . Narratives can inspire people to do terrible things, or to push back against those extremist voices" (Harman 2014). In fact, there are several attempts to launch counter-narrative campaigns online. For example, the "Think Again Turn Away" Twitter campaign is a $5 million effort by the U.S. Department of State to directly challenge the messages that Al-Qaeda promotes as justification for its radical causes (Schmitt 2013). It is hard to measure the effectiveness of these campaigns but they were heavily criticized by terrorism experts. Thus, for example, Rita Katz argued that "the Think Again Turn Away campaign has been anything but valiant—particularly on Twitter. This outreach by the U.S. government is not only ineffective, but also provides jihadists with a stage to voice their arguments" (Katz 2014).

To implement such a strategy and to identify appropriate tactics to counter terrorists' narratives, it is necessary to gain a deeper understanding of the role that these narratives play in seducing and persuading target audiences (Aly, 2014). Thus, it appears that a potentially effective way for Western democracies to counter terrorism is to monitor the emerging terrorist narratives and launch credible counter-narratives. The new media represents "an increasing continuation of war by other means," to adapt von Clausewitz's famous phrase. Cyberspace, with its numerous and emerging online platforms, presents new challenges and requires dramatic shifts in strategic thinking regarding national security and countering terrorism. Such shifts include the move from reacting to terrorist moves to anticipatory, preemptive measures (i.e., identifying emerging platforms and technologies and designing them with built-in limitations on potential use by terrorists), and the need for public-private partnerships (PPPs) in combating online terrorism (see further Weimann 2015). Strategic thinkers should look beyond current challenges to future developments and emerging social media resources, and the problems of anticipating and preempting terrorist abuse of these tools.

Notes

1 Omar Hammami used social media to recruit foreign fighters to join al-Shabaab before his death in 2013.
2 From Twitter.com/khorasan313, July 23, 2014.
3 Some of these self-policing regulations are presented in Weimann (2015).
4 However, an experimental study revealed that the effectiveness of the flagging system is rather limited: Out of 125 videos flagged, 57 (45.4 percent) were still online more than four months later. See Stalinsky and Zweig (2013).

References

Advertiser. (2008) "Facebook Terrorism Investigation," April 5, 2008.

Aly, A., Weimann-Saks, D. and Weimann, G. (2014) "Making "Noise" Online: An Analysis of the *Say No to Terror* Online Campaign" in *Perspectives on Terrorism*, vol 8, no 5, pp. 3–47.

Barrett, R. (2014) "Foreign Fighters in Syria." The Soufan Group Report, June 2, 2014.

Berger, JM. (2014) "How ISIS Games Twitter," *The Atlantic Monthly*. Available at: www.theatlantic.com/international/archive/2014/06/isis-iraq-twitter-social-media-strategy/372856/, last accessed January 10, 2015.

Daily Mail. (2014) "Three Teenage Denver Girls Stole $2,000 from their Parents and Ran away to Join ISIS—but Were Caught in Germany after FBI tip off," October 22, 2014. Available at: www.dailymail.co.uk/news/article-2802168/three-girls-way-join-isis-detained-germany.html, last accessed May 5, 2015.

Department of Homeland Security. (2010) "Terrorist Use of Social Networking Facebook Case Study," *Public Intelligence*, December 5, 2010. Available at: www.publicintelligence.net/ufouoles-dhs-terrorist-use-of-social-networking-facebook-case-study, last accessed January 10, 2015.

eMarket. (2013) "Social Usage Involves More Platforms, More Often." Available at: www.emarketer.com/Article/Social-Usage-Involves-More-Platforms-More-Often/1010019, last accessed January 10, 2015.

EUROPOL. (2012) "Annual Terrorism Situation and Trend Report." European Police Office. Available at: www.europol.europa.eu/sites/default/files/publications/europoltsat.pdf, last accessed January 10, 2015.

Harman, J. (2014) "Future Terrorists," *Los Angeles Times*, January 6, 2014. Available at: http://articles.latimes.com/2014/jan/06/opinion/la-oe-harman-terrorism-response-20140106, last accessed March 14, 2014.

Homeland Security Project. (2012) "Countering Online Radicalization in America." *Bipartisan Policy Center*, December 2012. Available at: http://bipartisanpolicy.org/sites/default/files/BPC%20_Online%20Radicalization%20Report.pdf, last accessed January 10, 2015.

Jost, J. and Weimann, G. (2015) "Neue Terrorismus and Neue Medien" in *Zeitschrift für Außen- und Sicherheitspolitik*, vol 8, no 3, pp. 369–388.

Katz, R. (2014) "The State Department's Twitter War with ISIS Is Embarrassing," *Time* September 16, 2014. Available at: http://time.com/3387065/isis-twitter-war-state-department/, last accessed January 10, 2015.

McCants, W. (2011) "Testimony: Jihadist Use of Social Media—How to Prevent Terrorism and Preserve Innovation," *U.S. House of Representatives: Subcommittee on Counterterrorism and Intelligence*, December 6, 2011. Available at: http://homeland.house.gov/hearing/subcommittee-hearing-jihadist-use-social-media-how-prevent-terrorism-and-preserve-innovation, last accessed January 10, 2015.

MEMRI. (2011) "In Interview, Taliban Commander Reveals Details of Their Print Magazines, International Media Operations: 'We Are Also Active on Facebook and Twitter, Where We Publish News Every Day'; 'Wars Today Cannot Be Won Without the Media'–The Media Is Directed at The Heart . . . [and] If The Heart Is Defeated, then the Battle Is Won." Special Dispatch Series No. 3598, February 18, 2011. Available at: www.memrijttm.org/in-interview-taliban-commander-reveals-details-of-their-print-magazines-international-media-operations-we-are-also-active-on-facebook-and-twitter-where-we-publish-news-every-day-wars-today-cannot-be-won-without-the-media-the-media-is-directed-at-the-heart, last accessed January 10, 2015.

MEMRI. (2012a) "Indonesian Militant Umar Patek Urges Muslims to Go to Palestine to Wage Jihad, Calls for Jihad On Internet: 'This Is Not the Stone Age . . . This Is the Internet Era, There Is Facebook, Twitter and Others.'" June 11, 2012. Available at: www.memrijttm.org/indonesian-militant-umar-patek-urges-muslims-to-go-to-palestine-to-wage-jihad-calls-for-jihad-on-internet-this-is-not-the-stone-agethis-is-the-internet-era-there-is-facebook-twitter-and-others.html, last accessed January 10, 2015.

MEMRI. (2012b) "Taliban Spokesman Discusses The Taliban's Media Strategy: 'I Use Computers and Have Accounts On Facebook, Twitter and YouTube; Winning over the Minds and Hearts of the Masses Who Visit the Websites' Is More Important." Jihad and Terrorism Threat Monitor Report, April 17, 2012. Available at: www.memrijttm.org/taliban-spokesman-discusses-the-talibans-media-strategy-i-use-computers-and-have-accounts-on-facebook-twitter-and-youtube-winning-over-the-minds-and-hearts-of-the-masses-who-visit-the-websites-is-more-important.html, last accessed January 10, 2015.

MEMRI. (2013) "In Exclusive Interview in Inspire X, American Al-Qaeda Operative Adam Gadahn Tells "Governments of the Crusader West" To Withdraw from Islamic Lands; Says Arab Spring, Economic Crisis Signs of Their Dwindling Power; Muslim's Ascendency." Special Dispatch Series No. 5210, March 1, 2013. Available at: www.memrijttm.org/in-exclusive-interview-in-inspire-x-american-al-qaeda-operative-adam-gadahn-tells-governments-of-the-crusader-west-to-withdraw-from-islamic-lands-says-arab-spring-economic-crisis-signs-of-their-dwindling-power-muslims-ascendancy.html, last accessed January 10, 2015.

Morgan, N., Jones, G. and Hodges, A. (2012) "Social Media: The Complete Guide to Social Media from the Social Media Guys." Available at: www.yumpu.com/en/document/view/5539277/the-complete-guide-to-social-media-the-social-media-guys, last accessed January 10, 2015.

Noguchi, Y. (2006) "Tracking Terrorists Online," *Washington Post*, April 19, 2006. Available at: www.washingtonpost.com/wp-dyn/content/discussion/2006/04/11/DI2006041100626.html, last accessed January 10, 2015.

Pew Research Center. (2014) "Social Networking Fact Sheet." Available at: www.pewinternet.org/fact-sheets/social-networking-fact-sheet/, last accessed January 10, 2015.

Schmitt, E. (2013) "A U.S. Reply, in English, to Terrorist's Online Lure." *The NY Times*, December 4, 2013. Available at: www.nytimes.com/2013/12/05/world/middleeast/us-aims-to-blunt-terrorist-recruiting-of-english-speakers.html?_r=0, last accessed January 10, 2015.

SITE. (2012) "Jihadist Gives Analysis of Electronic Jihad," January 6, 2012. Available at: https://news.siteintelgroup.com/index.php/19-jihadist-news/1462-jihadist-gives-analysis-of-electronic-jihad, last accessed January 10, 2015.

Statista Report. (2014) "Statistics and facts about Social Networks." Available at: www.statista.com/topics/1164/social-networks/, last accessed January 10, 2015.

Stalinsky, S. and Zweig, E. (2013) "YouTube Questioned in U.K. House of Commons over Keeping Terrorism-Promoting Videos Active on Its Website." MEMRI Inquiry & Analysis Series Report 956, April 9, 2013. Available at: www.memri.org/report/en/0/0/0/0/0/841/7121.htm, last accessed January 10, 2015.

Teich, S. (2013) "Trends and Developments in Lone Wolf Terrorism in the Western World: An Analysis of Terrorist Attacks and Attempted Attacks by Islamic Extremists." *International Institute for Counter-Terrorism*. Available at: http://i-hls.com/wp-content/uploads/2013/11/Lone-Wolf-Sarah-Teich-2013.pdf, last accessed January 10, 2015.

Weimann, G. (2004) *www.Terror.Net: How Modern Terrorism Uses the Internet*. Special Report, Washington, DC: United States Institute of Peace.

Weimann, G. (2006a) *Terror on the Internet: The New Arena, the New Challenges*, Washington, DC: United States Institute of Peace Press.

Weimann, G. (2006b) "Virtual Disputes: The Use of the Internet for Terrorist Debates" in *Studies in Conflict and Terrorism*, vol 29, no7, pp. 623–639.

Weimann, G. (2009) "When Fatwas Clash Online: Terrorist Debates on the Internet." In J. Forest (Ed.), *Influence Warfare: How Terrorists and Governments Fight to Shape Perceptions in a War of Ideas*. Westport, CT: Praeger.

Weimann, G. (2012) "Lone Wolves in Cyberspace," in *Journal of Terrorism Research*, vol 3, no 2, pp. 75–90.

Weimann, G. (2014) "Virtual Packs of Lone Wolves" *Medium.com*, February 25, 2014. Available at: https://medium.com/p/17b12f8c455a, last accessed January 10, 2015.

Weimann, G. (2015) *Terrorism in Cyberspace: The Next Generation*, New York, NY: Columbia University Press.

4 #Westgate

A case study – How al-Shabaab used Twitter during an ongoing attack

David Mair

Introduction

On 21st September 2013, four men entered the Westgate shopping mall in Nairobi, Kenya, armed with automatic weapons and grenades. Initially, police thought that they were dealing with an armed robbery gone wrong (Kabir 2014), and as such, the first police units on the scene were from the Kenyan flying squad. It wasn't until a Twitter account associated with Somalia-based terrorist group al-Shabaab took responsibility for the attack that law enforcement, the Kenyan government and the international media understood that a terrorist attack was developing at the Kenyan shopping mall. The Westgate attack lasted for four days, during which time 67 people were killed and 175 wounded. Throughout the entirety of the attack, al-Shabaab's press office generated Twitter content justifying the attack, creating fictional threats, providing news on hostages and mocking the police and military response. These accounts were often identified and suspended by Twitter, but the terrorist group merely created new accounts in order to continue producing and disseminating its propaganda and narratives. This chapter provides an analysis of these tweets and their composition, content and intended audience.

Little academic attention has been paid to al-Shabaab and the Westgate attack of 2013. Prior to Westgate, al-Shabaab was not a stranger to social media. In an analysis of sub-Saharan terrorist groups' Internet usage, Bertram and Ellison (2014) found that al-Shabaab was especially active on Twitter compared to other groups operating on the African continent. Historically, al-Shabaab operated a number of accounts, both quasi-official and unofficial. For example, foreign fighter Omar Hammami maintained an active Twitter account detailing his life as a member and commander of al-Shabaab up until his death in 2013 (Berger 2013). Al-Shabaab itself also maintained Twitter accounts, and though it never formally acknowledged their existence, these accounts provided information on previous attacks, justified its use of force and produced terrorist propaganda. Pearlman (2012) conducted a content analysis of one of these accounts, identifying that al-Shabaab primarily uses Twitter to reach a global audience, produce and disseminate propaganda and create counter-narratives in the form of news updates and information. This chapter will conduct a similar analysis to that of Pearlman's, allowing comparisons to be drawn between the motivating factors of terrorist use of Twitter during attack and non-attack phases. The legitimacy of these 'official' accounts will be examined in greater detail in the methodology section.

The Westgate attack was the first incidence of a terrorist organisation using Twitter to claim responsibility for an attack before live-tweeting throughout the ongoing operation (Weimann 2014). Prior to this event, Twitter may have been used as a tool to monitor the placement of police and military personnel during attacks, such as in the Mumbai terrorist attack of 2008 (Oh, 2011), and has since been used by Islamic State during the siege of Mosul (The Telegraph 2014). It is likely that Twitter will be used again by terrorist groups during attacks and, as such, live-tweeting by terrorist organisations should be studied by researchers in order to understand the underlying motivations for this activity and to examine the narrative created throughout these strategic online communications. Simon et al. (2014), have published on the Twitter data generated by the Westgate terrorist attack, collecting 67,849 tweets. However, the focus of this paper is not purely on al-Shabaab's tweets; it focuses on an analysis of how information is disseminated during emergencies and how governments and responders could better use Twitter during these situations. Furthermore, this paper only identified 258 tweets from three al-Shabaab Twitter accounts. Of these accounts, two are contained within this analysis and the third account was rejected from this analysis for reasons outlined in the methodology. Sullivan (2014) has analysed tweets on the Westgate attack, sent from an account purporting to be linked to al-Shabaab. However, Sullivan's analysis was limited to a single Twitter account, which was rejected from this analysis as it did not meet the criteria for inclusion, for reasons outlined in the methodology.

This chapter will outline how the Westgate tweets were collected and analysed, before presenting the findings on how al-Shabaab utilised Twitter to communicate throughout the Westgate attack. The first section of this analysis details the composition of these tweets, assessing the usage of external links, communication with other Twitter users and use of image and audio files. The second section of this chapter deals with the content of these tweets, exploring what overarching function and objective they were intended to meet. Finally, this chapter assesses the intended audience of the Twitter feed. This chapter concludes by discussing what the Westgate tweets indicate about al-Shabaab's overarching narrative and ideology, and encourages future empirical research to be conducted on terrorists' use of social media.

Methodology

Compiling the data set

This chapter will assess 556 tweets sent from eight al-Shabaab-affiliated Twitter accounts between 21st and 24th September 2013 – throughout the duration of the Westgate attack. These tweets were assessed in terms of their composition, content and intended audience. By assessing these three variables, it was possible to draw conclusions as to the reasons why terrorist groups choose to use social media during ongoing attacks and also provided an opportunity to draw conclusions as to the motivations and objectives of al-Shabaab itself and the way in which it frames itself while enjoying global government and media attention.

Before being included in this analysis, each Twitter account had to satisfy a number of conditions, the most important of which was that the account was able to demonstrate a reasonable level of evidence of having been affiliated with al-Shabaab in an official or quasi-official capacity. This was largely determined by an analysis of the content and context of the tweets sent from these accounts. While none of the tweeters behind these accounts directly expressed that they were al-Shabaab members, the content of their tweets indicated that they were in contact with the Westgate fighters, had access to senior figures of al-Shabaab leadership, viewed al-Shabaab activities in a sympathetic light and were able to express a high level of knowledge about al-Shabaab's history and motivation. In addition, each of the accounts identified had to adhere to a consistent profile. In all of the accounts, the Twitter handle was a variant of '@HSM . . .' and the profile picture was an al-Shabaab icon – a jihadi symbol involving a black background with white Arabic writing, known as the black flag of jihad, or the black standard. Having met this criteria, the accounts were then subject to content analysis during which the tone, sincerity and commitment to al-Shabaab's ideology were assessed. From this analysis, one account, @HSMPress, was identified and discarded from the analysis. The tone of this account was sarcastic and out of keeping with the other accounts, and as a result the author was judged to not be genuine but instead parodying al-Shabaab. The content generated by @HSMPress has been analysed by Sullivan (2014).

Data collection took place during two phases. The first data collection occurred between 21st and 24th September 2013, as the Westgate attack was happening. As such, these tweets were collected in real time. Collection consisted of a manual search of the '#Westgate' hashtag alongside variations of '@HSM' Twitter handles. As each Twitter account maintained a similar username, these accounts retained consistency, which allowed the researcher to identify and confirm potential terrorist Twitter feeds. Tweets were recorded by taking screenshots and entering their content into a database. A secondary search for data was conducted several months later. This search uncovered a large archive of tweets related to the Westgate attack, which were then collected and added to the database.

In phase one, six Twitter accounts were identified and 265 tweets were collected. In phase two, a further 289 tweets were identified across four accounts, two of which (@HSM_PRESS2 and @HSM_PressOffice) were new to the analysis. The original data collection identified two accounts that weren't present in the online archive (@HSM_SUPERSTARS and @HSM_official1). The original data collection also identified an additional eight tweets from @HSM_PR that weren't present in the online archive of that account. The final analysis therefore included 556 tweets from eight Twitter accounts. Throughout the analysis, where tweets are quoted, they have been produced as originally written, with original spelling and grammar.

68 David Mair

The Twitter accounts and numbers of tweets that make up the data set can be seen in Table 4.1 below.

Table 4.1 Number of tweets collected from each account during each phase of data collection

Twitter handle	Number of tweets collected (phase one)	Number of tweets collected (phase two)	Total number of tweets	Proportion of database (%)
@HSM_PRESOFFICE2	59	161	220	39.6
@HSM_PRESS2	0	115	115	20.7
@HSM_SUPERSTARS	98	0	98	17.6
@HSM_PR	42	0	42	7.6
@HSM_official1	26	0	26	4.6
@HSM_Press	21	4	25	4.5
@HSMPROffice	18	0	18	3.2
@HSM_PressOffice	0	12	12	2.2
Total number of tweets	264	292	556	100.0

Conducting the analysis

Each tweet was assessed in three respects: composition, content and the intended audience. This was an iterative process in which the data was read, considered and then categorised, ensuring that the categories created were the most appropriate ones possible.

Composition

When coding the content of each tweet, the data was assessed on a number of variables, such as inclusion of a link to an external website, how often each account interacted with other Twitter users and whether the tweets contained any picture or video files. Additionally, each tweet was assessed on whether or not it contained any threatening content, such as a direct threat to civilians or government, or promised future violence.

Content

The content of the tweets was assessed on three factors: their function, objective and any explicitly religious or political motivations present.

Terrorist groups use the Internet for a variety of purposes (Weimann 2004; Denning 2009). Macdonald and Mair (2015) summarised these uses into three overarching functions – outreach, logistics and attack – with each function further subdivided into publicity and propaganda, recruitment and radicalisation, and networking (outreach); online training, research and planning, command and control of attacks, and financing (logistics); and psychological warfare and cyberattacks (attack). In the present study, each tweet was coded, based on its content, as falling into one, or more, of these functions. For example, tweets that encouraged individuals to engage in jihad were classed as recruitment and radicalisation; tweets that contained instructions were coded as command and control; threats of upcoming attacks were classed as psychological warfare; and tweets that attempted to justify the attack or further al-Shabaab's ideology were classified as publicity and propaganda. Some tweets met the criteria for coding as more than one function, and in these cases they were coded as both. As such, at times, the number of tweets discussed in the analysis may sum to greater than 556.

Each tweet was then further assessed in terms of a specific objective. This was an iterative process during which the categories were informed and influenced by the tweets themselves. As such, rather than approaching the data set with preconceived hypotheses to test for, the classifications were created based on the content of the tweets. There was no minimum number of tweets that had to be present in the data set for a category to be created; the objective merely had to be distinct from the other categories identified. This was a process that required multiple readings of the data to ensure that all objectives had been identified. The identified categories were furthering of terrorist ideology, justification of attack, contempt for response, threats of future attack, news updates, praise for attackers, anti-Western rhetoric, celebration of attack and invitation to direct contact with al-Shabaab. As with the function variable, a number of tweets met the criteria for inclusion in multiple objective categories. Like earlier, they were coded for the number of objectives present in the content of the tweet and, as such, the total number of tweets discussed in the analysis in terms of objectives may sum to more than 556.

Finally, it was noted when tweets contained explicit political or religious content. This was done in order to better understand the group's ideology and identify empirical evidence to assess the claim that New Terrorism is largely religiously, not politically, motivated.

Intended audience

Terrorism is not just violence. It is a strategic communication that involves the use, or threat, of violence (Richards 2014). Being that the act of terrorism is in itself a communicative process, aimed at influencing some form of change, it is important to understand who this communication is aimed at in order to understand the terrorists' objectives. As Brian Jenkins (1974) famously wrote: 'Terrorism is aimed at the people watching, not the actual victims. Terrorism is theatre'. Since Twitter provides a platform within which terrorist groups can communicate with every form of participant – from government offices to eyewitness citizens – this data set provides an opportunity to assess the intended audience of the Westgate terrorist attack and the subsequent communications towards these individuals and groups.

For this reason, the tweets were assessed in terms of who they were intended to address. In total, six potential audiences were identified: the Kenyan Government, Kenyan citizens, the West, terrorist sympathisers, emergency responders and the media.

Limitations

The two principal limitations of the study are the extent to which the data collected could be considered a reliable and credible source of al-Shabaab affiliated tweets and the limitations imposed on collecting Twitter data in real time.

The first issue to address is the legitimacy of the accounts involved. The original Twitter account identified, @HSM_Press, had been in operation since December 2011. While it had never been officially linked to al-Shabaab, it had provided reliable information regarding al-Shabaab's activities, and did so in a pro al-Shabaab manner. The account created counter-narratives to African Mission to Somalia (AMISOM) security forces publicity, up-to-date information on current al-Shabaab operations and acted as a point of contact for journalists (Pearlman 2012). @HSM_Press often provided accurate information before legitimate news outlets, once evidencing that al-Shabaab had captured AMISOM soldiers by publishing pictures of military identity cards (Aljazeera 2011). It is clear that the author(s) of @HSM_Press had a high level of interest in the activities of al-Shabaab and if not an official spokesperson for the group, sympathised with its objectives and actions. In this respect, it is clear that @HSM_Press met the criteria for inclusion in this study. Having established the credibility of this account, it was necessary to ensure that each following account demonstrated a similar level of legitimacy. For example, all the Twitter accounts identified in this analysis presented themselves as speaking on behalf of al-Shabaab – some accounts even claimed to have had direct contact with the attackers. While these claims are not guarantees of legitimacy, the content of the Twitter accounts made it clear that the operators were very sympathetic to al-Shabaab's aims and objectives. Finally, the accounts all followed a similar naming and avatar-image pattern. Often, newly established accounts referenced previous accounts that had been suspended. The consistency of the content, in addition to the consistency in the branding of the accounts, suggests that the accounts were operated by the same individuals or group of individuals.

The second issue to address is the method of data collection. The tweets were collected in real time. As these tweets were authored by a designated terrorist organisation (United States of America State Department 2015) and contained hate speech, threats and abusive language, the accounts were in violation of Twitter's Terms of Service (Twitter 2015). As such, they were often reported and suspended by Twitter, making the tweets inaccessible. In addition, the '#Westgate' hashtag was trending worldwide at the time, with several thousand tweets being generated on the topic each minute. This made it very challenging to identify the accounts involved in tweeting terrorist content and to collect all of the tweets before they were flagged and suspended. Therefore, it was not possible to collect all of the tweets during the original collection. In order to mitigate the risk posed by this limitation, a secondary search for data was conducted. The author is now satisfied that the vast majority of content has been found and is present in this analysis.

This data was drawn from a single terrorist group's use of Twitter during a specific attack. While this study will draw conclusions on how and why al-Shabaab used Twitter during the Westgate terrorist attack, it should be viewed as a pilot study on terrorist groups' aims and motivations for social media usage. Further empirical research will need to be conducted to understand the extent to which these findings are of wider application.

Findings and analysis

Intended audience

Internet and Twitter metrics

Internet Live Stats (2015), which extrapolates data on global Internet connectivity from sources including the International Telecommunication Union (ITU), United Nations Population Division, Internet and Mobile Association of India (IAMAI) and the World Bank, states Somalia has approximately 163,183 Internet users (1.51 per cent of the country's population). Kenya, on the other hand, has 16,713,319 Internet users (30.7 per cent of the country's population). Exact numbers of Twitter users in each country are unavailable but it is reasonable to infer that al-Shabaab did not use Twitter in order to reach the 1.51 per cent of Somalians with an Internet connection as this would be a very inefficient method of communication. After all, of the 1.51 per cent of Somalians online, not all will be Twitter users. In addition, the Somalians with Internet access are likely to be in the top socio-economic bracket, and unlikely to be sympathetic to al-Shabaab's cause. In fact, to reach the non-Internet connected masses of Somalia, al-Shabaab operates a number of radio stations that broadcast in English, Arabic and Somali (Ploch 2010).

In addition, of the 556 Tweets, only 15 (2.7 per cent) were not in English. Of these, seven were in Arabic, four were in Somali and four were a mixture of languages, one being a mixture of English and Arabic and three being a mixture of Somali and English. As the national language of Somalia is Somali, it is unlikely that these English language tweets were aimed at Somalians. Kenya's official language, on the other hand, is English. As the Westgate attack took place in Kenya, the tweets were written in the national language of Kenya, and Kenya has a much higher incidence of Internet connectivity, it is more plausible that these tweets were aimed at the Kenyan population, though they may also have been aimed at other English-speaking groups following the events in Westgate.

Intended readership

Six audiences to the Westgate tweets were identified: the general Kenyan population, the Kenyan government, the West, the media, terrorist sympathisers and emergency responders.

The primary groups at which the tweets were targeted were the general Kenyan population, the Kenyan government and terrorist sympathisers. Emergency responders, the West and the media received far less attention from the account controllers.

72 David Mair

```
441 — General Kenyan population
256 — Terrorist sympathisers
215 — Kenyan Government
46  — The West
28  — Emergency responders
17  — Media
```

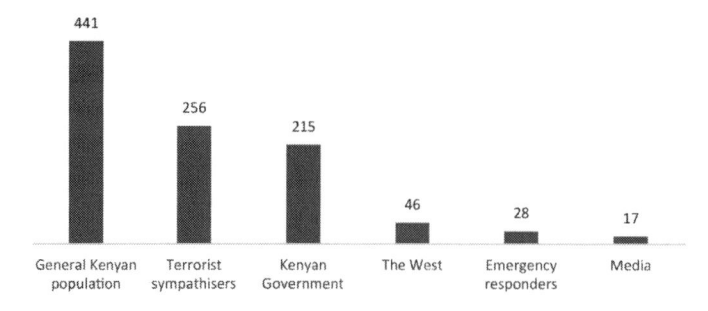

Figure 4.1 Intended readership of tweets

The reason that the Kenyan population and government were targeted by the tweets may be a very simple one. As terrorism is a strategic action aimed at generating an audience (Jenkins 1974), it is perhaps to be expected that the majority of tweets was directed at those most affected by the Westgate attack.

The West was the intended audience for forty-six tweets, 8.27 per cent of the data set, and the media were the intended audience for seventeen tweets, accounting for 3.05 per cent of the data set. Reasons why al-Shabaab did not appear to prioritise reaching the West or the media are explored later in this analysis.

Composition

This section details the composition of the tweets. This includes links to external websites, references to other Twitter users, use of images and other media files, and the extent to which threatening content was present.

Links to external websites

In addition to social media accounts, al-Shabaab maintained an official website (since taken down), has a number of unofficial blogs, produces an online magazine and hosts a number of online jihadist forums (Ploch 2010). These online environments have been credited with the recruitment of foreign fighters and the production of terrorist propaganda.

With such a large reliance on online platforms, it is perhaps surprising that the vast majority of tweets did not link out to an external website. Out of 556 tweets, only eight (1.4 per cent) contained a URL within the tweet. This is especially surprising when compared to Twitter content produced by Jabhat-al-Nusra. According to a study conducted by Prucha and Fisher (2013) of 76,000 tweets analysed, more than 34,000 links (44 per cent) were generated. The tweets involving URLs are quoted in Table 4.2 below.

A further finding is that only two of the eight identified accounts (@HSM_PR and @HSM_Press) directed users to external websites.

#Westgate: a case study   73

Table 4.2 Tweets involving external links

Twitter handle	Tweet
@HSM_PR	'TRANSCRIPT: Speech of HSM Leader, Shaykh Mukhtar Abu Zubayr, regarding the #Westgate Operation All praise is . . . [URL]'
@HSM_PR	'An English Audio interpretation of Shaykh Mukhtar Abu Aubayr's speech regarding #Westgate attacks. [URL]'
@HSM_PR	As above. Tweet published in Somali.
@HSM_PR	'A Swahili Nasheed of praise dedicated specifically to the Mujahideen inside #Westgate Mall. Kenyans, take note [URL]'
@HSM_PR	'As per Kafir testimony, Mujahideen gave women and children at #Westgate a safe passage before beginning their assault [URL]'
@HSM_PR	'Here's a short ARABIC statement by HSM spokesman, Sh Ali Dhere, regarding the #Westgate operation [URL]'
@HSM_PR	As above. Tweet published in Arabic.
@HSM_Press	'Verily, those who disbelieve spend their wealth to hinder (men) from the Path of Allah, and so will they (cont) [URL]'

In the first three instances, the tweets linked to archive websites – webpages that allow users to submit documents and data for the purposes of storage or for others to view. The Swahili nasheed of praise was uploaded to SoundCloud, the news article came from the Metro newspaper and the statement from Shaykh Ali Dhere was uploaded to gulfup.com (an Arabic language digital drop box type website). None of the links directed users to official or unofficial al-Shabaab websites.

This is surprising, as one might assume that terrorist groups, eager to capitalise on the publicity that their attack has generated, would be quick to divert audiences to their online communities or materials. However, this hasn't happened in this instance. Instead, the external links are to innocuous websites with no terrorist links or content. There are two possible explanations for this.

First, the groups operating the Twitter account wish to retain control of the narrative for as long as possible. By restricting the number of links on their accounts, the groups ensure a captive audience and do not have to rely on – or trust – journalists to provide positive publicity. In the one circumstance of linking to a newspaper article, the news item portrayed al-Shabaab positively. In it, the mujahideen can be seen to comply with hadiths that charge them not to harm women or children. This provides al-Shabaab with credibility when it discusses its moral superiority and nobility of its fighters in comparison with that of the Kenyan security forces it is fighting against, who – by al-Shabaab's narrative – often kill women and children.

Second, it is possible those operating the Twitter accounts understood that the majority of individuals reading the tweets would have been horrified by the atrocities committed at Westgate. Linking to a website that celebrated the actions at Westgate would have lost whatever sympathy or positive spin generated by the Twitter account. This links in closely with previous findings from Bertram and

Ellison (2014) who conducted a study into links generated from al-Shabaab Twitter feeds. They found that while al-Shabaab's Twitter feeds did link to external websites, they primarily linked to open source news content and not radical or extremist websites. Similarly, Pearlman (2012) found that al-Shabaab's Twitter usage was primarily focused around information generation, not signposting.

To this end, it can be concluded that al-Shabaab's aim in operating a Twitter account during the Westgate terrorist attack was not to act as a springboard or advertisement to other online content, but instead engage in information generation.

Conversations within Twitter

Twitter is inherently a communication tool, used to facilitate short conversation between individuals and organisations. By using Twitter during the Westgate attack, al-Shabaab had the opportunity to communicate widely to a global audience, or to engage in conversation with a specific individual, or group of individuals. In the vast majority of cases, however, al-Shabaab chose to communicate widely and shunned the opportunity to engage with individuals directly. Eleven tweets, just 2 per cent of the total data set, included a reference to specific Twitter users. These tweets are detailed in Table 4.3 below.

Of these 'direct' communications with other Twitter users, three could be argued to be contacting individuals for symbolic effect, as opposed to for genuine communication purposes. Twitter user @Ukenyata (ref 4) refers to the president of Kenya, whose political leadership of the military action in Somalia al-Shabaab claims to be responding to. When al-Shabaab links him or David Cameron (ref 9) in its tweets, it is not inviting them to engage in discussion, but merely inflating its own status to that of a world leader, pointing out how it has disrupted the activities of important people and focused global attention on the Westgate crisis. Should these tweets provoke a response from these world leaders, it further reinforces the impact that al-Shabaab has had globally. Similarly, when al-Shabaab communicates with Twitter (ref 4) in its tweets, it is not making a genuine complaint of harassment, but is mocking Twitter's response of suspending its accounts and showing how fruitless a task it is. This may have also been used as a tactic to increase the following of the Twitter account. When tweets are directed at users, they can appear in searches for that user. Any individual searching on Twitter for @kenyatta, @David_Cameron or @Twitter may have seen these tweets and been drawn into the narrative. As this is a fairly convoluted way of increasing followers and was only attempted a small number of times, however, it is unlikely that this was the main motivation in tweeting directly to these individual user accounts.

Two of the tweets did not respond or interact with individuals, but instead referred to other Twitter accounts operated by al-Shabaab (ref 5 + 10). The motivation behind this was either to publicise new accounts in expectation of suspension or to establish credibility in claiming to be the new account of a previously trusted, and now suspended, account.

Interestingly, five of the identified accounts did make genuine responses to specific individuals (ref 1, 2, 3, 6 + 11). Of those, one account is no longer active

#Westgate: a case study 75

Table 4.3 Tweets involving direct contact with other Twitter users

Reference	Twitter handle	Tweet
1	@HSM_official1	'Our comrades are in full of the #WestGate, let not enyat police tell you propaganda about what is happening inside.@xxx'
2	@HSM_official1	'The term "negotiatinn" was ruled out absolutely, what we are calling for tho is Kenya to withdraw its troops from Somalia. @xxx'
3	@HSM_official1	'Kindly tell us which news org do u work for and where are u tweeting us from?thanks @xxx'
4	@HSM_official1	'@Twitter @ukenyatta is threatening us thus violating your TOS, so we call upon you to suspend his account.thanks'
5	@HSM_PRESS2	'follow @HSM_PressOffice, @HSMPRESS2 @HSMPRESSOFFIC1 incase of suspension of any of the above accounts'
6	@HSM_PRESS2	'@xxx why would they trace us? Free speech bitch'
7	@HSM_PRESS2	'@kenya we are gonna bring you down to your knees! #westgate #AlShabaab'
8	@HSM_PR	'@Ukenyata and his govt are to be held culpable for #Westgate and for the lives of the 137 hostages who were being held by the Mujahideen'
9	@HSM_PR	'For #Woolwich, @David_Cameron cut short his trip to France to chair Cobra. For #Westgate he had to cut his trip to Balmoral to chair Cobra!'
10	@HSMPRESOFFICE2	'earlier tweets on our suspended acc @hsm_press2 we revealed the names of our mujahideen! And well tweet the rest #westgateattack #westgate'
11	@HSMPROffice	'@xxx @xxx @xxx Consider it done'.

Note: some usernames have been removed to protect the account holders.

(ref 1), two appear to be randomly contacted individuals (ref 2 + 6) and four identify themselves as journalists who report on security, Africa or a combination of both (ref 3 +11). This last group may have been contacted due to its intrinsic value to al-Shabaab. While al-Shabaab appears to have tried to retain control of the narrative of the attack as much as possible, it would have known that journalists would report on Westgate. Responding to journalists' enquiries could be interpreted as an attempt to generate positive publicity.

Overall, however, there was no real attempt to interact with Twitter users. Ninety-eight per cent of the tweets did not involve contacting users and none of the tweets that did led to a discussion. This can be explained as another attempt to preserve the audience's interest in the Twitter account. Had al-Shabaab engaged in discussions on its Twitter feed, it would have soon been overrun with either celebrations of the attack with sympathisers, or debates and justifications with detractors. In either case, al-Shabaab would no longer have had complete control over the narrative as it would be responding to the narratives imposed on it by others. As such, it was very selective in who it interacted with in order to ensure that it maintained its audience's interest while also retaining control of the overarching narratives.

Use of images

Images are intrinsically important to terrorist groups' publicity and propaganda campaigns. During the murder of Fusilier Lee Rigby in London, Michael Adebolajo and Michael Adebowale encouraged passers-by to film the assault on their phones and gave impromptu interviews that were later broadcast around the world. Similarly, the 9/11 attackers knew that their actions would make world news, accompanied by striking images of their attack. Terrorists have to ensure that their attack generates publicity in order to benefit from an audience. Ensuring that there are striking images of their event is an important consideration for all terrorist groups when planning, coordinating and carrying out an attack. The al-Qaeda magazine *Inspire* went so far as to provide potential jihadists with suggestions for targets and tactics that would guarantee maximum media exposure (Bosco 2013). Some researchers have even claimed that cyberterrorism – in the sense of catastrophic cyberattacks against critical national infrastructure – is unlikely to be of interest to terrorist groups, partly due to the lack of spectacular images that this would create (Conway 2014).

It is very surprising, then, that only two images were broadcast across the Twitter accounts. It was the same image, tweeted once in English and once in Arabic, portraying two of the mujahideen walking through the shopping mall with their weapons. In other words, less than 1 per cent (0.36 per cent) of the tweets had an accompanying image. This is surprising as recent research has indicated that a tweet is 35 per cent more likely to be retweeted if it contains an image (Twitter 2014).

It is possible that this image was used because it was widely circulated through social media during the Westgate attack and al-Shabaab wanted to put its own spin on it. However, this is the only image that was used, when there were many others available through social media and via news sources. There are perhaps two reasons why this image alone was disseminated. First, those that were responsible for tweeting were not in the Westgate mall with the attackers. As such, they had no access to live images from within Westgate and had to rely on the security services and news media to release images of the attack. Second, because of the tactics employed at Westgate, with point-blank executions of civilians, the images released of the attack at the Westgate mall were very graphic. Posting photos showing armed militants murdering unarmed civilians would result in al-Shabaab losing any positive publicity that it had generated and would not allow it to paint its mujahideen as heroically fighting the Kenyan security forces, despite being outmanned and outgunned. Instead, it would be portrayed as a vicious killer. It is

#Westgate: a case study   77

also likely that the graphic nature of the images would turn the audience of the Twitter feed away, leading to reduced numbers of people reading.

Threatening and non-threatening content

One of the defining features of terrorism is the use or threat of force, to advance a political or ideological cause. As such, it is unsurprising that al-Shabaab capitalised on the increased attention that its social media accounts were receiving to make some threats against the population.

While the majority of the tweets were non-threatening in nature, a quarter (24.6 per cent) of the tweets contained some form of threat against the hostages held at Westgate, the security forces outside the mall or the general Kenyan population. This made up 144 of the total number of tweets sent across all eight accounts. In addition, al-Shabaab used psychological warfare techniques to make fictional threats about imminent attacks and spread misinformation to ensure that no attempt was made to rescue any hostages lest they be harmed.

> '5th squad enroute to ther undisclosed location to carry our the next attack! Hoaaa-ah! #alshabaab #westgate' – @HSM_PRESOFFICE2

Despite the threat made in this tweet, there was no 5th squad and there was no next attack. Instead, al-Shabaab's Twitter account had been used to cause panic among the Kenyan population, put the security forces under strain as they responded to the new information and divert attention away from the Westgate mall. With this tweet, the audience is reminded that they are at direct risk of being subject to harm by the terrorist actors and that nowhere in Kenya is safe at that point.

> 'The Mujahideen inside #WestGateMall killed more than 100 kuffars so far. Mission yet to be fulfilled.#JihadDispatches' – @HSM_official1

In this tweet, the attackers highlight the human cost of the Westgate attack, but sign off by reminding the audience that their mission is not yet completed and that more bloodshed may follow. It is a stark reminder that al-Shabaab is prepared to kill a high number of individuals and will continue to do so until its mission is complete.

However, the majority of the tweets published by al-Shabaab were not threatening in nature. Over 70 per cent of these tweets contained no threatening content whatsoever. Instead, these tweets focused on the grievances that al-Shabaab claim to legitimately have, such as military involvement by the Kenyan military in Somalia, persecution of Somalian citizens and religious justifications for the attack (see next section). These tweets seek to provide justification for the attack, but do not promise future violence.

One reason that al-Shabaab may have published more innocuous than threatening tweets is to ensure that the Twitter accounts maintained their audience. An account that continually makes threats against its audience is likely to lose its readership. By subjecting its readers to threats, the account is likely to create high levels of fear and anxiety but will mean that the audience is less likely to read the updates that are published. As such, a balance between terrorising and maintaining the audience needs to be struck.

Moreover, when making threats against a population, the issue of credibility must be considered. When a terrorist group threatens attacks that do not materialise, that group loses its credibility. If al-Shabaab were to make a high number of threats that did not occur, it is likely that some of its other claims, such as having hostages strapped to bombs or being in a position to defend the mall from assault, would have been brought into question. This would ultimately lead to the accounts no longer being trusted as sources of useful and pertinent information.

Content

Function

In this section, tweets are assessed in terms of their function. This assessment was based on identified ways terrorist groups use the Internet such as engaging in publicity and propaganda, recruitment and radicalisation, networking, online training, command and control of attacks, financing, psychological warfare and cyberattacks (Weimann 2004; Denning 2009). Figure 4.2 below shows the number of tweets by objectives.

As evident, the primary reason for engaging with Twitter was publicity and propaganda (88.3 per cent). This is perhaps unsurprising, as Twitter itself is a publicity tool used the world over by organisations to promote products. In this respect, terrorist organisations share the same objective as legitimate businesses. This is in line with al-Shabaab's prior use of Twitter. Pearlman (2012) states that, prior to the Westgate attack, al-Shabaab's Twitter account was utilised for the creation of 'dynamic propaganda' – a communication that 'both defies an opponent and furthers another belief'.

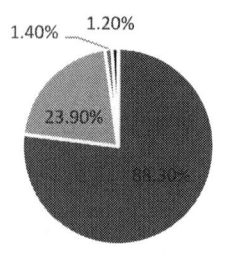

- Publicity and propaganda - 495
- Psychological warfare - 133
- Command and control - 8
- Recruitment and radicalisation - 7

Figure 4.2 Overarching tweet function

Of the tweets, 23.9 per cent were for the purpose of conducting psychological warfare. This is in line with the proportion of tweets that contained a threat (24.6 per cent). Examples of tweets made for the purposes of conducting psychological warfare include direct threats of future attacks and updates regarding imminent assaults elsewhere in Kenya.

Eight tweets were related to command and control of attacks, comprising 1.4 per cent of the tweets captured. These tweets pertained to messages allegedly from al-Shabaab's high command and usually centred on commands to begin strikes elsewhere in Nairobi. All eight command and control tweets were also examples of psychological warfare.

The seven tweets (1.2 per cent) relating to recruitment and radicalisation were not necessarily direct calls to join al-Shabaab, but were more general calls to take part in the global jihad. As one tweet put it:

'we received requests from our brothers across the world to join us fulfil our goals! Well look into it. Inshalah. Keep up the good spirits' – @HSM_PRESOFFICE2

In this tweet, no offer of recruitment into al-Shabaab is made. Previously al-Shabaab has actively recruited foreign fighters via the Internet. American jihadist Omar Hammimi, who was a senior commander in al-Shabaab until in-group fighting led to his death at the hands of his former colleagues, had prominently featured in videos, audio tapes and written statements released through Twitter inviting Westerners to join al-Shabaab's ranks (Anti-Defamation League 2013). This is particularly interesting as terrorist sympathisers were the second most targeted audience for the tweets (see Figure 4.1). In total, 256 tweets were aimed at terrorist sympathisers, but only seven tweets attempted to recruit these sympathisers to jihad. That al-Shabaab did not use the large scale and successful attack on the Westgate shopping mall to recruit more fighters to their cause may signify that al-Shabaab is moving away from recruiting foreign fighters. This ties in with changes in al-Shabaab's recruitment strategy. In 2011, the United States House of Representatives heard evidence that approximately 40 US and 20 Canadian citizens had been recruited to al-Shabaab since 2009 (United States of America Committee on Homeland Security 2011). By mid-2013, these recruitment efforts seem to have stopped. Pantucci and Sayyid (2013) point out that internal power struggles within the leadership of al-Shabaab, splits between foreign and local recruits, disruption of Western terror cells that had historical links to al-Shabaab and new battlefields emerging in Syria and other Arab Spring nations all led to decreased interest from Western jihadis in travelling to Somalia. The Westgate attack, occurring in late 2013, fell at a time where these issues were unresolved, providing an explanation for why there was not an English-language recruitment drive from the publicity this attack generated. Alternately, or additionally, al-Shabaab may be attempting to signal its strength by not showing a need for new volunteers.

80 David Mair

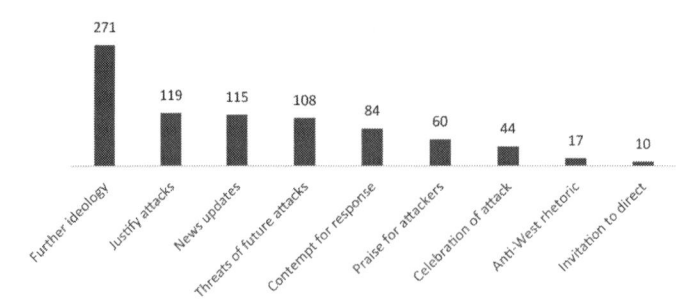

Bar chart with values: Further ideology 271; Justify attacks 119; News updates 115; Threats of future attacks 108; Contempt for response 84; Praise for attackers 60; Celebration of attack 44; Anti-West rhetoric 17; Invitation to direct 10.

Figure 4.3 Tweet objective

Objective

The previous section looked at what function the Westgate tweets were meant to perform. This section deals with the why of the matter – the intended purpose of each tweet. In total, nine objectives were identified from the content of the tweets. These are distinct from the overarching objectives that are applicable to all terrorist use of the Internet and more succinctly define the reasons why al-Shabaab was interested in using social media during the Westgate attack.

As can be seen in Figure 4.3, the primary tweet type that al-Shabaab used Twitter to convey during the Westgate terrorist attack was to further its ideology, accounting for almost half (48.7 per cent) of all tweets. This finding can be explained with reference to the level of publicity that this attack generated. As the attack against Westgate garnered worldwide media attention, it is reasonable to assume that al-Shabaab would wish to push its agenda as much as possible. The second and third most common tweet types were to justify the attack (21.4 per cent) and to produce news content (20.7 per cent). Again, this can be explained given that the tweets were sent while the attack was ongoing. As the attack against Westgate was the main motivating factor driving the Twitter feeds, it is understandable that a substantial portion of the tweets dealt with both updates as to developments at the mall and the reasons behind the attack, the most commonly cited of which were the military incursions into Somalia and human rights abuses by AMISOM troops.

19.4 per cent of the Twitter content was comprised of threats of future attacks. This would generally be expected in the context of the 24.6 per cent of tweets that were threatening in nature. These tweets made several references to the Westgate attack being a drill, and that further, grander attacks would occur unless Kenya responded to al-Shabaab's demands. However, it should be noted that these threats only accounted for a fifth of the total Twitter content. This can be explained, as noted earlier, by a desire to retain an audience base.

That there was contempt shown for the response to the Westgate attack (15.1 per cent) can be explained as the tweets were not only discussing the attackers' intentions at the mall, as in the furthering of ideology, justifications and news updates, but were responding to changes in the mall's environment, such as the

#Westgate: a case study   81

presence of security forces and any attempts made to rescue hostages or bring the siege to an end. This would be expected in any dynamic situation where events are constantly developing. That this comprised a minor volume of the Twitter content as a whole is perhaps indicative of al-Shabaab's desire to retain control of the narrative of the attack, and a desire to focus on its own actions at the mall, rather than those of others.

What is perhaps surprising is that very little attention was paid to encourage individuals to contact al-Shabaab. There was very little attempt at reaching out to journalists or government officials via the Twitter account; attempts of this nature only accounted for ten tweets (1.8 per cent of the data set). This may initially suggest that al-Shabaab was unwilling to give up the control of the narrative to others and wished to rely on its own communications for publicity. However, a small number of tweets directed towards journalists mentioned a mailing list that would shortly be disseminating a press release, so contact with journalists and maintenance of the Twitter accounts were activities that were kept distinct.

Also noteworthy is the lack of engagement in anti-Western rhetoric. Al-Shabaab officially merged with al-Qaeda in November 2012, eleven months before the Westgate attack happened. As al-Qaeda is a key player in the Global Jihad against the West, it was expected that a higher number of al-Shabaab's tweets would have engaged in anti-Western rhetoric or made threats directly against the West. However, as Figure 4.3 above shows, only seventeen tweets included anti-West rhetoric, comprising 3 per cent of the data set. When this figure is further assessed to identify what proportion of these seventeen tweets were threatening in nature, it becomes clear that al-Shabaab was not interested in producing threatening, anti-Western content.[1]

As can be seen from Figure 4.4, of the small fraction of tweets containing anti-Western rhetoric only four were threatening in nature. While this made up 23.5 per cent of all tweets involving anti-West rhetoric, it comprised less than 1 per cent (0.89 per cent) of the entire data set. The text of these four tweets was as follows:

> 'When you rise America will fall on its knees! When you understand, EU will disappear! When you act the world will notice you! #Westgate' – @HSM_SUPERSTARS

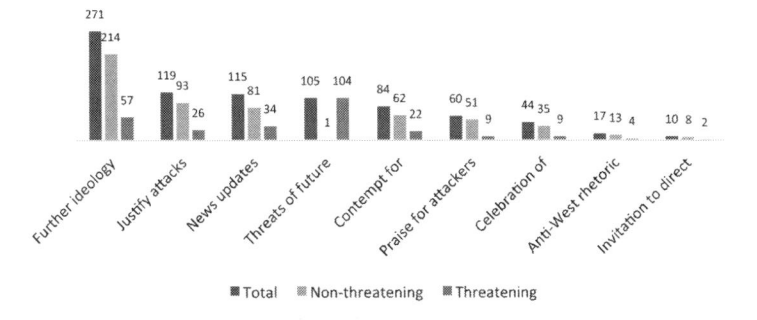

Figure 4.4 Tweet objective by threat content

'It's an eye for an eye and a tooth for a tooth' . . .' Remember Mujahid Adebolajo? This is what he meant. His was #Woolwich, #Westgate ours!' – @HSM_PR

'6 reckless American hostages are likely to execute point blank! #westgate #AlShabaab' – @HSM_PRESOFFICE2

'update: 6 americans execute point blank #westgate #AlShabaab' – @HSM_PRESOFFICE2

While sinister in nature, none of these statements amount to a direct threat against the West from al-Shabaab. While the @HSM_SUPERSTARS tweet attempts to incite others to a global crusade against Western superpowers, it does not fit with the normal message narrative and does not suggest that al-Shabaab will be the group that destroys America or the EU. This suggests that al-Shabaab is far more concerned with fighting against Kenyan intervention in Somalia than it is in engaging in global jihad. The two tweets relating to American hostages appear to be more antagonistic than threatening and are unlikely to cause concern to the vast majority of Americans who are unaffected by terrorism and instability in Africa. When we consider that the West was the intended audience for a mere forty-six tweets (8.27 per cent), it becomes clear that the publicity generated during the Westgate attack was not intended to intimidate or directly threaten the West.

For all categories, the number of non-threatening tweets was higher except for the threat of future attacks category. In fact, the proportion of threatening content was similar across all categories, and was similar to the 24.6 per cent figure of tweets involving threatening content.

Political versus religious content

There has been an ongoing discussion within academic literature on the underlying motivations of terrorist groups. Pointing to the manner in which many terrorist organisations have justified attacks, some researchers have argued that contemporary terrorism should be understood as religiously, not politically, motivated. This is one of the respects in which the New Terrorism thesis claims that contemporary terrorism is different from the 'old' terrorism of the past (Hoffman 1989; Laquer 2000; Neumann 2009). The 'four waves' theory goes even further, stating that the motivation behind terrorist groups can be tracked chronologically through four distinct generations: from anarchic, to anti-colonial, to extreme left wing, to religious – where we are now (Rapoport 2004). Others, however, reject this hypothesis, arguing that terrorists are as politically motivated today as they have always been, citing that the objectives of groups such as al-Qaeda have had little to do with religion and more to do with politics, territory and consolidating power (Duyvesteyn 2004; Abrahms 2009).

Despite this discussion, there has been little attempt at an empirical analysis of the narratives that have surrounded recent terrorist attacks (McAllister and Schmid 2011). Bowie and Schmid (2011) conducted a comprehensive analysis of twenty terrorism incident databases and found that none of these monitored or collected terrorist communications, allowing categorisation of terrorists' overarching motivations and narratives. To address this gap, this study conducted an analysis of the Westgate tweets in terms of explicit political and religious content present in the tweets.

The number of political tweets versus the number of tweets that were religious in nature were similar. Tweets with political content appeared 106 times (accounting for 19.1 per cent of the data set) and explicitly religious tweets accounted for eighty-seven tweets (15.6 per cent of the data set). Such figures make it very difficult to describe the Westgate attack as primarily motivated by either politics or religion. However, in the light of this finding, it is clear that the number of tweets containing religious content have not outflanked the number of tweets involving political content. This is an important finding, given, first, that it has been argued that the explicit reference in many legal definitions of terrorism to religious motivation is unnecessary, as these definitions also refer to political motives, and, second, that some researchers have argued that any reference to religion is not only offensive to members of the relevant faith – the majority of which are peaceful moderates – but is also unhelpful as it reinforces negative stereotypes associating Islam with terrorism and may lead to racial profiling, the creation of suspect communities and human rights violations (Hardy 2011).

Moreover, this finding resonates with a research report produced by the RAND Corporation that undertook an analysis into how terrorist groups end (Jones and Libicki 2008). The biggest contributing factor to the end of a terrorist group was found to be a political change in the environment in which the terrorist group operated. Of the 268 terrorist groups studied, 43 per cent came to an end through a process of politicisation, involving policy changes, territory changes or regime changes – acts that al-Shabaab claimed to be fighting for throughout its tweets. As previous terrorist groups have been ended through engagement in a political process, and al-Shabaab is evidenced to be calling for political change, it is submitted that it should be regarded primarily as a violent political force operating in the Horn of Africa, rather than as an apocalyptical religious cult with which no discussion or negotiation is possible.

Conclusions

Al-Shabaab's use of Twitter seemed to be characterised by a desire to retain control over the narrative of its attack. By not linking to external websites or inviting communication with others, al-Shabaab was able to focus on furthering its ideology, provide justifications for why it had carried out the attack, and, express contempt for the response made by Kenyan security forces and government officials. With this in mind, counterterrorism efforts that attempt to engage directly with terrorist propaganda teams on social media appear unlikely to gain any traction. One of the challenges identified by this research paper is that rather than engaging with the terrorist actors, counterterrorist narratives should be addressed to the intended recipients of the terrorist Twitter accounts.

In order to maintain its audience, one of al-Shabaab's primary motivations for tweeting was to deliver news updates. As these came from sources supposedly within the Westgate mall, al-Shabaab was able to claim credibility. In order to retain the audience garnered by these updates, al-Shabaab adopted an innocuous tone to its communications, shying away from presenting graphic images from within the mall. Furthermore, while psychological warfare tactics accounted for 23.9 per cent of tweets, al-Shabaab refrained from expressing a high number of threats of imminent attacks (n = 105; 18.9 per cent) in order to retain its audience – though it is likely that this was also done in order to maintain al-Shabaab's credibility when future attacks are genuinely planned. This provides worthwhile evidence for use in future counter-narrative campaigns where psychological warfare tactics are used to threaten fictional future attacks. Managing the public concern regarding these attacks should be a key component of any counter-narrative strategy to ensure that widespread panic does not emerge within civilian populations threatened through psychological warfare means.

The primary target audience of these tweets was found to be the Kenyan population and government. The West and the world's media were not found to be a priority audience. Furthermore, no evidence was found to support the idea that al-Shabaab may have been primarily motivated by religion when engaging in the Westgate attack. This suggests that al-Shabaab is not a global terrorist entity motivated by religion, but is rather a localised group with geographical aims and regional political objectives. This challenges the New Terrorism thesis, which states that modern-day terrorism is religiously motivated and transnational in nature (Neumann 2009). In the case of the Westgate attack, the arguments put forward by Duyvesteyn (2004) and Abrahms (2009) are supported: The Westgate attack had a geographically limited focus and was primarily motivated by political factors.

In conclusion, this study has opened up several possibilities for future research. In particular, future studies should expand on the content analysis presented here and analyse the meta-data of terrorists' publications, such as the reach of terrorists' Twitter accounts, the number of followers, the numbers of retweets and the number of favourites per tweet. Such work will complement the insights offered by studies such as this one, into why and how terrorist groups use Twitter by furthering the understanding of the impact that terrorists' use of social media has on local populations.

Note

1 This tweet stated that an additional squad of mujahideen had been stood down until further notice. While it threatened further attacks, it did not threaten that these attacks were imminent and thus was coded as non-threatening.

References

Abrahms, M. (2006) 'Why Terrorism Does Not Work'. *International Security*, vol 31, no 2, pp. 42–78.

AlJazeera. (2011) *Al-Shabab Starts Tweeting*. Available at: <http://blogs.aljazeera.com/blog/africa/al-shabab-starts-tweeting> [12/02/2015].

Anti-Defamation League. (2013) *Profile: Omar Hammami*. Available at: <www.adl.org/combating-hate/international-extremism-terrorism/c/profile-omar-hammami.html> [02/02/2015].

Berger, J.M. (2013) *Omar and Me: My Strange, Frustrating Friendship with an American Terrorist*. Foreign Policy. Available at: <http://foreignpolicy.com/2013/09/17/omar-and-me/> [11/02/2015].

Bertram, S. and Ellison, K. (2014) 'Sub-Saharan African Terrorist Groups' Use of the Internet'. *Journal of Terrorism Research*, vol 5, no 1, pp. 5–26.

Bosco, F. (2013) 'Terrorist Use of the Internet'. In: *Capacity Building in the Fight Against Terrorism*. NATO Science for Peace and Security Studies – E: Human and Societal Dynamics, vol 112, no 39, pp. 39–46.

Bowie, N. and Schmid, A. (2011) 'Databases on Terrorism'. In: Schmid, A. (ed.) *The Routledge Handbook of Terrorism Research*. New York: Routledge, pp. 339.

Conway, M. (2014) 'Reality Check: Assessing the (Un)likelihood of Cyberterrorism'. In: Chen, T., Jarvis, L. and Macdonald, S. (eds) *Cyberterrorism: Assessment, Understanding and Response*. New York: Springer, pp. 103–21.

Denning, D. (2009) 'Terror's Web: How the Internet Is Transforming Modern Terrorism'. In: Jewkes, Y. and Yar, M. (eds) *Handbook on Internet Crimes*. New York: Routledge, pp. 194–213.

Dhanji, K. (2014) *Westgate: A Photographer's Story*. Available at: <www.aljazeera.com/indepth/inpictures/2014/09/westgate-photographer-story-2014922135957197364.html> [12/03/2015].

Duyvesteyn, I. (2004) 'How New Is the New Terrorism?' *Studies in Conflict and Terrorism*, vol 27, no 5, pp. 439–54.

Hardy, K. (2011) 'Hijacking the Public Discourse: Religious Motive in the Australian Definition of a Terrorist Act'. *University of New South Wales Law Journal*, vol 34, no 1, pp. 333–50

Hoffman, B. (2009) *Inside Terrorism*. New York: Columbia University Press.

Jenkins, B. (1974) *International Terrorism: A New Kind of Warfare*. Santa Monica: RAND Corporation, No. P-5261.

Jones, S. and Libicki, M. (2008) *How Terrorist Groups End: Lessons for Countering AlQa'ida*. RAND Corporation.

Laquer, W. (2000) *The New Terrorism: Fanaticism and the Arms of Mass Destruction*. Oxford: Oxford University Press.

McAllister, B and Schmid, A. (2011) 'Theories of Terrorism'. In: Schmid, A. (ed.) *The Routledge Handbook of Terrorism Research*. New York: Routledge, pp. 233.

Macdonald, S. and Mair, D. (2015) 'Terrorism Online: A New Strategic Environment'. In: Macdonald, S., Jarvis, L. and Chen, T. (eds) *Terrorism Online: Politics, Law and Technology*. London: Routledge, pp. 10–34.

Neumann, P. (2009) *Old and New Terrorism*. Polity, 4.

Oh, O., Agrawel, M. and Rao, R. (2011) 'Information Control and Terrorism: Tracking the Mumbai Terrorist Attack Through Twitter'. *Information Systems Frontiers*, vol 13, no 1, pp. 33–43.

Pantucci, R. and Sayyid, A. R. (2013) 'Foreign Fighters in Somalia and Al-Shabaab's Internal Purge'. *Terrorism Monitor Volume*, vol 11, no 2, pp. 4–6.

Pearlman, L. (2012) 'Tweeting to Win: Al-Shabaab's Strategic Use of Microblogging'. *The Yale Review of International Studies*, vol 3, no 1, pp. 23–44.

Ploch, L. (2010) *Countering Terrorism in East Africa: The US Response*. Washington, DC: Congressional Research Service.

Prucha, N. and Fisher, A. (2013) 'Tweeting for the Caliphate: Twitter as the New Frontier for Jihadist Propaganda'. *CTC Sentinel*, vol 6, no 6, pp. 19–23.

Rapoport, D. (2004) *The Four Waves of Modern Terrorism. Attacking Terrorism: Elements of a Grand Strategy*. Available at: <http://international.ucla.edu/media/files/Rapoport-Four-Waves-of-Modern-Terrorism.pdf> [30/03/2015].

Richards, A. (2014) 'Conceptualising Terrorism'. *Studies in Conflict and Terrorism*, vol 37, no 3, pp. 213–36.

Sullivan, R. (2014) 'Live-Tweeting Terror: A Rhetorical Analysis of @HSMPress_ Twitter Updates During the 2013 Nairobi Hostage Crisis'. *Critical Studies on Terrorism*, vol 7, no 3, pp. 422–33.

The Telegraph. (2014) *How Terrorists Are Using Social Media*. Available at: www.telegraph.co.uk/news/worldnews/islamic-state/11207681/How-terrorists-are-using-social-media.html [02/08/2015].

Tomer, S., Golberg, A., Aharonson-Daniel, L., Leykin, D. and Adini, B. (2014) 'Twitter in the Cross Fire – The Use of Social Media in the Westgate Mall Terror Attack in Kenya'. *PloS one*, vol 9, no 8, e104136.

Twitter. (2014) *What Fuels a Tweets Engagement?* Available at: <https://blog.Twitter.com/2014/what-fuels-a-tweets-engagement> [05/08/2015].

Twitter. (2015) *The Twitter Rules*. Available at: <https://support.Twitter.com/articles/18311-the-Twitter-rules> [15/03/2015].

United States of America Committee on Homeland Security. (2011) 'Al-Shabaab: Recruitment and Radicalisation Within the Muslim American Community and the Threat to the Homeland'. In: *Compilation of Recent Hearings on Islamist Radicalisation – Volume 1*. Available at: <www.gpo.gov/fdsys/pkg/CHRG-112hhrg72541.pdf> pp. 277–348 [03/02/2015].

United States of America State Department. (2015) *Designated Foreign Terrorist Organisations*. Available at: <www.state.gov/j/ct/rls/other/des/123085.htm> [10/04/2015].

Weimann, G. (2004) *www.terror.net: How Modern Terrorism Uses the Internet*. vol 31. DIANE Publishing.

Weimann, G. (2014) *New Terrorism and New Media*. Washington, DC: Wilson Centre, p. 8.

5 Violent extremism online and the criminal trial

Keiran Hardy

Introduction

Speculation continues over whether terrorist organisations are likely to use the Internet to launch devastating cyber-attacks against critical infrastructure (Conway, 2003, 2014; Stohl, 2006), but it is clear that terrorists already use the Internet for a variety of other purposes including financing, recruitment, propaganda and communication (Walker, 2005/6; Weimann, 2005; Carlile and Macdonald, 2014; Macdonald and Mair, 2015). In particular, the risk that individuals will become radicalised by viewing violent extremist material on the Internet remains a key issue for governments aiming to prevent domestic terrorism. The dangers of accessing violent extremist materials online have been heightened by the rise of Islamic State, which has been using the Internet to promote its activities and recruit young Muslims from around the globe. The wide and successful use of social media by Islamic State – including through Facebook, Twitter, Instagram, YouTube and even tailor-made smartphone applications – has led the conflicts in Iraq and Syria to be dubbed the 'twitter jihad' (Richards, 2014).

This chapter examines how evidence of violent extremism online is used in the criminal trial to convict individuals for offences under counterterrorism laws. Since the 9/11 attacks on New York and Washington, and more recently in response to the threat of foreign fighters returning from Iraq and Syria, Western governments have enacted a wide range of laws in response to the threat of terrorism. These laws have expanded the powers of law enforcement and intelligence agencies, and created a range of new offences for terrorism-related activity (see generally Roach, 2011; Williams, 2011, 2013; Ramraj *et al.*, 2012).

For the purposes of this chapter, evidence of violent extremism online means evidence that an individual has used the Internet to access information and resources that can play a role in radicalisation. This includes accessing radical religious literature, bomb-making instructions and videos of beheadings and other violent acts. Evidence of this online behaviour might be available because the person has stored that information on a computer hard drive, addresses of websites they have visited are listed in their web browsing history or they have printed hard copies of the material. The chapter does not address other forms of online behaviour in which terrorist groups might be involved, such as posting extremist propaganda, financing attacks, communicating with each other or recruiting new members.

This inquiry differs from previous literature, which has considered how counter-terrorism laws apply to the use of computer and Internet technology (Hardy, 2011; Carlile and Macdonald, 2014; Hardy and Williams, 2014). That literature outlines the circumstances in which the use of computer and Internet technology could constitute a criminal offence under counterterrorism laws, and it considers on that basis whether the offences are appropriately defined. This chapter delves a step deeper by examining how the prosecution uses evidence of violent extremism online in the criminal trial to prove that a terrorism offence has been committed. It questions the appropriateness of using evidence of violent extremism online for this purpose.

The chapter considers these questions through case studies of two major terrorism trials in Australia. Both trials resulted from Operation Pendennis, a large-scale counterterrorism investigation in which police uncovered terrorist cells in Melbourne and Sydney as well as stockpiles of guns, ammunition and bomb-making equipment. The first trial is the Benbrika (or Melbourne) trial, in which twelve men were charged with being members of a terrorist organisation and related offences. The second trial is the Elomar (or Sydney) trial, in which nine men were charged with conspiracy to do acts in preparation for a terrorist act.

The sections below explain the offences with which these individuals were charged before setting out the evidence of violent extremism online put forward by the prosecution in each case. They consider some important issues raised by the admission of this evidence in court, and question the appropriateness of relying on this evidence to prove the relevant offences. While most of this content is specific to Australian law, similar issues are raised in other jurisdictions. In particular, the United Kingdom has similar offences because Australia looked towards that jurisdiction when drafting its own counterterrorism laws (see Terrorism Act 2000, Sections 11, 57, 58; Terrorism Act 2006, s 5; Roach, 2009).

The key aim of the sections below is to assess the role that evidence of violent extremism online played in the trial process: *which offences* was it relevant to, *how was it used* to support the prosecution's case, *how significant* was it in securing the relevant convictions and *how appropriate* was it for the convictions to be secured on the basis of that evidence? In particular, these trials demonstrate that evidence of violent extremism online is used to build cases against groups of individuals on the basis that they are preparing, or have agreed to prepare, a terrorist act. Some key issues raised are whether accessing violent extremist materials online should constitute preparation for terrorism, whether it is appropriate to infer from such materials that a group is likely to commit a terrorist act at some future time and whether showing these materials to juries is likely to impact a defendant's right to a fair trial.

The Benbrika trial

In late 2005 and early 2006, thirteen men were arrested in Melbourne for their ties to a terrorist organisation led by Abdul Nacer Benbrika. Benbrika was an

Algerian migrant and former aviation engineer who became known for his radical religious teaching in various mosques and Islamic organisations. Prior to his arrest, he began teaching smaller religious classes ('dars') to a group of young men. He met informally and socially with some of these men, and it was this group that was alleged to be an organisation preparing a terrorist act. The target of the attack may have been the Australian Football League Grand Final or Melbourne Grand Prix, although this was never confirmed. The main objective of this alleged attack was to influence the Australian government into pulling its troops out of the Iraq War.

After one man pleaded guilty, the remaining twelve faced twenty-seven charges during a trial that lasted more than 6 months. The main charge for all twelve men was being a member of a terrorist organisation. This is an offence under Section 102.3(1) of the Criminal Code Act 1995 (Cth) (Criminal Code) and is punishable by up to 10 years' imprisonment. Some of the men were also charged with providing support or resources to a terrorist organisation (Criminal Code, Section 102.7) and possessing things connected with preparation for a terrorist act (Criminal Code, Section 101.4). As the organisation's leader, Benbrika faced an additional charge of directing the activities of a terrorist organisation (Criminal Code, Section 102.2).

The meaning of 'terrorism', for the purposes of these offences and others, hinges on a statutory definition of a terrorist act (Criminal Code, Section 100.1). This section defines terrorism as conduct or a threat that is: (1) designed to advance a political, religious or ideological cause; (2) intended to coerce a government, influence a government by intimidation or intimidate a section of the public and (3) causes or is intended to cause one in a list of specified harms, including death, serious bodily injury or creating a serious risk to health or safety (Criminal Code, Section 100.1).

Section 102.3 of the Criminal Code sets out three elements that must be proved for the offence of being a member of a terrorist organisation. Each of these elements needs to be established by the prosecution beyond reasonable doubt. First, the person must be a member of the organisation. This includes 'informal' members and those who have 'taken steps' to join the organisation (Criminal Code, Section 102.1). Second, the organisation must be a terrorist organisation. Third, the person must know that the organisation is a terrorist organisation.

A key issue in the Benbrika trial was whether the prosecution had satisfied the second element: that the group of individuals was a terrorist organisation. To establish this, the prosecution must convince the jury that the group of individuals is an 'organisation', and that the organisation is 'directly or indirectly engaged in, preparing, planning, assisting in or fostering the doing of a terrorist act' (Criminal Code, Section 102.1). An alternative is that the Attorney-General has previously declared the organisation to be a terrorist organisation (Criminal Code, Section 102.1). In early 2015, there were twenty organisations on the list of proscribed terrorist organisations maintained by the Australian government. These include al-Qaeda, Jemaah Islamiya, the military wing of Hezbollah, Boko Haram and Islamic State (Australian National Security, 2015). However, the proscription process was not relevant in this case as Benbrika's organisation was not a 'recognised' terrorist group.

The prosecution put forward several points to convince the jury that the group of individuals led by Benbrika was an organisation that was fostering or preparing a terrorist act (see *Benbrika*, 2010: [6]). Many of these were designed to show that the twelve men were an organised group: for example, the men referred to themselves collectively as the 'jema'ah' (a 'group' or 'association'), some of the men took on specific roles and responsibilities and they contributed money to fund the organisation's activities. This supported the prosecution's case because it was necessary to show that the defendants were an 'organisation' (as opposed to an ad hoc or informal grouping of individuals). To support these claims, the prosecution relied on a large body of transcripts from telephone intercepts and listening devices, which had recorded conversations among the men.[1]

Other points put forward by the prosecution were designed to show the radical religious nature of the group and their preparation for a terrorist act. The men received religious instruction from Benbrika, who taught 'the pursuit of violent jihad as a religious obligation' (*Benbrika*, 2010: [6]). The group members frequently discussed the need to engage in violent jihad against the West, and Benbrika encouraged the other group members to commit acts of violence, such as by killing people and destroying buildings (*Benbrika*, 2009: [38]).

To support these last points, the prosecution admitted into evidence a large quantity of extremist and instructional material, most of which the defendants had downloaded from extremist websites (*Benbrika*, 2010: [10], [25]). Police had seized this material in the Operation Pendennis raids, as it was held by the defendants either on computer hard drives, CDs or printed hard copies. The material included:

- videos of beheadings;
- footage of acts of violence carried out in the Iraq War and other conflicts (including a video of a hostage being shot in the head at close range);
- bomb-making manuals (including *The Terrorist's Handbook* and *The Car Bomb Recognition Guide*);
- combat literature (including *The White Resistance Manual*);
- speeches by Osama bin Laden and other terrorist leaders.

Evidence from telephone intercepts and listening devices shed light on how the group used this material after downloading it from the Internet. According to this surveillance evidence, the extremist and instructional material was circulated among the group members, who viewed it on a communal laptop computer and discussed it at different members' homes (*Benbrika*, 2010: [11]). Viewings of the violent videos were 'accompanied by expressions of delight upon seeing kuffar [non-believers] killed at the hands of the Muslim brothers' (*Benbrika*, 2010: [11]).

Evidence of violent extremism online was therefore put forward by the prosecution in the Benbrika trial in order to establish that the defendants were members of a 'terrorist organisation' for the purposes of s 102.3 of the Criminal Code. To some extent, this evidence demonstrated a degree of formality to the group structure, as the defendants collected and viewed the material together and used it as a bonding exercise (*Benbrika*, 2010: [11], [278]). More importantly, the evidence of violent extremism online was said to demonstrate that the organisation was engaged in preparing a terrorist act (Criminal Code, Section 102.1). The sharing of extremist material obtained on the Internet was designed to motivate the group into committing a terrorist act, to desensitise them against the violence and to train them in killing techniques (*Benbrika*, 2010: [276]–[278]).

The jury was satisfied beyond reasonable doubt that the group of individuals led by Benbrika was an organisation that was preparing a terrorist act. It found seven of the defendants (including Benbrika) guilty of being members of that organisation. Four of the defendants were acquitted of that charge, and the jury was unable to reach a verdict in relation to one defendant.

For the membership offence, the seven men received sentences ranging between 4 and 5 years.[2] Three of these men received total sentences of between 7 and 8 years, as they were also found guilty of providing resources and attempting to provide funds to the organisation (Criminal Code, Sections 102.6, 102.7). Benbrika, who was also found guilty of directing the activities of the organisation (Criminal Code, Section 102.2), received the longest total sentence of 15 years' imprisonment.

On appeal, the defence counsel raised several arguments suggesting that the evidence of violent extremism online may have impacted the defendants' right to receive a fair trial. The first argument was that the videos of beheadings and other violent acts should not have been admitted into evidence because their gruesome contents were likely to sway the jury by emotion rather than logic. In a criminal trial, the court must refuse to admit evidence adduced by the prosecution if the probative (that is, rational or instrumental) value of that evidence is 'outweighed by the danger of unfair prejudice to the defendant' (Evidence Act 1995 (Cth), Section 137). This is to ensure that the law operates to the maximum extent possible in a rational and objective way, so that individuals are punished fairly and consistently and are not convicted out of bias, prejudice or presumption. In other words, there was a risk that a jury would simply assume that the defendants must be terrorists because they enjoyed watching such horrific violence.

The Victorian Supreme Court did not accept this argument, and held that the probative value of the video evidence outweighed any danger of unfair prejudice to the defendants. While the court recognised that the video evidence in itself would not likely have been sufficient to mount the case, it stressed that the videos were part of a large body of extremist and instructional material that had significant probative value (*Benbrika*, 2010: [272]). This body of material was considered highly relevant to demonstrating 'both the existence and nature of the organisation, and the common commitment of the applicants to the cause of violent jihad' (*Benbrika*, 2010: [276]).

The second argument raised by the defence was that it was unfair to admit the evidence of violent extremism online, because hundreds of other individuals would likely have viewed the same material online without being charged with any offence. During cross-examination, one Muslim cleric gave evidence that 'it is not uncommon for ordinary young Muslims to access websites containing the sort of material found by investigators in the possession of some of the prisoners' (*Benbrika*, 2010: [26]). If this is the case, there is a strong argument that such evidence should not support serious criminal charges for being a member of a terrorist organisation. It suggests an element of discrimination in the choice to prosecute certain individuals who access violent extremist materials online, and not others.

The court also denied this argument, reasoning that the evidence of violent extremism online should be viewed alongside the social interactions of the group and particularly the influential role of Benbrika. It held that

> [p]ossession of such material takes on a much more sinister complexion when it is realised that those who have it are being encouraged by someone they regard as worthy of emulation and respect to engage in ... acts of terrorism. (*Benbrika*, 2010: [27])

A parallel might be drawn here with research suggesting that social processes are still the crucial factor in radicalisation, even though the Internet is taking on an increasingly important role (see Home Office, 2011: [8.21]; von Behr *et al.*, 2013). It appears that the Victorian Supreme Court approached this issue in a similar way: it did not consider evidence of violent extremism online *in itself* to be sufficient to support the charge, but in combination with evidence of 'offline' radicalisation, it helped to trigger liability.

A third argument was that the evidence of violent extremism online was not capable of demonstrating that Benbrika's organisation was 'preparing' a terrorist act (Criminal Code, Section 102.1). The defendants had not taken any physical steps to prepare a terrorist act, other than pooling funds and collecting and circulating extremist material. They had not, for example, purchased bomb-making equipment or even scoped out a particular target for the attack. Indeed, the Victorian Supreme Court referred to the prosecution's case as 'largely circumstantial' (*Benbrika*, 2010: [6]).

The Victorian Supreme Court nonetheless confirmed that Benbrika's organisation was preparing a terrorist act, and that the online materials were capable of demonstrating this. The materials obtained online had not been viewed solely out of curiosity or for entertainment purposes: according to the prosecution's case, the material had been circulated among the group in order to motivate its members, train them in killing techniques, and desensitise them against violence so that they would be more likely to follow through with an attack (*Benbrika*, 2010: [277]). The court also considered that the online material provided evidence of preparation for terrorism because it helped with the 'forging of bonds' between group members (*Benbrika*, 2010: [278]). Despite the lack of physical acts of preparation, the court stressed that '[a]n organisation may become a ... terrorist organisation long before it selects a target, obtains bomb-making or similar materials, or plans an attack' (*Benbrika*, 2009: [44]). In other words, the court equated the viewing of online material with preparation for terrorism because those resources were used as a motivating, training and desensitising tool.

The court was therefore quick to dismiss some major concerns with introducing the evidence of violent extremism online. Videos of beheadings and other violent acts may sway a jury by emotion rather than logic, many other young Muslims may have viewed the same material without becoming a target for the authorities and viewing extremist material does not necessarily equate to preparation for terrorism. And yet, evidence of this online behaviour provided a key basis on which seven defendants were found guilty of an offence punishable by up to 10 years' imprisonment.

The online materials were not the only important evidence put forward by the prosecution. As noted above, the men referred to themselves collectively as a 'jema'ah', they pooled funds to spend on group activities, they discussed the need to engage in violent jihad against the West and Benbrika encouraged the group members to commit violent acts (*Benbrika*, 2009: [21], 2010: [6]). They also participated in group bonding and training sessions, and some of the men were involved in other criminal activity, such as car rebirthing and credit card fraud, to raise additional funds for the organisation (*Benbrika*, 2010: [6]). It is therefore clear that the group's activities went beyond the collection and viewing of violent extremist materials. Without this other evidence, it is unlikely that the convictions would have been successful.

At the same time, the evidence of online behaviour was arguably the most important factor in securing the convictions. As jury deliberations are kept secret, it is impossible to know the exact weight that the jury members gave to that evidence in reaching the guilty verdicts. However, that evidence provided a large body of visual and written material suggesting the motivations of the group and the kinds of violent acts they might carry out. As the court noted, it was highly relevant to demonstrating both the existence of the organisation and its intention to engage in acts of terrorism (*Benbrika*, 2010: [276]). Were it not for that evidence, the defendants would have been a group of individuals who discussed violent jihad and were involved in some petty criminal activity. This might have legitimately drawn the attention of the police and security services, but it would have been extremely difficult for the prosecution to secure multiple successful convictions on the basis that the group was a 'terrorist organisation'. It is therefore fair to say that the evidence of violent extremism online proved extremely important – and likely crucial – in determining the outcome of the Benbrika trial.

In particular, the online materials were crucial in establishing that Benbrika's organisation was preparing acts of terrorism. As discussed above, the court was satisfied on appeal that the online materials demonstrated preparation for terrorism because it was used to motivate, desensitise and train the group members (*Benbrika*, 2010: [77]). The pooling of funds by group members (amounting to some $7,000) was also arguably important in demonstrating preparation for terrorism, although this appeared to be given less weight by the court. In response to submissions by defence counsel that Benbrika's organisation had not been preparing acts of terrorism, the court pointed to the online material rather than the collection of funds as the reason why the organisation's activities could be characterised as preparation (*Benbrika*, 2009: [45]).

Given this, there are serious questions as to whether the court's approach to admitting the evidence of violent extremism online was adequate. In cases where there is physical evidence directly suggesting that an organisation is preparing a terrorist act (such as weapons and explosive devices), or evidence of physical steps taken to obtain or build such items (such as purchasing large quantities of chemicals from hardware stores), it would be appropriate for the prosecution to adduce evidence of violent extremism online to demonstrate the intentions of the group. For example, the prosecution might admit evidence that a group of individuals had accessed bomb-making instructions in order to demonstrate that they intended to combine different items (such as fertiliser, detonators and electronic timers) into an explosive device. In such a case, the online materials would play a secondary role in proving preparation for terrorism. Preparation for terrorism would primarily be established by physical evidence such as weapons or explosive devices, or steps taken to obtain such items.

The problem in the Benbrika trial is that the online materials took on the primary role in proving preparation for terrorism. There was no evidence, for example, that the group had purchased chemicals for making explosive devices or conducted reconnaissance on a potential target for an attack. In these circumstances, the potential unfairness in relying on the evidence of those online materials – as outlined above – should have been given much greater weight by the court.

From *Benbrika* and other cases, it is clear that a person or group can be preparing an act of terrorism even if they are yet to select a particular date, target or method for the attack (*Lodhi*, 2006: [66]; *Benbrika*, 2009: [44]; *Elomar*, 2010: [79]). However, the *Benbrika* judgements are significant because the defendants were said to be preparing acts of terrorism at a point in time before they had engaged in any physical acts of preparation (such as purchasing items to use in the attack, taking photos of a potential target or building an explosive device). Of course, in a strict sense, the defendants had committed physical acts by using computers to download extremist and instructional material. However, the court held this to be preparation for terrorism not because their conduct was significant, but because they were training themselves *intellectually* and *psychologically* for a future attack (by reading about how to make explosive devices, and by watching videos of beheadings to desensitise themselves to those acts) (*Benbrika*, 2010: [277]).

This appears to be justified from a legal perspective on the grounds that a terrorist organisation may be 'indirectly' engaged in preparing terrorism (Criminal Code, Section 102.1). However, it nonetheless gives a very wide interpretation to the concept of preparation. If researching violent extremist materials online may be characterised as preparation for terrorism, the terrorist organisation offences could ensnare groups whose plans to commit a terrorist act are little more than aspirational. A group may be inspired by terrorist attacks committed elsewhere, and access extremist materials online to research how they might emulate such an attack. However, that group might have no realistic prospect (for psychological or organisational reasons) of ever carrying out that attack successfully. Arguably, Benbrika's organisation fell into this category (see Hughes, 2008). Or, indeed, the group might later decide against carrying out the attack out of good conscience or fear of prosecution. Such organisations should rightly attract the attention of the police and security services to ensure that their activities do not become dangerous to the community, but they should not – at that point in time – be prosecuted as terrorist organisations alongside a list of others including al-Qaeda and Islamic State.

Prosecuting groups like Benbrika's as terrorist organisations may also have a wider chilling effect on religious organisations that pose no danger to the community and that might otherwise cooperate with the government to develop a meaningful community dialogue about terrorism. An organisation may fear being prosecuted as a terrorist organisation for circulating radical religious teachings among its members, even if the group has no aspirations to commit a terrorist act and none of its members have ever downloaded any bomb-making or other instructional manuals. Such groups will be discouraged from talking to the government when a constructive dialogue between communities and government is precisely what is needed to develop innovative and effective approaches to countering violent extremism online.

Organisations that only research radical religious teachings online and do not access bomb-making or other instructional manuals will not likely fall within the definition of a terrorist organisation. In *Benbrika*, it was the presence of both radical religious teachings and bomb-making instructional manuals, combined with a discussion about committing a terrorist act and other evidence of criminal behaviour, which allowed for a successful prosecution. However, the court did little to stress this point. If a wider chilling effect on religious organisations is to be avoided, the next court to hear a case for terrorist organisation offences should clarify the combination of online materials and other factors that are necessary for a group to cross the line into criminality. To do this, the court could draw a clearer distinction between different types of online materials and the level of criminality they imply. Such categories, ranging from less to more serious, might include:

- religious literature that is conservative and controversial but is not necessarily connected with terrorism;
- images and videos that were originally produced for a legitimate purpose but can be used to radicalise individuals by desensitising them to violence and motivating them to commit terrorist acts (such as images and video footage from news reports on foreign conflicts);
- radical or fundamentalist religious teachings (including those from the leaders of known terrorist organisations) that explicitly support or encourage terrorism;
- images and videos that demonstrate the kinds of acts a group seeks to emulate, and that can also be used to desensitise and motivate group members (such as videos of bombings and beheadings);
- Documents that have some objective connection to preparing terrorist acts (such as bomb-making instruction manuals).

A typology along these lines would assist the court in determining which groups of individuals should be categorised as terrorist organisations on the grounds that they are preparing acts of terrorism. The first category, for example, should not of its own attract liability for terrorist organisation offences. The last category would most clearly suggest that an organisation is preparing an act of terrorism. Difficult questions will remain, however, as to what volume and combination of online materials should be sufficient to cross the line into criminality. The answer in a particular case will also depend on the availability of other evidence, including evidence of a formal group structure and physical steps taken to prepare a terrorist act.

In addition to supporting the convictions for membership of a terrorist organisation, the online materials supported charges of 'possessing a thing connected with preparation for a terrorist act' (Criminal Code, Section 101.4). This and similar offences raise their own unique concerns, such as whether it should be an offence to possess violent extremist material without an intention to commit a terrorist act (in the United Kingdom, see Terrorism Act 2000, Section 58; *R v G*). However, only Benbrika and one other group member were charged with this offence, and those convictions were overturned on appeal (see *Benbrika*, 2010: [357], [392]).

It is therefore striking that the primary use of the online material in the Benbrika trial was not to convict individuals for possessing that material (Criminal Code, Section 101.4), but to build a larger case against a group of individuals on the grounds that they were members of a terrorist organisation preparing a terrorist act (Criminal Code, Section 102.3). A similar approach can be seen in the Elomar trial considered below, in which evidence of online behaviour was used to prosecute a group of individuals for conspiring to prepare an act of terrorism.

The Elomar trial

In November 2005, nine men were arrested in Sydney as part of the same counterterrorism operation that led to the arrests of the Benbrika organisation. The leader of this group was Mohamed Elomar, the uncle of the Mohamed Elomar who is, at the time of writing, fighting with Islamic State in Syria. There were links between the men arrested in Melbourne and Sydney, although these links were only confirmed later, with the New South Wales Supreme Court using a pseudonym (Sheikh Bakr) to refer to Benbrika during the Sydney trial. As Benbrika's organisation had already been convicted by the time the Sydney trial took place, this was to avoid the risk that a jury would assume the Sydney defendants to be guilty via association.

Four of the men arrested in Sydney pleaded guilty, and the remaining five faced an 11-month trial for conspiring to do acts in preparation for a terrorist act. The relevant substantive offence, found in Section 101.6 of the Criminal Code, provides a maximum penalty of life imprisonment where a person does 'any ... act in preparation for a terrorist act'. The defendants were charged with conspiring to commit this offence (Criminal Code, Section 11.5).

Conspiracy is a longstanding element of the criminal law, and will be made out where there is an agreement between two or more people to commit an unlawful act (*LK & RK*, 2010). Under federal law in Australia, it requires that at least one party to the agreement has done an overt act in pursuance of the agreement (Criminal Code, Section 11.5).[3] In other words, the defendants were charged with agreeing to prepare a terrorist act, and taking some steps towards fulfilling that agreement.

This combination of conspiracy and Section 101.6 is a key example of the 'pre-crime' logic underlying counterterrorism laws (see Zedner, 2007; McCulloch and Pickering, 2009). Under the ordinary criminal law, a person can be charged not only with completing a substantive offence (such as theft or murder) but also with an attempt or conspiracy to commit a substantive offence. This is referred to as 'inchoate liability'. It extends criminal liability 'back in time' so that the police do not need to wait until harm is caused for a person to be arrested and charged with an offence.

Counterterrorism laws extend criminal liability even further back in time, before the laws of attempt or conspiracy would normally be triggered. For example, it would not be an offence for a person to *prepare* to commit murder (such as by lawfully purchasing a gun). The person would have to do something 'more than merely preparatory' to committing murder (Criminal Code, Section 11.1; Criminal Attempts Act 1981 (UK), Section 1(1)), such as firing the gun and missing his target (see Alexander and Ferzan, 2012).

By contrast, under Section 101.6 of the Criminal Code, it *is* an offence to prepare an act of terrorism (such as by purchasing weapons or bomb-making material). For this reason, terrorism offences are sometimes referred to as 'pre-inchoate' offences (Tulich, 2012). Remarkably, inchoate liability can then be applied to one of these pre-inchoate offences, meaning that it is an offence *to agree to prepare* to commit a terrorist act. This is what the defendants were charged with in the Elomar trial. As Justice Whealy noted in sentencing the offenders, '[t]he legislation is designed to bite early, long before the preparatory acts mature into circumstances of deadly or dangerous consequence for the community' (*Elomar*, 2010: [79]).

This pre-crime logic is justified on the basis that it is preferable to imprison somebody before a terrorist attack occurs rather than waiting until an attack happens and prosecuting whoever was responsible (if indeed he or she is still alive). This is understandable in terms of protecting the public from serious harm, but it poses a significant challenge for longstanding principles of the criminal law. In particular, individuals are exposed to lengthy prison sentences for acts, which, at that stage, cause no direct harm to others (such as purchasing chemicals from a hardware store). These problems with pre-inchoate offences have led counterterrorism laws to be described as a form of 'enemy criminal law', in which individuals are exposed to severe penalties and their procedural rights reduced in order to prevent future harms (see Macdonald, 2015).

The difficulty in conspiracy cases can lie in proving the existence of an agreement between the defendants: either the agreement needs to be witnessed by another person (or recorded by a listening device) or there needs to be physical evidence demonstrating some kind of criminal plan to be carried out. In the Elomar trial, the prosecution put forward a large body of evidence to demonstrate an agreement between the defendants to prepare a terrorist act, including:

- recordings from telephone intercept and listening devices, in which the defendants voiced extremist views and used code words to disguise their names and actions;
- firearms, nearly 20,000 rounds of ammunition for assault rifles, 10 litres of hydrogen peroxide and laboratory equipment;
- orders placed in false names and some deposits paid to hardware stores for large volumes of chemicals (including acetone and sulphuric acid);
- evidence of attendance at survival and sniper-style training camps in remote locations, where some shooting of firearms took place.

In addition, the prosecution submitted to the court a large quantity of electronic documents similar to those admitted in the Benbrika trial. It appears that much of this material was accessed on the Internet, although some of the group members received it from others and downloaded it to their computer from CDs, apparently out of concern that their online behaviour would be tracked by the authorities (*Elomar*, 2010: [122]). As in the Benbrika trial, this material fell into two general categories. The first was a range of extremist material (see *Elomar*, 2010: [43]–[55]), including:

- images of injured or deceased Muslim civilians and soldiers;
- images of the destruction of the Twin Towers on 9/11;
- slogans and images glorifying the 9/11 hijackers;
- pictures of Osama bin Laden, Abu Musab al-Zarqawi and other prominent Islamist identities;
- images of Americans and their Allies being killed or wounded in combat;
- videos showing hostages and prisoners being executed by Mujahideen fighters.

The second category of electronic documents was a large body of instructional material (see *Elomar*, 2010: [38]–[42]), including:

- recipes for making explosives from nitro-glycerine, hexamine, acetone, sulphuric acid, ammonium nitrate and mercury fulminate;
- instructions for making a detonator from acetone and peroxide;
- manuals on surveillance techniques, sabotage, kidnapping and assassination;
- military handbooks on sniper and survival techniques.

This evidence of violent extremism online supported the conspiracy charges because it revealed a 'shared mindset' on behalf of the defendants (*Elomar*, 2010: [62]). It was said to be a 'reflection of each offender's ideology, his inspiration and motivation in the pursuit of the extremist cause of violent jihad' (*Elomar*,

2010: [62]). This shared mindset involved hatred of non-Muslims, intolerance towards the democratic Australian government and its policies, and a conviction that Muslims are obligated to pursue violent jihad in order to overthrow Western societies and replace them with Islamic rule and Sharia law (*Elomar*, 2010: [63]). In other words, the online material demonstrated the existence of an agreement between the defendants with respect to their pursuit of violent jihad and their intention to prepare a terrorist act.

Two characteristics of the online material were important in demonstrating this shared mindset: first, the 'sheer volume' of the material, and second, the fact that it was 'held in commonality among the offenders' (*Benbrika*, 2010: [62]). If the defendants had accessed a much smaller amount of material, or if they had each accessed different documents independently rather than sharing it among the group, it would have been more difficult for the prosecution to use that material to prove an agreement between the defendants.

Another important factor for the court was that the evidence of violent extremism online revealed an 'extremist zeal' (*Elomar*, 2010: [64]). The law of conspiracy has long been considered problematic, as it attaches criminal liability to mere agreements between individuals (which might amount to little more than a conversation) rather than their actions. It has therefore been justified as a matter of legal policy on the grounds that it targets group-based violence, which is considered more serious than violence by individuals. While the grounds for this distinction are disputed, group-based violence is treated more seriously by the criminal law because groups can inflict greater harm than individuals acting alone, and because individuals may be more likely to follow through with their actions after they have made a commitment to others (see Abbate, 1992).

In the Elomar trial, the evidence of accessing violent extremist materials played into these policy justifications, because it suggested that the defendants were fanatical about the cause of violent jihad, and therefore more likely to follow through with a terrorist attack. In sentencing the offenders, Justice Whealy stated that 'the overall extremist zeal of a group venture is more enduring, more fanatical, more determined, more resourceful and ultimately likely to be more successful than an individual acting alone' (*Elomar*, 2010: [64]). Thus, the online material supported the charge of conspiracy in an immediate practical sense because it demonstrated the existence of an agreement between the defendants, but it also helped to justify that charge on a conceptual or policy-based level.

On the basis of the evidence outlined above, the five defendants were found guilty of conspiring to prepare a terrorist act and sentenced to prison terms of between 23 and 28 years. The online materials played an additional important role in delivering these severe sentences. Justice Whealy believed on the basis of the extremist material that 'an intolerant and inflexible fundamentalist religious conviction was the principal motivation for the commission of the offence' (*Benbrika*, 2010: [63]). He was convinced that 'each of the men was unequivocally committed to an outcome that . . . would have been very likely to cause devastation in the community' (*Benbrika*, 2010: [65]). He concluded that the 'the criminality of each offender is at a very high level indeed' (*Benbrika*, 2010: [89]).

In late 2014, the New South Wales Court of Criminal Appeal (CCA) upheld these sentences despite the unfairly prejudicial impact that some of the online material may have had on the jury (*Elomar*, 2014). Similar to the appeals in the Benbrika trial, counsel for Elomar and his co-accused contended that the unfairly prejudicial effect of the gruesome images and videos (including pictures of mutilated bodies and videos of beheadings) outweighed their probative value (Evidence Act 1995 (Cth), s 137). To support this, the appellants relied on two items of evidence: (1) a report by an associate professor of psychology that concluded that the images and videos were likely to 'exacerbate juror stress', reduce their capacity to focus on other evidence and make them more likely to convict the defendants; and (2) a statement by a member of the Australian Federal Police that the videos and images had been designated by a joint team of state and federal police as 'psychologically hazardous' (see *Elomar*, 2014: [410]–[415]). Counsel for the appellants also noted that, while the evidence was being shown to the jury, one juror was not watching the screen and later moved seats so that the screen was no longer in front of her, and two other jurors held their notepads and folders in front of their eyes to obscure the screen from view (*Elomar*, 2014: [428]).

The CCA was quick to acknowledge the 'graphic and confronting' nature of that online material (*Elomar*, 2014: [404]), but otherwise gave little weight to the impact that evidence had or was likely to have on the jury. The court held that the appellants' argument was flawed because they would need to show that the evidence was misused in some way, and not merely that it had an emotional impact on the jury or police (*Elomar*, 2014: [444]). It held that the question of whether there had been an error of law in admitting the evidence could not be determined by its impact on the jury after it had been admitted (*Elomar*, 2014: [443]).

The CCA also placed significant weight on the restrictions that Justice Whealy placed on showing the evidence in court. For example, only one of six beheading videos was shown, the footage of the actual beheading was edited out of that video and the images were displayed on a screen for a relatively short period of time (8–9 seconds per image) (see *Elomar*, 2014: [409], [422]). These restrictions would certainly have reduced the unfairly prejudicial impact that the uncensored evidence would have had on the jury, but it is doubtful that they reduced it sufficiently to ensure a fair trial.

For example, the jury was still provided with chilling descriptions of the contents of the video footage that was not shown – including one video in which a victim could be seen and heard 'gurgling through his throat' as his head was completely severed, placed back on his body and turned towards the camera (see *Benbrika*, 2014: [434]). Given their horrific contents, written descriptions like these could still be sufficient to influence a jury by emotion rather than logic. And while each image of a dead or mutilated body might not be sufficiently disturbing to generate unfair prejudice (see *Elomar*, 2014: [418]), the cumulative effect of watching hundreds of these images – one after another, for up to 45 minutes at a time – would certainly be significant. In these circumstances, it is doubtful that Justice Whealy's directions to the jury members, such as instructions that they 'avoid reacting to this evidence in an emotional or irrational manner' (*Elomar*, 2014: [424]), were adequate. Indeed, the very fact that the court censored the most gruesome footage might have led some jurors to assume that the defendants were involved in conduct of a violent and criminal nature.

Certainly, the convictions would not have been successful if the prosecution had not put forward other crucial evidence, including weapons, ammunition, laboratory equipment and attempts to buy large volumes of chemicals. This is where the Elomar trial differs from the Benbrika trial, as there was significant evidence demonstrating that the Sydney accused had taken physical (as opposed to merely intellectual or psychological) steps towards preparing a terrorist act. The evidence of violent extremism online was still significant, as it is unlikely that the prosecution would have succeeded in proving a conspiracy without the online material to demonstrate a 'shared mindset' between the offenders (*Elomar*, 2010: [62]). The online material also played a significant role in increasing the severity of the sentences delivered by the court. However, that evidence played a secondary rather than primary role in allowing the court to find that the defendants had agreed to prepare a terrorist act.

This suggests that evidence of violent extremism online was used in a more appropriate way in the Elomar trial compared to the Benbrika trial. However, the case against the Sydney accused was still largely circumstantial, as the group had not decided on the nature or target of the attack (*Elomar*, 2010: [58]). The imposition of sentences around 25 years' imprisonment seems particularly severe given that it is not clear what attack, if any, the group would have carried out.

The court's use of the online material was therefore particularly problematic in that it convinced the sentencing judge that the defendants were 'very likely to cause devastation in the community' (*Benbrika*, 2010: [65]). Because a terrorist attack had not yet occurred, there was no evidence of the harm that the defendants *had* caused, but the online materials provided an insight into the harm that the defendants *were likely* to cause to the Australian community. This provides further evidence that risk management processes are playing an increasingly important role in terrorism trials, such that the courts are imagining 'potential violent futures' and ascribing guilt on that basis (de Goede and de Graaf, 2013: 314). It supports de Goede and de Graaf's (2013: 314) conclusion that the terrorism trial is a '*performative* space where potential future terror is imagined, invoked, contested, and made real, in the proceedings and verdict'.

Certainly, the online material contained gruesome images, footage of violent acts and a range of instructions on how to commit acts of terrorism. This was clearly of some relevance in indicating the types of attack that the defendants wished to carry out. It is problematic, however, to substitute the conduct and words of those who authored the online materials for the defendants' possible future actions – in other words, to rely on the extremist and instructional material as an indicator of the level of harm the defendants were likely to cause. As defence counsel for Elomar and his co-accused submitted to the court, 'a person is not what he reads' (*Elomar*, 2010: [62]).

Conclusion

These two Australian terrorism trials demonstrate how evidence of violent extremism online can be used to convict individuals for criminal offences under counterterrorism laws. In particular, what emerges from these trials is that individuals are not simply prosecuted for possessing extremist and instructional material they have downloaded from the Internet. Rather, evidence of violent extremism online provides a foundation for building cases against large groups of individuals on the grounds that they are preparing, or have agreed to prepare, terrorist acts.

In both the Benbrika and Elomar trials, evidence of violent extremism online played a significant and likely crucial role in securing the relevant convictions. However, it was not merely the fact that each group of defendants accessed violent extremist materials online, but rather that they accessed those online materials *as a group*. The courts appear to have given significant weight to this evidence because of the role violent extremist materials play in developing a common extremist mindset in groups of individuals, in desensitising those groups to violence against innocent civilians and in training those groups in how to commit terrorist acts. This provides further evidence that the criminal law treats more severely those who would engage in violent acts with others, compared to those acting alone (see Abbate, 1992).

Each case raises a key concern with how evidence of violent extremism online is used by the courts. In the Benbrika trial, accessing violent extremist materials online was said to constitute preparation for terrorism because those resources served a training and motivational purpose within the organisation. This expanded the concept of 'preparation' for terrorism beyond physical conduct (such as surveilling a potential target, or purchasing the components of explosive devices) to intellectual and psychological preparation – in other words, *preparing oneself* for future action. As a result, the terrorist organisation offences operate back in time to a point where it is difficult to distinguish those who aspire to committing terrorist acts from those who pose a real and immediate danger to the community. The activities of groups like Benbrika's – which may aspire to committing a terrorist act but have little realistic prospect of doing so – are equated with those of established terrorist organisations like al-Qaeda. If groups like Benbrika's continue to be prosecuted as terrorist organisations on the grounds that they are preparing terrorist acts, this may have a wider chilling effect on religious organisations that might otherwise cooperate with the government to develop a meaningful community dialogue about terrorism.

In the Elomar trial, evidence of violent extremism online played a key role in delivering severe sentences of around 25 years' imprisonment when the defendants had not yet decided on the details of their plan. This pre-crime logic, of convicting individuals for very early preparatory acts, is understandable from the perspective of protecting the public from serious harm. However, as criminal liability is triggered at such an early stage, well before a successful attack has occurred, there is little direct evidence available to demonstrate the kind of attack the defendants would have carried out. Evidence of violent extremism online fills this gap by providing an insight into the minds of the offenders. It allows the courts to extrapolate on the kind of attack the defendants would have carried out and the kinds of damage that might have been caused. The 'extremist zeal' demonstrated by that material also suggests to the courts that the offenders were likely to follow through with their intended actions (*Elomar*, 2010: [64]). In other words, the precrime nature of terrorism offences necessitates the use of online materials as a major source of evidence suggesting the courses of action the defendants were likely to take.

Using evidence of violent extremism online in this way is problematic, as it equates the words and conduct of those who authored the online materials with the defendants' possible future actions, which cannot be known for certain. Of course, videos of beheadings and other gruesome acts are relevant, in that they demonstrate the kinds of activities that the defendants were seeking to emulate. However, those materials are not a reliable indicator of the defendants' future actions, and should not be treated as such. The approach of the Victorian and NSW courts to date suggests that significant weight is given to the contents of the online material in predicting the defendants' future actions, while little consideration is given to the fairness of this predictive exercise.

Both cases also raise serious questions about the potential prejudice of admitting evidence of violent extremism online in court. There is a very real danger that jurors will assume defendants to be involved in violent and criminal conduct if they are shown large quantities of gruesome material – such as images of mutilated bodies and videos of hostages being beheaded by foreign fighters. It is doubtful whether restrictions on showing this evidence in court, or directions to the jury that it should not react to that evidence in an irrational way (*Elomar*, 2014: [424]), are adequate to protect against the danger of unfair prejudice to the defendants. Indeed, the special treatment given to this material may in itself contribute to unfair prejudice: if the defendants possessed online materials so gruesome that those materials cannot be shown to jurors and the general public, or can only be shown in an edited format, the jury may assume that the defendants were involved in sufficiently serious conduct to justify that material being treated differently by the court.

The evidence of violent extremism online was not the only important evidence put forward by the prosecution in each case. In the Benbrika trial, the successful convictions also depended on the fact that the group members had referred to themselves collectively as an 'association', that they had pooled funds to spend on group activities and that Benbrika had encouraged the group to kill innocent people. In the Elomar trial, the defendants had purchased laboratory equipment and thousands of rounds of ammunition, and they had attempted to buy much larger volumes of dangerous chemicals. Both groups of defendants, and particularly the Sydney accused, were involved in potentially dangerous behaviour that should rightly have attracted the attention of the police and security services.

However, there is a serious question as to whether the evidence of violent extremism online should have turned what was otherwise suspicious behaviour into successful convictions for serious criminal activity. Groups of individuals who are vulnerable to extremist ideas may view fundamentalist literature online, express their dissatisfaction with democracy and even talk about or agree to commit acts of terrorism – but to criminalise their actions at that point in time, when their plans may be little more than aspirational, poses significant problems for the criminal law and for counterterrorism policy. To do so risks marginalising those who might otherwise work with the government to develop considered, innovative and effective approaches to countering violent extremism online.

Notes

1 This contrasts with the United Kingdom, where intercept evidence is not allowed to be used in the courtroom (see Home Office, 2014; Macdonald, 2014).
2 The sentences were originally set between six and seven years, but were reduced on appeal (see *Benbrika*, 2010).
3 This differs from UK law, where no overt acts are required: Criminal Law Act 1977 (UK), s 1.

References

Cases

Benbrika v The Queen (2010) 29 VR 593 (*Benbrika*, 2010).
Elomar v R (2014) 316 ALR 206 (*Elomar*, 2014).
R v Benbrika (2009) 222 FLR 433 (*Benbrika*, 2009).
R v Elomar & Ors (2010) 264 ALR 759 (*Elomar*, 2010).
R v G (2009) UKHL 13.
R v Lodhi (2006) 199 FLR 354 (*Lodhi*, 2006).
The Queen v LK; The Queen v RK (2010) 241 CLR 177 (*LK & RK*, 2010).

Articles and Reports

Abbate F (1992) 'The conspiracy doctrine: A critique', in: Gorr M and Harwood S (eds) *Controversies in Criminal Law: Philosophical Essays on Responsibility and Procedure*, Westview, Colorado.
Alexander L and Ferzan K (2012) 'Risk and inchoate crimes: Retribution or prevention?' in: Sullivan GR, and Dennis I (eds) *Seeking Security: Pre-Empting the Commission of Criminal Harms*, Oxford: Hart.
Australian National Security (2015) *Listed Terrorist Organisations*. www.nationalsecurity.gov.au/Listedterroristorganisations/Pages/default.aspx
Carlile A and Macdonald S (2014) 'The criminalisation of terrorists' online preparatory acts', in: Chen TM, Jarvis L and Macdonald S (eds) *Cyberterrorism: Understanding, Assessment, and Response*, London: Springer.
Conway M (2014) 'Reality check: Assessing the (un)likelihood of cyberterrorism', in: Chen TM, Jarvis L and Macdonald S (eds) *Cyberterrorism: Understanding, Assessment, and Response*, London: Springer, pp. 103–122.
de Goede M and de Graaf B (2013) 'Sentencing risk: Temporality and precaution in terrorism trials', *International Political Sociology*, vol 7, pp. 313–331.

Hardy K (2011) 'WWWMDs: Cyber-attacks against infrastructure in domestic anti-terror laws', *Computer Law and Security Review*, vol 27, pp. 152–161.

Hardy K and Williams G (2014) 'What is "cyber-terrorism"? Computer and Internet technology in legal definitions of terrorism', in: Chen TM, Jarvis L and Macdonald S (eds) *Cyberterrorism: Understanding, Assessment, and Response*, London: Springer, pp. 1–24.

Home Office (2014) Intercept as Evidence. Cm 8989.

Home Office (2011) Prevent Strategy. Cm 8092.

Hughes G (2008) 'Stupid and inept, but not terrorists: lawyer', *The Australian*, 10 July.

McCulloch J and Pickering S (2009) 'Pre-crime and counter-terrorism: Imagining future crime in the "war on terror"', *British Journal of Criminology*, vol 49, pp. 628–645.

Macdonald S (2015) 'Cyberterrorism and enemy criminal law', in: Ohlin JD, Finkelstein C and Govern K (eds) *Cyber War: Law and Ethics for Virtual Conflicts*, Oxford: Oxford University Press.

Macdonald S (2014) 'Prosecuting suspected terrorists: precursor crimes, intercept evidence and the priority of security', in: Jarvis L and Lister M (eds) *Critical Perspectives on Counter-Terrorism*, Abingdon: Routledge.

Macdonald S and Mair D (2015) 'Terrorism online: a new strategic environment', in: Chen TM, Jarvis L and Macdonald S (eds) *Terrorism Online: Politics, Law and Technology*, Abingdon: Routledge, pp. 10–34.

Ramraj VV, Hor M, Roach K and Williams G (2012) *Global Anti-Terrorism Law and Policy*, (2nd ed.). Cambridge: Cambridge University Press.

Richards D (2014) 'The twitter jihad: ISIS insurgents in Iraq, Syria using social media to recruit fighters, promote violence', *ABC News (Online)*. 21 June 2014. www.abc.net.au/news/2014-06-20/isis-using-social-media-to-recruit-fighters-promote-violence/5540474

Roach K (2011) *The 9/11 Effect: Comparative Counter-Terrorism*, Cambridge: Cambridge University Press.

Roach K (2006) 'The post-9/11 migration of Britain's Terrorism Act 2000', in: Choudhry S (ed.) *The Migration of Constitutional Law*, Cambridge: Cambridge University Press, pp. 374–402.

Stohl M (2006) 'Cyber terrorism: A clear and present danger, the sum of all fears, breaking point or patriot games?', *Crime, Law and Social Change*, vol 46, pp. 223–238.

Tulich T (2012) 'A view inside the preventive state: Reflections on a decade of anti-terror law', *Griffith Law Review*, vol 21, pp. 209–244.

von Behr I, Reding A, Edwarda C and Gribbon D (2013) *Radicalisation in the Digital Era: The Use of the Internet in 15 Cases of Terrorism and Extremism*, Brussels: RAND.

Walker C (2005/6) 'Cyber-terrorism: Legal principle and law in the United Kingdom', *Penn State Law Review*, vol 110, pp. 625–665.

Weimann G (2005) 'How modern terrorism use the Internet', *Journal of International Security Affairs*, vol 8, pp. 91–105. www.securityaffairs.org/issues/2005/08/weimann.php

Williams G (2013) 'The legal legacy of the war on terror', *Macquarie Law Journal*, vol 12, pp. 3–16.

Williams G (2011) 'A decade of Australian anti-terror laws', *Melbourne University Law Review*, vol 35, pp. 1136–1176.

Zedner L (2007) 'Pre-crime and post-criminology?', *Theoretical Criminology*, vol 11, pp. 261–281.

6 Brothers, believers, brave mujahideen

Focusing attention on the audience of violent jihadist preachers

Anne Aly

Introduction

In his critique on the stagnation in terrorism research, Marc Sageman (2014, pp. 1–16) laments the lack of progress towards understanding terrorism or political violence. Sageman notes the focus in both government and some academic circles on the role and influence of the Internet in political violence, and draws attention to the dearth in both quantity and quality of research into the Internet and its relationship to political violence. In response to Sageman, Jessica Stern (2014) defends the turn in terrorism research towards narratives and Internet propaganda, arguing that 'there are so many examples of extremists who have been influenced by "preachers of hate" and Internet propaganda that is hard to understand why Dr Sageman belittles their importance'. Stern highlights key examples of jihadists for whom violent extremist online narratives played at least some role in their trajectory towards violence. Stern's response, though astute, does not fully respond to Sageman's (2014) point that, contrary to the silver bullet approach that is driven by 'an implicit assumption that mere exposure to material on jihadi websites radicalises naive Muslims and turns them violent', 'online jihadists' are active participants who each have their own reasons for seeking out and engaging with violent extremist online narratives. While both Sageman and Stern acknowledge that the Internet plays a role in the radicalisation process, the exchange highlights a contemporary problematic in the field of terrorism studies: the lack of empirical evidence to support assumptions of causality between online narratives and radicalisation to violent extremism.

Just how directly online violent extremist propaganda is connected to the reality of terrorist violence is still a source of confusion and subject to conjecture and hypothesising. A study by the RAND Corporation (von Behr *et al.* 2013) that tested five assumptions about Internet radicalisation in the literature found that empirical evidence existed to support the assumption that the Internet creates more opportunities to become radicalised and serves as a space for individuals to find support for their ideas among like-minded individuals. The study also found that assumptions that the Internet accelerates the process of radicalisation and promotes self-radicalisation without physical contact were not supported. Conroy *et al.* (2012) assert that a connection does exist, stating that 'participation in online political groups is strongly correlated with offline political participation, as a potential function of engaging members online'. Pauwels and Schils (2014, pp. 1–29) contend that active participation, as opposed to passive consumption, is key, and argue that a strong correlation does exist between offline social interaction with like-minded peers and self-activated online engagement with extremist violence:

> The statistical association between measures of extremism through [new social media] and self-reported political violence remains significant and fairly constant. The most persistent effects are found for those measures where individuals actively seek out extremist content on the Internet, as opposed to passive and accidental encounters using NSM. Furthermore, offline differential associations with racist and delinquent peers are also strongly and directly related to self-reported political violence, as are some mechanisms from rival perspectives.

Research on terrorism and the Internet is characterised by a focus on examining how terrorists use the Internet for various purposes including fundraising, recruitment and indoctrination, by analysing (both quantitatively and qualitatively) terrorist activity online and, as Sageman (2014) points out, open source data sets comprising communications and documents found on violent extremist websites. Much of the research applies methods of textual analysis to deconstruct the terrorist narrative in order to make recommendations for the construction of counter-narratives, to shed light on the motives and drivers of terrorist actors or to provide some clues to the process of radicalisation. While studies on the terrorist discourse are useful for developing an understanding of master narratives that terrorists use to influence and motivate action, they tend to ignore a vital element in the communication process – the audience – who receive, decode, internalise and in some cases act on the messages embedded in these narratives. The audience plays a central role in media and communication models. Yet analysis and empirical studies of terrorism tend to assume that the terrorist messages reach and influence a submissive audience primed for radicalisation – often by virtue of cursory traits such as demographics or religious belief. Where the literature does give some consideration to the audiences of violent extremist narratives – defined here as those members of public that terrorists seek to communicate with and influence – the audience tends to be constructed into rudimentary and broad categories of government/victim and supporters. A more comprehensive approach would also give consideration to the contexts, social situations and extraneous factors that impact the ways in which different individuals and groups receive, construct, deconstruct and reconstruct the terrorists' message as active consumers, and producers, of terrorist messaging.

Focusing attention on the terrorists' audience and the social and political contexts in which the audience and the terrorist message interact can add significant value to counterterrorism efforts – particularly the development of counter-narratives. It can also highlight why different audiences receiving the same messages through the same mediums respond differently, thus assisting an understanding of why a minority of people in relatively homogenous groups will act upon terrorist messaging received through online mediums while the majority do not.

This chapter proceeds by first rationalising the terrorists' audience, drawing on conceptualisations of the audience that have emerged in the field of media studies. The idea of an audience is not without problems and the topic has been hotly debated among media theorists for decades. Among the various models and deconstructions of the audience is a fundamental assumption that the audience in fact does exist as real people in real situations. It is with this assumption that one may then begin to construct a conceptualisation of the audience for the purpose of research. Following the analysis of the terrorists' audience, this chapter then expounds some methodological approaches and dilemmas to studying the audience and proposes a research framework for researching the terrorists' audience as active participants in the reception and construction of meaning from online violent extremist messaging.

Conceptualising the audience: the contribution of media theory

There are estimated thousands of violent jihadi websites currently operating on the Internet. They vary in their content, purpose and origin, ranging from sympathetic websites dedicated to 'inciting believers' to those run by militant Islamist groups that openly advocate the use of violence. While they all contribute to an overarching discourse, they also vie for attention in an increasingly competitive marketplace of ideas by adopting communication behaviours that aim to establish their religious authority and authenticity. The Islamic State of Iraq and al-Sham (ISIS) is just one example of a violent jihadi group that has a substantial and comprehensive social media presence. ISIS operates a media campaign comparable to some of the world's largest multinationals. Before being shut down, it had its own official Arabic language Twitter app 'The Dawn of Glad Tidings', which offered users a convenient way to stay up to date with the group's activities. The app's posting activity had reached close to 40,000 tweets in a single day. ISIS also boasts Facebook pages in almost every language. The ubiquity of ISIS online is, at least partly, implicated in the phenomenon of foreign fighters. Although actual numbers vary, the estimated number of foreign fighters who have travelled to take up arms alongside ISIS runs into tens of thousands. The popularity of the group's social media campaign is much higher suggesting that assumptions about the influence of the ISIS discourse on the number of foreign fighters may be flawed. In previous work, this author has argued that the Internet presents a new frontier for the decentralisation of traditional structures of religious authority in Islam. In the Islamic tradition, religious authority is conferred upon opinion leaders who are considered to be knowledgeable about religious matters, who have status within their social networks and who elicit community trust through their communication behaviours. Thus, epistemic authority in Islam is highly dependent on the perception and acceptance of authority by a social network as opposed to being embedded in an institutional order (Aly 2012). Weimann makes this point in relation to the issuing of jihadist fatwas (religious edicts) on the Internet:

> The authors of jihadist fatwas come from diverse backgrounds. Some are scholars, some are religious authoritative figures, and others are political leaders of radical movements who are not seen in the wider Islamic world as having authority to provide fatwas, but are accepted as authorities by their followers.
>
> (Weimann 2011)

As such, researchers should consider not only loci of religious authority but also the power of Muslim audiences to prefer one religious authority over another.

It is fair to say that the concept of audience often eluded early media researchers, resulting in various deconstructions and attempts to devise new ways of imagining what an audience (if indeed the audience does exist at all) might look like and how it might be studied. These attempts converged into three basic models of the audience that occasionally overlap to accommodate more complex conceptualisations: audience-as-mass, audience-as-outcome and audience-as-agent (Webster 1998).

Audience-as-mass views the audience as a 'large collection of people scattered across time and space who act autonomously and have little or no immediate knowledge of one another' (Webster 1998, p. 191). This model allows for a construction of the audience as an aggregate defined by their shared contact with the media and is not concerned with individual cases. The disciplinary traditions associated with mass marketing, such as public relations and advertising, also conceptualise the audience as mass as a means to understanding and managing outcomes. Here, the audience is 'a mass of isolated individuals who are inherently susceptible to manipulation, though they may fail to recognise the hegemonic processes at work' (Webster 1998, p. 195). The audience-as-outcome model perceives the audience as passive receivers of media messages and is most closely associated with the media effects tradition in communication research. This model reflects a concern about the impact of the media on individuals and, in turn, on society.

For the most part, research into terrorism and the Internet that focuses only on the elements, qualities and construction of the terrorist message locates the audience somewhere between mass and outcome. Such a concept of the audience as primed for radicalisation, constant and receptive discounts the unpredictable, changeable and often unstable social world in which actual audiences operate and how these conditions affect the interactivity between sender, receiver and message. It is this very conceptualisation of the audience as solid and unwavering that underpins the assumption of vulnerability that Sageman, among others, is critical of.

Since the early 1970s, the audience-as-agent model has developed as an alternative conceptualisation of the audience, conceiving people as active agents in the media communication process whose choices and actions are influenced by social and cultural variables. The audience-as-agent model spawned qualitative models of investigation, most notably audience ethnographies and academic inquiry into reader response theory and interpretive communities. The juncture of audience-as-outcome and audience-as-agent houses the limited effects perspective, which conceptualises people as members of social networks actively involved in selecting and interpreting the media messages they encounter. Interpretive studies, cultural studies, reception analysis and social semiotics are also located here, perceiving the audience as not just receivers but also active interpreters of media messages that may carry certain embedded meanings and attributing individuals with the capacity to accept, negotiate or reject these meanings (Webster 1998).

Locating the terrorists' audience within this juncture offers the most useful approach for turning the spotlight from how the message is constructed to how the message is received and the dynamics of radicalisation in this context. This means researching online terrorist messaging from the point of view of actual audiences – both intended and unintended – taking into account the contexts and experiences in which these actual audiences interact with violent extremist online content and how these variables may (or may not) influence how they engage with the terrorists' message.

The terrorists' audience

Despite the lack of attention to the terrorists' audience in terrorism literature, a few studies do make some attempts to construct an understanding of the individuals and groups with whom terrorists try to communicate beyond the usual binary of victim/supporter. One of the earliest is Price's (1977) model of the audience in a hostage-taking incident. Price, who was writing before terrorism took to the international stage, proposed three categories of audiences to a hostage-taking incident:

1 the immediate victim – the hostage;
2 the identification group – those responsible for the welfare of the hostage;
3 the resonant mass – the broader victim population.

Writing a decade later, Cordes (1987) analysed the communiqués of Euroterrorists and distinguished between two different aspects of terrorist communication: propaganda that is intended to influence an external audience and auto propaganda that is intended to self-influence. According to Cordes, terrorist communiqués are intended to reach four audiences:

1 the government they intend to coerce;
2 the constituency – those the terrorists claim to represent in order to inform them about their purpose, engender support or mobilise;

3   members of like-minded groups in order to demonstrate solidarity;
4   the terrorists themselves – in this case, the message is auto propaganda, which restructures behaviour and provides self-exoneration.

Gressang (2001) suggests that identification of the terrorists' audience should be informed by an analysis of the terrorists' intentions and expectations. Gressang distinguishes between two core audiences of terrorist messaging in written and spoken communiqués and actions that are often violent: human audience and ethereal audience. These core audiences play a central role in determining the boundaries of violence that are acceptable. Terrorists address an ethereal audience, or a deity, through actions that can be considered sacrificial or serving a higher purpose. In terrorist propaganda, suicide acts framed as martyr missions extol the religious virtues of the martyr who is driven to act by his absolute submission to Allah. Suicide missions are constructed as otherworldly acts of divine providence (Aly 2009). Acts that emphasise the deity or ethereal audience tend to have a greater propensity for violence because

> an ethereal primary audience allows the terrorist to rationalize and justify exceeding existing behavioural and social barriers by citing divine will or other unverifiable criterion. Those groups which, on the other hand, seek to establish a dialogue with a human audience are more likely to accept self-imposed limits to the level of violence used to further their ends.
>
> (Gressang 2001, pp. 94–95)

While these three studies of the terrorists' audience yield very different conceptualisations of the audience, they all approach the problem of defining the audience through an analysis of the message – whether this message is embedded and communicated through the act itself (e.g. hijacking) or in the communication protocols used by terrorists to frame their cause and their actions. This involves deconstructing texts into their discursive elements but pays little heed to the structural relations between the texts, their senders and their receivers, which give texts their meanings. The underlying assumption is that through the message, one can also know the sender and the audience. Such an approach has been criticised for producing understandings of the audience based on an erudite reading of the text (e.g. Nightingale 1993). Stuart Hall argued that careful analyses of texts are nonetheless necessary in order to understand how the text was meant to be interpreted – its preferred meaning (Morley 2006). Recognising that the readers of violent extremist online narratives constitute not one but multiple audiences that construct different meanings from a single text in different ways necessarily shifts the focus onto the audience and how their meanings are formed.

A research framework for studying the audience of online narratives

The Internet shares much of the same features as traditional mass media such as television and radio, particularly its ability to reach mass audiences across time and space. It also incorporates unique features and offers a platform for almost any mode of transmission associated with discrete activities of traditional media – reading a newspaper, watching a television show or film, listening to the radio as well as for participation either through peer-to-peer or user-to-content interaction and production. The rise of the Internet as the most all-pervading medium of interpersonal communication has spawned a host of research on the effects of the Internet on personal relationships and social identity. These studies highlight that the personal identity and social interaction functions that the Internet provides play an important role in influencing behaviour. One study by Bargh and McKenna (2004) found that the influence of the Internet on the formation of personal relationships, group membership and social identity was not only dependent on the reasons why individuals use the Internet but also on the unique qualities of the Internet, including anonymity. Centola's (2010) study on the spread of health behaviours through online mediums found that reinforcement from online social networks was conducive for the adoption of individual behaviours.

In the field of terrorism research, cases where terrorist actors have been found to have used Internet forums to express their views or publicise their intent has led some researchers to believe that markers of violent intent could be detected by disaggregating the communications of such actors to linguistic cues of radical violence (Cohen *et al.* 2013). The exponential growth in the popularity of online social networking services such as Twitter and Facebook has motivated research interest into social media interactions and patterns of influence. Research produced by the International Centre for the Study of Radicalisation and Political Violence (ICSR) applied quantitative techniques to the analysis of American white supremacist accounts on Twitter in order to identify which social media accounts were most likely to influence or be influenced. Their approach measured interactions whereby users who inspired the most responses (replies or retweets) were deemed to be influential (Berger and Strathearn 2013). Further research by the ICSR (Carter *et al.* 2014) compiled a database of social media profiles of Western and European foreign fighters in Syria affiliated with al-Qaeda-inspired violent extremist groups. The database was used to develop an understanding of how foreign fighters in Syria receive information and are influenced. The research found that foreign fighters do not receive information about the conflict through official channels but that information is mediated through disseminators. Control of information about the conflict and the ability to influence resides not with the organised violent jihadist groups, but with individual opinion leaders who are primarily based in the West and who may not be physically involved in the conflict.

These kinds of research certainly yield some useful insights, but provide very little evidence as to why certain users and certain content are more influential than others or indeed what having influence actually means. Measuring influence by the number of responses, retweets or Facebook likes assumes that influence is the ability of the message producer to inspire fairly passive online behaviours in the message receivers (to make them reply, retweet or like a page) and that the message is therefore crafted in ways that persuade audiences towards these benign behaviours. The question of how influential online opinion leaders are in mobilising audiences in ways that matter *offline* remains unanswered. It is here that media theory can potentially make the most contribution. The content-focused approach to studying terrorism communication means that we can know who the message is intended to reach and what the terrorists intend to communicate. But we can never really understand these audiences or the cultural discourses, lived experiences and social networks that shape how they make meaning from the message. Nor can we understand how this meaning-making process shapes the range of behavioural responses, from Facebook likes to retweets to actually joining a violent extremist group or taking up arms. Further questions need to be asked about how and why the terrorist message becomes meaningful to certain people, their media habits and the contexts within which they consume, engage with and decode the terrorists' message.

A research framework for studying the terrorists' audience

The study of audiences has developed over the past three decades or so to reflect an interest in how users of mass media make sense of mediated messages in their everyday lives. Prior to these recent trends, early audience research tended to focus on the effects of media, and viewed the audience as passive, vulnerable and homogenous receivers of linearly transmitted media messages. This one-step process of transferring the media message from sender to receiver is also known as the 'silver bullet theory' and the 'hypodermic needle model' (Newbold *et al.* 2012).

A more advanced theory that emerged largely out of a study of the 1940 US Presidential election is Katz and Lazarsfeld's (1995) two-step flow model of mass media and personal influence. The main assumption of this model is that people do not react to media messages as socially isolated individuals but as members of social groups. This more holistic approach to mass media research offered a better understanding of the extraneous factors that intervene in the communication process between media and audience. Katz and Lazarsfeld identified interpersonal relations as an intervening variable. This approach suggests that audiences should be studied within the context of the groups to which they belong and the interpersonal relationships within these groups that bear on their constructions of meaning. The two-step model approaches the transmission of communications within groups in terms of the roles that people play in group interactions to locate critical points – namely the origin, the relay points and the terminal points – of intra-group communication. Today, media theory and the study of audiences accept that audiences are active participants in the meaning-making process and that this process is influenced by a range of internal and external factors. Thus, the study of the media and its influence on audiences is grounded in theories that place a fundamental emphasis on context and the understanding of actions as they occur within the dynamics of contemporary culture.

A research framework for studying the terrorists' audience based on media theories should focus on the message, its producers and its consumers as well as the relationships among these three elements. Such a framework involves three levels of analysis – each yielding different insights that collectively inform an understanding of how and why violent extremist online narratives are constructed and deconstructed in different ways by different people.

The first level of analysis is already prevalent in the terrorism and Internet literature. This level of analysis involves examinations of violent extremist online content in order to develop an understanding of what terrorists are saying and who they are speaking to. It also involves quantitative measures of who is actually receiving these messages. Such measures may not produce anything more insightful than broad demographics but potentially, like the body of research being produced by the ICSR, could yield empirical observations about the characteristics and habits of users who are participating in interactive relationships around violent extremist online content.

Researchers who are interested in the audience are also interested in how the people who make up the audience construct meaning from the messages they receive and how the social and cultural realities of their lives impact these meanings. Thus, a research framework for developing an understanding of the terrorists' audience should also incorporate a second level of analysis that answers questions about why and how individuals seek out and engage with violent extremist online content in the first place and why the violent extremist narrative fulfils a particular purpose or need for such audience members.

In media theory, the approach that focuses on how audiences use the media – their media needs – is known as the uses and gratifications model. The uses and gratifications approach attempts to understand why particular audiences are attracted to particular kinds of media and how media content satisfies their social or psychological needs. Media use is driven by needs that are generated by a combination of psychological, sociological and environmental factors. Decades of research into media uses and gratifications have yielded several classifications of user needs broadly based on the informational and entertainment functions of the media. Contemporary approaches recognise the following four needs:

1 information – relates to the cognitive needs and the desire for understanding, which are served by the surveillance function of the media;
2 personal identity – relates to strengthening confidence and credibility and value reinforcement;
3 social integration and social interaction – relates to personal relationships and the need to strengthen social contact and affiliate with a group; and
4 entertainment – relates to the need to escape and release tension (Katz *et al.* 1973; McQuail 1983).

The application of uses and gratification to social media has yielded research demonstrating that social media primarily gratifies needs that are driven by social factors through its features that facilitate self-disclosure and interaction across geographical boundaries (Ellison *et al.* 2007). Self-disclosure enables users to represent themselves in a controlled environment and strengthens interpersonal relationships (Whitty 2008; Dunne *et al.* 2010). Wang and Tchernev's (2009) study of the social media use, needs and gratifications among college students found that social media use was driven by four needs: emotional, cognitive, social and habitual. Leung's (2009) study identified a further three needs in addition to social needs: recognition, cognition and entertainment that correlated with how much time users devoted to online content generation (blogging, posting, uploading information). In a later study, Wang et al. (2012) tested the relationship between needs and social media gratifications, and found that social media use only gratifies some needs. Ungratified needs had a cumulative effect that drove further social media use.

As a useful concept for studying the relationship between the Internet and violent extremism, the uses and gratifications model describes how needs motivate media use but only gives cursory consideration to the psychological dispositions, sociological factors and context in which media use occurs. As such, it does not, in itself, offer more than a preliminary analysis of how a social situation may be involved in the generation of needs that drive engagement with online violent extremist messaging. Questions therefore remain about how and why emotional, cognitive, social and habitual needs develop in the first place and, importantly, how and why violent extremist content and engagement online gratify those needs. What is the actual appeal of violent extremist content and why does it appeal to some but not to others?

In developing a research framework for the audience of online violent extremist narratives, it is necessary to position Internet use (or indeed any use of any media) within a broader context that takes into account the social and environmental realities that create needs in the first place and that drive media usage – particularly if they drive usage of a particular medium of communication over another. This might explain why, for example, thousands of supporters of violent jihadist extremism in Syria have taken to Twitter to find out news and information and also participate in the communication through tweeting behaviours. To some extent, the precursors to media need and use are individual, although attempts by sociologists, psychologists and social scientists to explain why some individuals are more vulnerable to the militant propaganda of jihadi terrorist groups such as al-Qaeda have concluded that it is impossible to psychologically profile a terrorist. There are, however, identifiable factors that characterise the contemporary context of Muslim audiences and their media needs that should form part of a research framework for the study of violent jihadist extremism on the Internet and the audience. Aly (2012) argues that the contemporary social situation of Muslim audiences that generate their media needs and uses is characterised by six factors: transnationalism and the emergence of a Muslim diaspora; the presence of a shared identity among Muslims around the globe grounded in victimhood and validated by the concept of brotherhood; a widely held perception among Muslims in the diaspora that the Western media is a complicit actor in a conspiracy to undermine Islam and subsequent disengagement with the Western media as a source of news and information; waning Western soft power; the presence of personal and communal crisis and access to new media. Weimann and von Knop (2008) also propose that the social situation of diaspora communities that may be socially alienated, disenfranchised and in search of social bonding creates a condition of emotional need that is served by the violent extremist narrative. The authors allude to a uses and gratifications approach to understanding the interface of sender, message and receiver:

> To be seduced by terrorist messages and narratives, the user must be in a condition of emotional need. To be persuasive, the narratives have to suggest goal fulfilment, namely the achievement of a sense of identity. To provide that identity, personal motivation must become influenced by a higher motivation, which in turn determines the goal formation. (p. 889)

Weimann and von Knop (2008) identify several stages of engagement with violent extremist narratives online: each motivated by a different set of needs that are in turn gratified by online functions and content. The 'Searching Phase' involves users looking for answers out of a particular interest or curiosity that leads them to visit extremist websites. The 'Seduction Phase' sees users being introduced to extremist narratives as they continue to visit specific websites. In the 'Captivation Phase', users start to visit blogs, forums or chat rooms though they do not participate in their interactive features. In the 'Persuasion Phase', users begin to participate in communicative exchanges as members of online communities. The final phase, 'Operative Phase', occurs when users are introduced to the operational activities of the group and this may translate to real-world activities. Weimann and von Knop's model presents a useful approach to the process of online radicalisation. In this model, uses and gratifications can be used as an organising concept for examining how media use at each phase is generated by different needs and how these interact with the social realities of users. The 'Searching Phase' for example may be prompted by informational needs causing the user to search for specific content on the Internet. This need might arise for a number of reasons including personal contact or exposure to new information. Uses and gratifications however falls short of offering a way of understanding how users in the searching phase make meaning from the content they find and why some users will continue from one phase to the next, while others will simply walk away from the narrative. In order to develop this comprehensive understanding of meaning making, a third level of analysis is required.

In the early 1980s, Stuart Hall and colleagues at the Centre for Contemporary Cultural Studies in Birmingham proposed a dynamic model of the relationship between media and the audience. Hall's (1980) encoding/decoding model identified the media communicative process as beginning with the construction of a message that is framed by producers of media texts to reflect ideologies and assumptions about the audience. This is the encoding phase of communication. The encoded messages are then communicated via meaningful discourse that can then be meaningfully decoded. Encoded messages are not always decoded in the same way that they were intended. The differences between encoded message and decoded meanings are formed by the social relations between the two sides of the communicative exchange – the producer of the message and the audience. Thus, a single message may actually produce various meanings according to factors such as socio/economic status, past experience and the context and ways in which the message is consumed. When audiences decode texts in ways that correspond with their intended or 'preferred' meaning, they assume the dominant hegemonic position. This position results in 'perfectly transparent communication'. The negotiated position acknowledges the dominant hegemonic code but negotiates the application of this code according to local or contextual conditions. The oppositional position occurs when a message is decoded contrary to the preferred code in its totality (Hall 1980, p. 136). According to Hall's model, it is not the encoded messages that impact audiences but their decoded meanings that 'influence, entertain, instruct or persuade' (p. 130). This final point, that the meanings taken from messages, not the meanings intended in messages, are all important is perhaps the most compelling argument for a focus on the audience in terrorism studies.

In applying Hall's model, Morley (1980) maintained that differences in decodings and constructions of meaning cannot simply be attributed to individual personality differences. Rather, they can also be related to sociocultural differences in the way in which social backgrounds equip people with different cultural tools and conceptual frameworks through which messages are decoded and meanings constructed. Morley theorised that whether or not a text succeeds in sending messages that are preferred will depend on whether or not there are readers whose codes and ideologies, influenced by other social institutions, correspond and work with those of the text. Members of particular subcultures inhabit similar codes and ideologies and hence share cultural orientations that influence whether they take a preferred, negotiated or oppositional position in relation to a media text.

To apply encoding/decoding to the study of the terrorists' audience requires some re-conceptualisation of the model to take into account the nature of online interactions between violent extremist producers of terrorist content and their audiences. The underlying theoretical assumption is that the violent extremist narrative contains embedded messages that intend to influence audience members through preferred readings. The relationship between the audience member and the text will determine whether the messages are decoded from a preferred, negotiated or oppositional position. This relationship is determined by a number of demographic factors but also the broader contexts in which media needs for information, social identity and personal identity are generated and gratified by media use. It is also determined by personal influence: who crafted the message and whether the message is interpreted by opinion leaders in the audience member's social reality. Thus, a reconceptualised model for the third level of analysis would also take into account social or political critical points that influence how meaning is constructed and the influence of opinion leaders who mediate meanings and can exert influence on how messages are read.

Audience-focused research framework in practice

Despite the focus on violent extremist narratives and messaging in much of the terrorism research, some research has emerged that takes into account the need for studying how audiences respond to mediated messages in order to illuminate the relationship between online messaging and behaviours. Aly's (2010a, 2010b, 2012) study on audience responses to the Australian media discourse on terrorism focused on audience reception and interpretations of mediated messages of the terrorism threat. Applying a methodological framework that combined both discourse analysis of mainstream news media reports with focus groups and in-depth interviews with a sample of 180 audience members, Aly demonstrated that audience constructions of terrorism were subject to critical points of meaning making. She argued that decoding of media messages about terrorism is a cumulative and fluid process that is subject to changes in the broader socio-political influences and the introduction of new 'truths' in the individuals' interpretations of messages. Accordingly, Aly argued that audience behaviours in response to mediated messages about terrorism cannot be determined by looking at the messages in isolation. Rather such responses are mediated by factors external to the immediate and instant interaction between audience and message, and subject to personal, social and environmental conditions and changes to those conditions.

Recent work on media ecology offers useful concepts to understanding questions of what drives online media needs and the relationship between these needs and the social and environmental contexts in which they occur. Scolari (2012) defines media ecology as being primarily concerned with 'what roles media force us to play, how media structure what we are seeing or thinking, and why media make us feel and act as we do'. Media ecology scholars argue that the influences of new media interactions must be understood within the broader context of media as a whole. As such, online violent extremist producers and mainstream news media producers are operating within broader ecology in which messages are produced, disseminated and interpreted. Al-Lami *et al.* (2012) applied a media ecology approach to their study of two case studies in which different groups mobilised and justified acts of violence. Their study traced the discourses produced by violent jihadists that legitimised violence as well as mainstream media discourses. In accordance with the research framework proposed in this chapter, their focus was not on the discourses themselves but on the dynamic between emergence and agency. Accordingly, Al-Lami and associates incorporated three levels of research into their study: an examination of online jihadist media, a discourse analysis of mainstream news media reports on jihadist violence, and a qualitative study of the audience to identify how such audiences interpret concepts of jihadist violence and radicalisation.

At the Countering online Violent Extremism Research (CoVER) program, researchers are developing research projects based on operationalising the concepts of audience and online radicalisation. The Counter Narratives to Interrupt Online Radicalisation (CNOIR) project[1] incorporates elements of Weimann and von Knop's (2008) online radicalisation model with current research on social media uses and gratifications and textual analysis of self-generated content online. Utilising data sets collected through a project that sought to explore how Internet users interpret and reproduce messages embedded in violent extremist propaganda, the project applied a discursive analysis of user-generated content derived from the research of Frank *et al.* (2014) and Matsumoto *et al.* (2013) into emotive indicators of political aggression and that of Cohen *et al.* (2013) on linguistic markers indicating warning behaviours of radial violence.

The CNOIR project identified five behavioural profiles of users who engage with radicalising narratives online. The profiles highlight levels of online engagement with extremist ideologies differentiated along three scales: social media needs (emotional, cognitive, social and habitual), online behaviours (self-disclosure, content generation, liking and reposting) and message engagement (thematic and emotive).

Table 6.1 Profile of online engagement with radicalising narratives

Profile	Description	Media needs	Behaviours	Engagement
Seeker	The Seeker describes the type of online behaviour demonstrated by a user in the searching phase.	Emotional Cognitive	Passive	In-group favouritism and victimhood.
Lurker	The Lurker is a user who is in the seduction phase. Lurkers are starting to narrow the information they seek to sources they are still appraising and/or beginning to trust.	Cognitive Emotional	Social Habitual Passive	Superficial engagement with in-group symbols and figures.
Inquirer	The Inquirer is a user in the captivation phase. Inquirers demonstrate an increased desire for making social connection with like-minded people.	Social Emotional Cognitive	Active questioning Self-disclosure	Superficial engagement with in group ideology. Out group contempt
Advocate	The Advocate is a user who is in the persuasion phase of the process.	Social Emotional	Self-disclosure Content generation Highly visible	In group ideology Self-identification as soldier/warrior. Out group anger and contempt.
Activator	The Activator represents a user in the operative stage. Activators may possess a latent but combustible mix of emotional aggression and warning behaviours.	Social Emotive	Self-disclosure	Fixation on violence. Out group intolerability and disgust. Declaration of intent.

Conclusion

The absence of the audience in studies that explore terrorism as a form of communication has resulted in a body of research that emphasises violent extremist narratives and makes assumptions about the ways in which these narratives influence. Studies that attempt to construct an understanding of the audience by carefully analysing the messages embedded in violent extremist narratives ignore the fact that these messages are received by active audiences: audiences who exercise agency in the ways in which they interact with the messages and whose interpretations of messages are also influenced by a range of factors. Previous research into terrorism and the Internet has served terrorism studies well by identifying the ways in which terrorists use the Internet. The more recent focus on social media and terrorism has argued for patterns of influence among and between users of social media services. Yet questions about the audience remain unanswered. A media theory approach that conceptualises communication as an interactive and dynamic process between message producers, the message and the receivers of the message provides a useful framework for exploring the terrorists' audience. The process by which terrorists' audiences make meaning from the violent extremist narrative and the variables – demographic, contextual, individual and group related – that affect these meanings can help to ensure that counter-narratives are equally as effective as the violent extremist narrative appears to be.

In an address to the Royal United Services Institute, Sir Richard Dearlove, former chief of MI6, surmised that the threat of Islamist terrorism had been greatly exaggerated by the focus on the Internet messages of 'misguided young men, rather pathetic figures' adding that it was 'surely better to ignore them'(Norton-Taylor 2014). He makes a valid point. On the same day that Musa Cerantonio's Twitter message announcing his arrival in the Islamic State made front-page headlines, pop star Miley Cyrus's tweet about 'wrinkly hands' received 3.9 thousand retweets and was favourited 7.5 thousand times. In comparison, Cerantonio's tweet, his most popular to date, was retweeted 636 times and favourited 509 times. Questions about the assumptions of influence need to be asked, especially when these assumptions form the basis for determining guilt in court trials or for assessing threat. What is the level of influence that online violent extremist messaging wields beyond responses that require little or no investment such as retweets and Facebook likes? This question can be answered by approaching the problem through an understanding that the message itself is limited in its power without a receptive and active audience. Applying media theories of uses and gratifications, opinion leaders and encoding/decoding can shed light of the conditions under which preferred readings of terrorist propaganda are constructed and the kinds of behaviours (both online and offline) they motivate. Findings can then be applied to more accurate risk assessments about the threat of Islamist terrorism.

Note

1 The CNOIR project is funded by the Australian Government Department of the Attorney General and was conducted in partnership with All Together Now and the Institute for Strategic Dialogue.

References

Al-Lami, M, Hoskins, A and O'Loughlin, B (2012), 'Mobilisation and Violence in the New Media Ecology: The Dua Khalil Aswad and Camilia Shehata Cases', *Critical Studies on Terrorism*, vol. 5, no. 2, pp. 237–56.

Aly, A (2009), 'The Terrorists' Audience: A Model of Internet Radicalisation', *Journal of Australian Professional Intelligence Officers*, pp. 3–19.

Aly, A (2010a), *A Study of Audience Responses to the Media Discourse About the 'Other': The Fear of Terrorism Between Australian Muslims and the Broader Community*, Lampeter, Edwin Mellen Press.

Aly, A (2010b), 'Shifting Positions to the Media Discourse on Terrorism: Critical Points in Audience Members' Meaning Making Experiences', *Media International Australia incorporating Culture and Policy*, vol. 134, no. 1, pp. 31–46.

Aly, A (2012), 'An Audience Focussed Approach to Examining Religious Extremism Online', *Australian and New Zealand Journal of Communication*, vol. 39, no, 1, pp. 1–17.

Bargh, J.A and McKenna, K.Y (2004), 'The Internet and Social Life', *Annual Review of Psychology*, vol. 55, pp. 573–90.

Berger, J.M and Strathearn, B (2013), *Who Matters Online: Measuring Influence, Evaluating Content and Countering Violent Extremism in Online Social Network*, Developments in Radicalisation and Political Violence, London: ICSR.

Carter, J.A, Maher, S and Neumann, P. R (2014), *Greenbirds: Measuring Importance and Influence in Syrian Foreign Fighter Networks*. Developments in Radicalisation and Political Violence, London: ICSR.

Centola, D (2010), 'The Spread of Behavior in an Online Social Network Experiment', *Science*, vol. 329, no. 5996, pp. 1194–7.

Cohen, K, Johansson, F, Kaati, L and Mork, J.C (2013), Detecting Linguistic Markers for Radical Violence in Social Media, *Terrorism and Political Violence*, vol. 26, no. 1, pp. 246–56.

Conroy, M, Feezell, J.T and Guerrero, M (2012), 'Facebook and Political Engagement: A Study of Online Political Group Membership and Offline Political Engagement', *Computers in Human Behavior*, vol. 28, no. 5, pp. 1535–46.

Cordes, B (1987), 'When Terrorists Do the Talking: Reflections on Terrorist Literature', *Journal of Strategic Studies*, vol. 10, no. 4, pp. 150–71.

Dunne, A, Lawlor, M and Rowley, J (2010), 'Young People's Use of Online Social Networking Sites: A Uses and Gratifications Perspective', *Journal of Research in Interactive Marketing*, vol. 4, pp. 46–58.

Ellison, N. B, Steinfield, C and Lampe, C (2007), 'The Benefits of Facebook "Friends": Social Capital and College Students' Use of Online Social Network Sites', *Journal of Computer-Mediated Communication*, vol. 12, pp. 1143–68.

Frank, M, Matsumoto, D and Hwang, H (2014), 'Intergroup Emotions and Political Aggression: The ANCODI Hypothesis' in J. P. Forgas, K. Fielder and W. D. Crano, (eds), *The Sydney Symposium of Social Psychology: Social Psychology of Politics*, Sydney, Psychology Press.

Gressang, D (2001), 'Audience and Message: Assessing Terrorist WMD Potential', *Terrorism and Political Violence*, vol. 13, no. 3, pp. 83–106.

Hall, S (1980), 'Encoding/Decoding', in S. Hall, D. Hobson, A. Lowe and P. Willis, (eds), *Culture, Media, Language*, London: Hutchinson, pp. 128–39.

Katz, E and Lazarsfeld, P.F (1955), *Personal Influence: The Part Played by People in the Flow of Mass Communications*, Chicago, IL: The Free Press.

Katz, E, Gurevitch, M and Haas, H (1973), 'On the Use of the Mass Media for Important Things', *American Sociological Review*, vol. 38 (April), pp. 164–81.

Leung, L (2009), 'User-Generated Content on the Internet: An Examination of Gratifications, Civic Engagement, and Psychological Empowerment', *New Media and Society*, vol. 11, pp. 1327–47.

McQuail, D (1983), *Mass Communication Theory*, (1st edn), London: Sage.

Matsumoto, D, Hwang, H and Frank, M (2013), 'Emotional Language and Political Aggression', *Journal of Language and Social Psychology*, vol. 32, no. 4, pp. 452–68.

Morley, D, (1980) *The 'Nationwide' Audience*, London, BFI.

Morley, D (2006), 'Unanswered Questions in Audience Research', *Compos*, pp. 1–25.

Newbold, C, Boyd-Barrett, O and Van Den Bulck, H, (eds) (2002), *The Media Book*, London: Arnold.

Nightingale, V (1993), 'What's "Ethnographic" About Ethnographic Audience Research?' in J. Frow and M. Morris, (eds), *Australian Cultural Studies: A Reader*, St Leonards, NSW: Allen & Unwin, pp. 149–61.

Norton-Taylor, R (2014), 'Islamist Terror Threat to West Blown Out of Proportion- Former MI6 Chief', *The Guardian*, 8 July 2014, accessible at www.theguardian.com/uk-news/2014/jul/07/islamist-terror-threat-out-proportion-former-mi6-chief-richard-dearlove

Pauwels, L and Schils, N (2014), 'Differential Online Exposure to Extremist Content and Political Violence: Testing the Relative Strength of Social Learning and Competing Perspectives', *Terrorism and Political Violence*, pp. 1–29.

Price, H. E (1997), 'The Strategy and Tactics of Revolutionary Terrorism', *Comparative Studies in Society and History*, vol. 19, no. 1, pp. 52–66.

Sageman, M (2014), 'The Stagnation in Terrorism Research', *Terrorism and Political Violence*, pp. 1–16.

Scolari, C (2012), 'Media Ecology: Exploring the Metaphor to Expand the Theory', *Communication Theory*, vol. 22, pp. 204–25.

Stern, J (2014), 'Response to Marc Sageman's "The Stagnation in Terrorism Research"', *Terrorism and Political Violence*, vol. 26, no. 4, pp. 607–13.

von Behr, I, Reding, A, Edwards, C and Gribbon, L (2013), *Radicalisation in the Digital Era: The Use of the Internet in 15 Cases of Terrorism and Extremism*, Brussels: RAND.

Wang, Z and Tchernev, J (2012), 'The "Myth" of Media Multitasking: Reciprocal Dynamics of Media Multitasking, Personal Needs, and Gratifications', *Journal of Communication*, pp. 1460–2466.

Wang, Z, Tchernev, J. M and Solloway, T (2012), 'A Dynamic Longitudinal Examination of Social Media Use, Needs, and Gratifications Among College Students', *Computers in Human Behavior*, vol. 28, pp. 1829–39.

Webster, J.G (1998), 'The Audience', *Journal of Broadcasting and Electronic Media*, vol. 42, no. 2, pp. 190–208.

Weimann, G and von Knop, K (2008), 'Applying the Notion of Noise to Countering Online-Terrorism', *Studies in Conflict and Terrorism*, vol. 31, pp. 883–902.

Weimann, G (2011), 'Cyber-Fatwas and Terrorism', *Studies in Conflict and Terrorism*, vol. 34, no. 10, pp. 765–81.

Whitty, M.T (2008), 'Revealing the "Real" Me, Searching for the "Actual" You: Presentations of Self on an Internet Dating Site', *Computers in Human Behavior*, vol. 24, pp. 1707–23.

7 Determining the role of the Internet in violent extremism and terrorism

Six suggestions for progressing research

Maura Conway

Introduction

The 'slick' and 'glossy' nature of the online content of the so-called 'Islamic State' (IS) and its resultant potential attractiveness to, and resonance with, discontented 'digital natives' (i.e. young people who have grown up with the Internet) has been widely reported upon in the world's press and is now a source of considerable public and governmental anxiety. There is as yet no proven connection between consumption of and networking around violent extremist online content and adoption of extremist ideology and/or engagement in violent extremism and terrorism (McCants 2011; Rieger *et al.* 2013). Some scholars and others remain sceptical of a significant role for the Internet in processes of violent radicalisation (Githens-Mazer 2010; Bouhana and Wikström 2011; Benson 2014).[1] There is increasing concern on the part of other scholars, and more so policymakers and publics, that high and increasing levels of always-on Internet access and the production and wide dissemination – and thence easy availability – of large amounts of violent extremist content online may have violent radicalising effects (Stenersen 2008; Gray and Head 2009; Berger and Strathearn 2013; Edwards and Gribbon 2013; Carter *et al.* 2014; United Nations 2014, p. 4), which certainly appears to be one of the main purposes of its producers. Determining the significance of the role of the Internet in contemporary extremism and terrorism is not the goal of this article however and, indeed, is unlikely to be able to be adequately addressed in any single journal article given the scope of the issues necessary to be addressed. This article has a narrower remit: it contextualises research and discussion in this area to-date and proffers six suggestions for progressing research on the role of the Internet in violent extremism and terrorism, so that we may be better placed to make a determination as to the significance of the Internet's role in the latter going forward. The article is composed of three sections. The first section provides context via summary of the nature of the research produced to-date on the role of the Internet in violent extremism and terrorism.

Section two composes a brief recap of a variety of arguments for and against the Internet having a significant role in contemporary violent extremism and terrorism. Section three, the article's longest, identifies two core questions regarding the interaction of violent extremism and terrorism and the Internet, particularly social media, which have yet to be adequately addressed, and supplies a series of six follow-up suggestions, flowing from these questions, for progressing research on violent online extremism and terrorism. These suggestions are with respect to the necessity for researchers in this area to widen our research beyond violent online jihadism, engage in more comparative analysis, consider virtual ethnography as a viable approach while at the same time not dismissing upscaling techniques, draw from Internet studies and engage in interdisciplinary research and consider gender as an important category. The conclusion reiterates that while ours is a burgeoning research field, it lacks a sound theoretical and evidential base.

Research to-date

A useful distinction may be drawn between descriptive research and explanatory research. Broadly, descriptive research asks '*What* is going on?' while explanatory approaches ask '*Why* is it going on?' Much descriptive research is scene-setting; it involves providing historical and/or contemporary overviews of some research topic or issue area by drawing together and synthesising the available data. Abstract questions are not ruled out however. 'Is the role of the Internet in contemporary terrorism increasing?' is a descriptive research question, for example. Explanatory research, on the other hand, largely develops causal explanations. Instead of asking whether the Internet has an increased role in contemporary terrorism, explanatory research might ask 'Why is the Internet playing an increased role in contemporary terrorism?' It is one thing to show that the Internet is of greater significance in contemporary terrorism, in other words, but another thing altogether to explain *why* this is so. Research of both sorts is 'fundamental to the research enterprise' (De Vaus 2001, p. 1); adequate amounts of neither have been undertaken on the role of the Internet in contemporary violent extremism and terrorism. It is impossible to adequately answer the question of *why* the Internet is playing a greater role in contemporary violent extremism and terrorism, without prior knowledge of *what* role, if *any*, the Internet is playing in the latter. Unfortunately, basic descriptive research is largely missing from this field, along with more complex theory-informed approaches seeking to show causal connections (Archetti 2013, pp. 21–22).

This is pretty astounding given the treasure trove of data now available online. It allowed William McCants, in testimony before the US House of Representatives Homeland Security Subcommittee on Counterterrorism and Intelligence in December 2011, to raise the following in relation to *what* questions:

> There is little research to go on, which is striking given how data-rich the Internet is. In hard numbers, how widely distributed was Zawahiri's last message? Did it resonate more in one U.S. city than another? Who were its main distributors on Facebook and YouTube? How are they connected with

one another? This sort of baseline quantitative research barely exists at the moment.

Aaron Zelin observed as recently as 2013 that:

> More than 11 years after the attacks of 9/11 and nearly a decade since the rise of popular online jihadi Internet forums, there is strikingly little empirical research on the manner in which jihadi activists use the Web to propagate their cause. Whereas researchers and policy analysts have systematically collected and analyzed the primary source material produced by al-Qaeda and its allies, very little work has been done on the conduits through which that information is distributed – and even to what extent anyone is accessing that propaganda other than counterterrorism analysts. (p. 1)[2]

Missing, in other words, are analyses of individual Internet users' online activity and experiences in extremist cyberspaces, in addition to research on the online structures within which the latter are operating – even constrained – and the different workings and therefore functions of these. Neither *what* or *why* questions are being addressed, in other words.

Given these and other difficulties with the available research, it's unsurprising that there is ongoing debate among scholars about the significance of the Internet in contemporary violent extremism and terrorism, particularly its role in processes of violent radicalisation.

Arguments for and against a significant role for the Internet in violent extremism and terrorism

Scepticism that the Internet might have a role to play in violent extremism and terrorism is not new. Walter Laqueur in 1999, an early and influential figure in Terrorism Studies, made the following observation

> No amount of email sent from the Baka Valley to Tel Aviv, from Kurdistan to Turkey, from the Jaffna peninsula to Colombo, or from India to Pakistan will have the slightest political effect. Nor can one envisage how in these conditions virtual power will translate into real power. (p. 262)

This is an interesting statement from a number of perspectives, chief among them being that just a few lines previously, on the very same page in fact, Laqueur says that audio cassettes of Khomeini smuggled into Iran during his exile in Najaf and subsequently Paris significantly impacted the Iranian revolution.[3] So Laqueur readily admits of the fact that audio cassettes changed the course of Iranian history, but cannot see how Internet technologies could fundamentally change anything in relation to terrorism. His initial impetus, to assign a role to information and communication technologies in political violence movements, is in keeping with David Rapoport's (2002) wave theory of terrorism, an often overlooked aspect of which is the way technology, especially communications technology, can influence the types, timing and spread of terrorism.

Laqueur's sceptical view nonetheless persists. Over a decade later, journalist Jason Burke (2011) made the following observation about social media and its effects in terms of contemporary terrorism:

> Twitter will never be a substitute for grassroots activism. In much of the Islamic world, social media is only for super-connected local elites or supporters in far-off countries. Neither are much use on the ground, where it counts. Social media can bring in donations or some foreign recruits. It can aid communication with some logistics and facilitate propaganda operations, but it is not much use in a firefight ... Twitter won't help al-Shabaab retake Mogadishu or the Taliban reach Kabul in any meaningful way.

Startlingly, Burke seems to think social media activity cannot be a substantive form of 'grassroots activism', which he seems to imply must be 'real world' activism. Second, he appears to think that not a great many people in the Arab and Muslim world(s) are social media users, which was untrue, even in 2011; five Arab countries (UAE, Lebanon, Jordan, Kuwait and Tunisia) had greater than 25 per cent Facebook penetration at the end of 2011, for example (Arab Social Media Report 2011). Third, Burke says that Twitter is 'not much use on the, ground, where it counts', while at the same time admitting that it can bring in donations, so it has a financing aspect; can attract so-called 'foreign fighters', so it has a recruitment function; and can also aid in communication, logistics and propaganda. An alternative viewpoint is that a single free online platform that can be employed for fundraising, recruitment, information dissemination and intra-group communications seems likely to be quite an important tool in arriving at, ultimately, the 'firefight'.

This privileging of 'real world' activity is shared by diverse commentators. Assertions that 'most jihadists need to actually meet recruiters offline to be convinced to make the trip overseas' (Bartlett 2015) or 'physical contact, in addition to online communication and propaganda, is essential' (Rogan 2006, p. 30) are quite commonplace. An implicit privileging of the 'real world' may also explain the contention contained in a UK House of Commons' Home Affairs Committee's counterterrorism report:

> The process of radicalisation will continue: the ideology which has come to be associated with al-Qa'ida will be more resilient than al-Qa'ida itself. Extremist material on the Internet will continue to motivate some people to engage in terrorism but will rarely be a substitute for *the social process of radicalisation*
>
> [italics mine] (House of Commons Home Affairs Committee 2014, pp. 6–7)

Thence, in 2014, there were – likely still are – those in the UK government who think that the Internet isn't social. They are either unaware of or have misunderstood the 'social' aspects of 'social media'. Today's Internet does not simply allow for the dissemination and consumption of 'extremist material' in a one-way broadcast from producer to consumer, but also high levels of online social interaction around this material. It is precisely the functionalities of the *social* Web that causes many scholars, policymakers and others to believe that the Internet is playing a significant role in contemporary radicalisation processes.

This is not to say that there are not more convincing arguments for the role of the Internet in contemporary violent radicalisation having been oversold; these arguments take two main forms. One position holds that most, though not all, contemporary violent online extremists are dilettantes, in the sense that they restrict themselves to using the Internet to support and encourage violent extremism, but pose no 'real world' threat. Put another way, there is the possibility that extremists' virtual 'venting' or 'purging' satisfies their desire to act. Their online activity, on this analysis, rather than becoming an avenue for violent radicalisation and potentially ultimately 'real world' action including, in the most extreme instances, terrorism, instead becomes for many a mechanism to dissipate the desire for violent action (Ramsay 2009, p. 35; Awan *et al.* 2012, pp. 58–59, 64–65). An associated argument is that many of those using the Internet to profess a dedication to or desire for violent action are engaged in a type of grandstanding common to the Internet, without ever having had any real commitment and/or intention to engage in violence at all. Even the UK's GCHQ has acceded that true intent can be very difficult to discern from online communications and activity (Intelligence and Security Committee of Parliament 2014, p. 131). The 'online dis-inhibition effect', in its 'toxic' form (Suler 2005; see also Bartlett 2015, pp. 41–42), means that discussion of violent action and even direct threats of violence are so prevalent online that were all social media companies to share all postings of a violent extremist nature with authorities, the latter would be deluged with information and potentially rendered unable to function; the ultimately benign – or at least not directly resulting in 'real world' violence – nature of most such vitriolic trolling is seen to make this unnecessary however.

A second sceptical approach is to argue that claiming violent extremist online content violently radicalises individuals is senseless given that other consumers of the same content are not similarly affected. In fact, large and growing numbers of researchers, journalists and others are regularly exposed to substantial amounts of violent extremist content over long periods of time, but are not radicalised, never mind caused to engage in terrorism. On the contrary, the latter experience may even increase these consumers' abhorrence of violent extremism and terrorism, which may be supposed to be the opposite effect than intended by its producers (Archetti 2015, p. 50). There's no reason to expect that this isn't also the experience of large segments of the general public. This is not the same thing, on the other hand, as saying that consumption of violent extremist content has negligible effects on all those who consume it. MI5 asserts that *Inspire* magazine was 'read by those involved in at last seven out of the ten attacks planned within the UK since its first issue [in 2010]' as quoted in Intelligence and Security Committee of Parliament 2014, p. 60 (see also Meleagrou-Hitchens 2011, p. 56). The direction of causation remains unknown however: Did reading *Inspire* cause the attack planners to plan the attacks? Did they begin attack planning and were then exposed to the magazine? Or did *Inspire* have different roles for different (groups of) attackers? Overall, the issue of the ratio of downloads/views to attacks causes some to argue that while violent extremist content can buttress an already sympathetic individual's resolve to engage in violence, it is not generally the originating cause of such a commitment (Sageman 2004, p. 163; Stevens and Neumann 2009, ch. 2; Githens-Mazer 2010; Hussain and Saltman 2014). This may make intuitive sense, but is it borne out by the evidence?

It is estimated that Internet penetration in North America is c. 88 per cent, in Europe is c. 70.5 per cent, and in the Middle East is c. 48 per cent (www.internet worldstats.com/stats.htm). Most scholars are inclined to agree, in this context, that along with all the other changes that it has wrought, the Internet is also affecting the conduct of contemporary violent extremism and terrorism. 'Terrorism cases in the UK without a "digital footprint" are increasingly rare', for example (Von Behr *et al.* 2013, p. 3). The former Chief Constable of West Yorkshire and UK Association of Chief of Police Officers (ACPO) head of 'Prevent', Norman Bettison, observed in 2012 that 'the Internet features in most, but not all, terrorism cases' (Von Behr *et al.* 2013, p. 5). This is a far cry however from Marc Sageman's assertion that 'face-to-face radicalisation has been replaced by online radicalisation' (Sageman 2008a, p. 41).[4] The vast majority of researchers grappling with the role of the Internet in contemporary violent extremism and terrorism – whether sceptics for a significant role, convinced of same, or located somewhere in between – now agree that the question is no longer *if* the Internet has a role to play in contemporary violent extremism and terrorism, but the more pertinent issue is determining its level of significance in contemporary violent radicalisation processes. How do we *know* that most jihadis still need to meet recruiters offline to be convinced to travel overseas? This is no more likely, in the absence of sound data and analysis, than young women being 'Brainwashed in their Bedrooms' via Twitter (Greenwood *et al.* 2015). Both could be true, in fact; perhaps gender is a determining factor. We just don't know enough at this stage as this whole research area is bereft of established empirical findings.

Where do we go from here? Six suggestions for progressing research

It is suggested that at least two foundational questions regarding the role of the Internet in violent extremism and terrorism are yet to be adequately addressed, never mind answered. These are:

1 Is it possible for persons to be radicalised online? In particular, can online interactions and/or consumption of violent and/or non-violent online content cause some individuals to become violently radicalised?
2 If violent online radicalisation[5] can be shown to occur, what are the contours of these processes? In particular, does the significance of the Internet in violent radicalisation processes differ according to users' ideology, location,

proximity to a given conflict, gender, types of online activity, preferred online platforms and/or other factors?

There is little difficulty in finding appropriate cases or anecdotes to illustrate the array of arguments both for and against a decisive role for the Internet in contemporary radicalisation processes. The reality however is that insufficient substantive empirically grounded social science research has been undertaken to-date in order to allow us to convincingly answer these questions. The work that has been done is largely focused on analysing digital content and not its producers or consumers (i.e. the audience), distribution mechanisms, or its functioning and effects.

Even if one accepts, in the absence of sound research – and many people do including, importantly, policymakers – but on the basis of common sense, anecdote and the like that violent online radicalisation is actually occurring, how can effective counter strategies be developed, if we don't know *how* it's occurring? This has not stopped a chorus of national leaders (e.g. Rawlinson 2015; Watt and Wintour 2015), government ministers (e.g. the Joint Statement of EU Ministers of the Interior and/or Justice 2015) and intelligence chiefs (e.g. Hannigan 2014; Brennan 2015), from calling on social media companies to do more to rid their platforms of violent extremist and terrorist content. This raises a host of potential difficulties not least what exactly constitutes 'terrorist content' and others around freedom of speech. Instead of wholesale removals of 'terrorist content', it could be possible if better analysis was available to do quite a targeted deletion of content shown to be directly implicated in violent radicalisation and terrorism. Content control and/or deletion measures are often advocated in conjunction with online countering violent extremism (CVE), in which more resources are promised to be invested by governments.[6] But how can we develop and deploy effective online CVE projects without knowing who precisely these should be targeted at, what types of content are attractive to them and what platforms are trafficked by these users? These are the kinds of answers that nobody appears to have at present.

How can we begin to remedy this? Below are six suggestions – there are surely a great many others; this is certainly not an exhaustive accounting, merely a first attempt – for progressing research and knowledge on the role of the Internet, especially social media, in violent extremism and terrorism.

Widen

Academics, media, policymakers and others have a tendency to lose perspective when it comes to violent jihadi online activity, particularly that of IS. The amount of violent political extremist online content is increasing all the time and is not limited to purveyors of any one political ideology. Research on the role of the Internet in violent extremism and terrorism therefore needs to be widened beyond the present narrow focus on violent jihadi online content and interactions. In order to determine whether violent online radicalisation is occurring, academic research needs to extend enquiry into the whole range of contemporary violent extremists and terrorists and their online activities. This includes so-called 'old' terrorist organisations that still maintain an online presence, all variants of the violent extreme right, and a range of others. This widening is necessary, if for no other reason than to allow for comparative research (of which more below), to ask how what the jihadis do is different from – but also how it may share similarities with – what other violent extremists are doing online and to come up with explanations for these, especially as pertaining to the alleged effectiveness of violent jihadis' online radicalisation strategies.

The extreme right is particularly worth consideration as, along with a history of violence, it has a very long online history, dating to the earliest days of the public Internet in the mid-1980s (Anti-Defamation League [ADL] 1985). The Stormfront online forum, which has proudly described itself as 'the first White Nationalist site on the Web' (Oldham 1998) has well over 11 million posts. As early as 1996, Stormfront's Don Black asserted that 'organizations have recruited through Stormfront, and through their Web pages that we've linked to' (Kanaley 1996), while a report by the Southern Poverty Law Center (SPLC) alleges that in 2010–2014, almost 100 murders could be attributed to registered Stormfront users (Beirich 2014, pp. 2–6). Stormfront recorded an average of some 5,800 threads per month between August 2012 and February 2015, which amounts to some 70,000 new threads per year.[7] By way of comparison, the top-tier jihadi forum al-Shumukh al-Islam showed some 150 new threads per day in Spring 2012 for an average of approximately 55,000 new threads per year (Zelin 2013, p. 8; see also Hegghammer 2014, p. 5).

Stormfront's longevity, size and notoriety means that it has attracted a certain amount of scholarly attention (e.g. De Kostera and Houtman 2008; Bowman-Grieve 2009; Meddaugh and Kay 2009). In fact, researchers' attention to the extreme right's online presence (e.g. Burris *et al*. 2000; Chroust 2000; Gerstenfeld *et al*. 2003; Bostdorff 2004; Adams and Roscigno 2005; Tateo 2005; Weatherby and Scoggins 2005; Chau and Xu 2007; Caiani and Wagemann 2009; Cammaerts 2009; Caiani and Parenti 2013), while not vast, dwarfs the analysis conducted on the 'new' media activity of 'old' terrorist groups. These groups are still very much in existence and maintain a presence on 'new' media, which has received very little attention from researchers in recent years. 'The IRA is unquestionably the most heavily studied terrorist organisation of the past forty years' (Silke 2007, p. 84), and yet there are only a handful of analyses addressing (dissident) Irish Republican online activity, despite these being considered a real and ongoing threat and having a plethora of websites, forums and social media accounts associated with them (Dartnell 2001; Bowman-Grieve 2010; Nalton *et al*. 2011; Reilly 2011; Bowman-Grieve and Conway 2012; Frenett and Smith 2012). This dearth of attention extends to other 'old' groups with very lengthy and active online presences including, for example, the Revolutionary Armed Forces of Colombia (FARC), whose lengthy online presence does not appear to have a single article or chapter dedicated to it, and the Kurdistan Workers' Party (PKK), the online presence regarding which I could find only two chapters (see also Conway 2005b; Çelebi 2008, 2010). Even Hamas and Hizbollah, both of which have proved themselves profoundly media-savvy and have a highly resourced and extensive online presence, have been largely overlooked (Conway 2005a, 2007; Friberg Lyme 2009; Mozes and Weimann 2010).

Compare

Widening our present narrow focus on violent online jihadism to encompass a variety of other contemporary violent online extremisms will allow us to engage in much-needed cross-ideological analysis. This is the minimum necessary level of comparative research however; comparison within and across a number of other categories is also vital. These categories are: (a) groups, (b) countries, (c) languages and (d) platforms.

Violent jihadism is an ideology to which a large number of widely dispersed groups subscribe. Today, most journalists, policy analysts and researchers are focused on the online activity of just one group that subscribes to this ideology: IS. A host of other violent jihadi groups are active online however and thus also warrant attention. Research on the role of the Internet in the Syria and Iraq conflicts largely omits analysis of the online activity of violent Shi'a groups, which are definitely not absent from the Internet, for example (Smyth 2015).[8] Africa-based jihadi groups, including al-Shabab and Boko Haram, are also under-researched (Meleagrou-Hitchens *et al.* 2012; Pearlman 2012; Ishengoma 2013; Bertram and Ellison 2014; Sullivan 2014). Boko Haram's online presence was, until quite recently, fairly low level and amateurish, but this appears to be changing (BBC Monitoring 2015). What influence will the latter's pledge of *Bay'ah* to IS have on the former's online activity and what, if any, will be the 'real world' impact of these?

Some types of violent extremism and terrorism are strongly linked with specific regions, countries or locales – varieties of nationalist-separatism or ethnic-separatism, for example (e.g. Irish Republicanism, Ulster Loyalism) – whereas others are more diffuse in character (e.g. violent jihadism, neo-Nazism) having both national and transnational components and links. Consider the European Union: different Member States face different levels of threat from these different types of violent extremists and terrorists, with some states facing significant difficulties from just one or a small number of types of extremism and others routinely dealing with violence perpetrated in the name of a wide variety of different extremisms. Germany, for example, has experienced recent violence on the part of violent jihadists, the extreme right and the extreme left; Ireland, on the other hand, has a long history of terrorism associated with the Northern Ireland conflict, but has suffered no terrorism on the part of violent jihadists, the extreme right or the extreme left. Interesting questions arise regarding the role of the Internet in more local extremisms versus those of a more transnational or even global character: Is the Internet more effective in one setting than the other? Does social media have different functions for extremists with a specific geographic affiliation versus those subscribing to more diffuse ideologies? How do the specific dynamics of local conflicts play out online? (Campana and Ducol 2014). The significance of the Internet in violent extremism and terrorism in specific locales has received scant scholarly attention to-date, much less comparison across these.

Should an emphasis on geography be avoided when researching the Internet? The Internet is oftentimes portrayed as inherently global in character; rather than geography playing a determining role therefore, might language be a more important factor? In some cases, language and geography map onto each other, but in many instances they do not. Clearly many people beyond those in Arab countries are consumers of Arabic language jihadi online content; not enough research into this content and activity surrounding it has yet been produced and this needs to change. Studying violent online political extremism within the EU context without considering Arabic language content would be redundant therefore as would studying IS's online activity only in the context of its Arabic language content and not the host of content produced in or translated into other languages. The French language 'jihadisphere', for example, is composed of contributors from France, Belgium and other francophone countries, particularly those in North Africa (Ducol 2012). The issue of translation is also relevant. Questions that have not yet even been raised in this domain include: What types of extremist online content is produced by extremist and terrorist groups in multiple languages simultaneously and why? What type of extremist content is routinely translated by fans, into what languages and why? This translation work might prove to be of particular importance if an analysis of interactions within and between extreme right communities on Twitter that found that linguistic and geographical proximity were highly influential factors was to play out similarly in the jihadi 'Twittersphere' and more widely (O'Callaghan *et al.* 2013).

Finally, in terms of top-level comparison, a lot more comparative research needs to get underway within and across online platforms, particularly social media platforms. Violent extremists and terrorists are active on not just one online platform but, like the rest of us, increasingly operate across multiple platforms. The Pew Research Centre found that multi-platform use was on the rise in 2014, with 52 per cent of online American adults using two or more social media sites, an increase of 10 per cent from 2013 (Duggan *et al.* 2015). Violent extremist and terrorist groups and individual extremists and fans may be expected, likewise, to maintain multiple official online presences, including dedicated websites, blogs, forums and assorted social media accounts. Researchers need to be cognisant of this and enquire into specific violent extremist groups/ideologies and how they operate across different social media platforms, websites and forums, on the one hand, and also consider how a diversity of violent extremist groups/ideologies operate on specific platforms. Different social media platforms have different functionalities; how are these different functions exploited by violent extremists? What are the affordances of Twitter that make it so attractive to jihadis, for example, and how does their Twitter activity differ from, but also integrate with, their YouTube activity? What, on the other hand, does the broad violent extremist landscape on Facebook look like? What does the violent extremist landscape of YouTube look like? And so on. It's worth noting here too that it's not just high-profile social media platforms that are integral to violent extremist online networks, but a host of other file, text, and video upload sites[9] are also crucial nodes as are a diversity of other platforms such as, for example, lower profile social media[10] and the Internet Archive. Analyses of the latter are worthwhile not just in themselves, but also because '[t]he dominance of Twitter as the "model organism" for social media big data analyses ... skews analyses of mechanisms' (Tufekci 2014, p. 2), particularly with respect to violent online jihadism.

Deepen

In addition to casting a wider ideological net and engaging in more comparative research, drilling downwards is also necessary. A great deal of the research that has been done in this area to-date is focused on (mainly jihadi) online content, whether drawn from websites, forums or social media. Von Behr *et al.* are therefore correct to underline that:

> [T]here has been little attention to the individual internet users' experience online and usage of the internet in the process of radicalisation, that is, whether and how the internet is associated with a person coming to support terrorism or forms of extremism leading to terrorism. When academic accounts do analyse these individuals' engagement with the internet, they often do so by examining secondary sources or anecdotal evidence. The largely secondary and/or anecdotal basis of knowledge in this field points to a key gap in the academic research on radicalisation – namely access to and analysis of primary data on terrorist 'users' of the internet.
>
> (Von Behr *et al.* 2013, p. 8)

Von Behr and colleagues liaised with British police for the purposes of their study, and this may be a route open to other UK researchers and those in other jurisdictions also. For those unable or unwilling to adopt this approach, collection of primary data will require some old-fashioned social science research, including interviewing, probably especially online interviewing (Salmons 2014) given that some of the currently ongoing conflicts that have significant terrorism and online components are not conducive to on-the-ground research.

Interviewing could allow us to gain a deeper and more contextualised understanding of who is behind varieties of violent extremist online content, what they believe their purposes are and why they are so invested in this particular pursuit. We need to ask users producing and disseminating this content: What are the content's production processes (i.e. how is it produced)? Why it is they are producing and disseminating the content? Who are they targeting? Who do they believe they are influencing and to what end? And to the consumers: How and where do they locate violent extremist content online? Why are they consuming it or what causes them to do so? What, precisely, is its attractiveness? How do they feel it has affected them? A particularly salient question would be whether a majority or minority of those encountered by interviewers are so-called 'prosumers', that is at the same time both producers and consumers of violent extremist online content. Given that the Internet is no longer a 'new media', there are also increasing numbers of former extremists able to speak to the role (or not) of the Internet in their (de-)radicalisation (Köhler 2014/15).

At the group as opposed to the individual level, virtual, online or digital ethnography is an underutilised approach for digging deeper. 'The objective of ethnography is to describe the lives of people other than ourselves, with an accuracy and sensitivity honed by detailed observation and prolonged first-hand experience' (Ingold 2008, p. 69). Rather than individual lives however, ethnographers are concerned with the systematic exploration of particular cultures, including particularly subcultures and countercultures. 'Virtual ethnography' or 'netnography' simply refers to the conduct of ethnographic research in online spaces (Hine 2000; Kozinets 2009). Employing the latter in research into violent online extremist spaces is doubly attractive because not only would it allow researchers to develop embedded understandings of the 'real' and 'online' day-to-day lives of particular countercultural groups, but in fact is being undertaken by many of us albeit largely unknowingly already:

> It took me a long time to even notice these things . . . but it didn't really register – it was background noise to me, stuff I needed to shove aside to get to the hard information about people and events.
>
> (Hegghammer 2015, p. 2)

Hegghammer is referring here to the way in which cultural products (i.e. music, poetry, etc.) and practices (i.e. clothing, beard styles, gestures) are largely overlooked by those studying extremism and terrorism because they are not immediately and obviously instrumental. Hegghammer's interest is in jihadi culture generally and so he laments that 'it was not possible to do participant observation with groups this radical. Fortunately, though, the internet has made available a large amount of high-granularity primary sources that allow for a form of "ethnography by proxy"' (2015, p. 8).

For those of us whose primary interest is in violent extremist online cultures however, the Internet *is* the 'field' and online participant observation is a staple of our daily lives; we just need to make this work for us to a greater extent than presently. Why? Because the successfulness of IS's (online) strategy is probably at least partially predicated on a steady stream of attack footage, including beheading videos, but what if an additional important ingredient of its online 'successfulness' is precisely the selfies, cat pictures and food 'porn' so prevalent across social media accounts of IS fighters? What virtual ethnographic approaches allow us to tap into is the soft power of the latter and thereby a potential explanation for why some violent extremists' online strategies are more effective than others. Certainly, for youthful online jihadi 'fanboys' and 'fangirls', al-Qaeda's online content was (and is) probably apprehended as remote, undirected and boring, while IS's is familiar, interactive and 'cool' displaying as it does many of the signs of everyday youth online culture albeit with a violent jihadi twist. This is not to say, of course, that virtual ethnographic approaches are inclined to take online pronouncements and portrayals at face value; much of what happens online is, following Irving Goffman, 'frontstage': 'normative, conventional, and expected behavior meant for public viewing'. A key advantage of deep and prolonged participant observation however, including in the online 'field', is that it provides access to the 'backstage' of groups' social lives: 'Backstage behavior is meant to be hidden from the public eye, it occurs behind the scenes, and only intimates can participate in or witness it' (De Munck 1998, p. 43). A clash of 'frontstage' and 'backstage' becomes fairly quickly apparent to observers of female involvement and portrayals in the violent jihadi online milieu, for example, of which more is discussed below (Pearson 2009).

Upscale

At the same time that the above-suggested deepening is taking place, some large-scale data – I hesitate to use the term 'big data' – collection and analysis also needs to be ongoing. There is a huge amount of 'born digital' data now publicly available online; this data along with available tools for its analysis and visualisation ought to be harnessed by violent online extremism researchers. Much of this data has a high level of ephemerality associated with it however and thus needs to be subject to continuous collection, formatting and archiving, so that it may be readied for immediate quantitative and qualitative research and retained for future comparative analyses. Such analyses would provide, at a minimum, a big picture view of the contemporary violent online extremist scene and its various corners and allow us to identify areas in which to excavate further. What explains the lack of studies employing large datasets culled from violent extremist online spaces? I suggest it's because most researchers in this area are social scientists and thus don't have the necessary skills to easily collect, store, and analyse truly large quantities of online data. There are at least four ways to seek to hurdle this obstacle however: (a) work with computer scientists, (b) learn how to undertake basic online data collection and analysis ourselves, (c) build data archives and develop bespoke tools and (d) use commercial data brokers. Collaborating with colleagues from other disciplines, including computer science, is addressed in the next section, so let me briefly address (b), (c) and (d) here.

It's not impossible for social scientists to learn how to use basic online data collection and analysis tools, especially freely available open source software accompanied by clear 'How To' documentation and online tutorials. Gephi data visualisation software is one such accessible tool. This option is made more attractive when researchers have the opportunity to learn how to use these tools in dedicated 'real world' tutorials and workshops, preferably tailored for social scientists.[11] Another option is to build, maintain and make accessible archives of violent extremist online content for use by researchers. An example of this is the University of Arizona's Dark Web Forum Portal, which collected and makes available to researchers the content of twenty-eight jihadi forums that together comprise nearly 13,000,000 messages.[12] This is an excellent resource, which has not been widely drawn upon; one reason for this may be the inability of social scientists, as already mentioned, to handle not just collection but also analysis of such 'big data' (another reason may be the shift of focus from forums to social media in recent years). The relatively low level of Dark Web take-up could be altered, it is suggested, by making available easy-to-use analysis tools alongside data on a single platform, which is a planned outcome of the EU-funded VOX-Pol project.[13] The final option is to employ the services of commercial social media data brokers, such as GNIP or DataSift,[14] which allow researchers to buy data from a multiplicity of social media platforms from a single supplier. Some downsides of this are the cost and the inability to freely share the data for replication and other purposes post-publication.

The difficulties of upscaling are not just of a practical sort however. One of the most obvious difficulties is the issue of representativeness. Analyses drawing on large or even huge amounts of violent extremist content from the Internet and using it to explain violent online extremism have the propensity to be treated as 'true' precisely because of the 'hugeness' of the data and thereby its alleged representativeness. Selecting data on the basis of meeting a criteria and then using that data as evidence for the criteria (i.e. selecting on the dependent variable) is problematic however. In the case of violent online extremism research, this is exacerbated by a recent further narrowing of focus to Twitter because of its particular affordances (e.g. ease of data collection due to its publicness) and thus introducing further sample selection bias. Layered atop all of this must be the further realisation that

> [s]ocial media data almost solely captures 'node-to-node' interactions, while 'field' effects – events that affect a society or a group in a wholesale fashion either through shared experience or through broadcast media – may often account for observed phenomena.
> (Tufekci 2014, p. 1)

Put another way, there needs to be greater awareness among violent online extremism researchers that IS's Twitter activity, for example, while unlikely to be having no impact in terms of, say, attracting 'foreign fighters', may be less impactful than IS's (and other violent jihadis') overall Internet-based campaign(s) that may, in turn, be much less impactful than other factors, such as IS's declaration of the caliphate, as an attraction factor. One of the only ways of determining this, to revert to an earlier point, would be to interview (former) 'foreign fighters' and ask them about what influenced their decision-making because '[s]ometimes, the only way to study people is to study people' (Tufekci 2014, p. 6).

Outreach

The original interest of most of those currently researching the intersection of violent extremism and terrorism and the Internet is violent extremism and/or terrorism rather than the Internet. This is easily remediable by, for example, exposing ourselves to new literatures beyond terrorism studies and/or direct outreach to colleagues in other disciplines. A literature that researchers in our field could usefully familiarise themselves with is Internet Studies, while disciplines that we could perhaps most usefully collaborate with colleagues from include computational linguistics, computer science, information systems and statistics.

It is pertinent to ask about media and communication studies in general and Internet Studies in particular what Richard Jackson asked about conflict analysis and peace research and its relationship to terrorism studies. 'How is it', Jackson enquired,

> that the 'known' knowledge of the causes and resolution of violent political conflict (including conflicts where terrorism was present), which has accumulated from decades of conflict analysis and peace research, among others, remains largely 'unknown' within the terrorism studies field? Why is it that within terrorism studies research continues apace on questions related to terrorism's causes and effective responses without reference to the key scholars and existing studies of peace and conflict studies?
>
> (Jackson 2012, p. 12)

Reformulating Jackson's question then: How is it that knowledge of the intersections of media and conflict (including conflicts where terrorism was present), which has accumulated from decades of media and communication research, among others, remains largely 'unknown' within the terrorism studies field? Why is it that within terrorism studies research there has been a surge of research on questions related to terrorism and the Internet, especially social media, without reference to the key scholars and existing studies of media and communication research generally and Internet studies particularly?

A ready answer to this question, which basically queries our lack of knowledge of other social scientists' research, is much more difficult to supply than, say, a convincing answer to the question of why collaboration between social scientists and computer scientists or statisticians is not more prevalent.

Christina Archetti has contributed a book detailing the merits of a communication studies approach to *Understanding Terrorism in the Age of Global Media* (2013); I want to emphasise here the necessity of drawing from Internet studies to enrich research on violent online extremism and terrorism. There is a large and increasing body of work done by Internet researchers that is germane to this particular sphere. Internet researchers have, for example, generated a significant amount of work on credibility and trust online, none of which deals directly with violent extremism or terrorism, but is nonetheless straightforwardly relevant in that it engages deeply with questions like how credibility is built online, how credibility is lost online, etc. (e.g. Nissenbaum 2001; Wang and Emurian 2001; Naquin, and Paulson 2003; Bryce and Fraser 2014; Bowen and Bowen 2015). Hegghammer's (2014) analysis of jihadi online forums is clearly enriched by his drawing from this literature; few other terrorism researchers have followed his lead however. Take another area of Internet research in which there are strongly consistent findings: the way in which discussion forums and other online spaces are generally dominated by a few 'super contributors' (Leimeister and Krcmar 2005, pp. 140–41; Silverstone 2005, pp. 66–70; Ducol 2012, pp. 58–59). Berger and Morgan made a similar finding in their recent work on IS-related Twitter activity (i.e. of the network of 40,000+ user accounts analysed, approximately 1,500–3,000 were prolific tweeters) (2015, p. 29), but omitted discussion of the way in which this is at least partially explainable by previous research on non-extremist online environments and thus is not unique to IS, albeit the latter have also been known to 'game the system' (Berger and Morgan 2015, p. 25). Having said this, *The ISIS Twitter Census* is an excellent example of a beneficial collaborative relationship between an extremism researcher and a technologist/data scientist, which does the important job of answering some of the *what* questions regarding IS' Twitter presence.

Truly interdisciplinary research is easier said than done; collaborating with colleagues from other disciplines, including computational linguistics and computer science, among others, is distinctly different than drawing from other social science fields like Communication Studies or Internet Studies. Research into the role of the Internet in violent extremism and terrorism is an area that would benefit hugely from the latter however. It was suggested in Section 4 above that social scientists educate ourselves in the use of basic online data collection and analysis tools; for more sophisticated analyses, we need to work with those who not only have knowledge of the available tools and their deployment, but can tailor these further. This is not a one-way relationship with computer scientists benefiting their social science colleagues in the absence of benefit to themselves; the best outcomes are obtained by computer scientists collaborating with domain experts, in this case those with knowledge of the ideologies prevalent within and day-to-day workings of online extremism. Increased collaboration between social scientists, especially terrorism studies scholars, and computer scientists is the most pressing, but there are a host of other colleagues we could doubtlessly benefit from collaborating with as well (e.g. law, criminology, psychology).

Gender

The preceding five subsections dealt largely with broad-brush methodological or 'how to' issues; this subsection is somewhat different. In it I want to emphasise both how some of my earlier points apply and how the study of gender is particularly pertinent in violent online extremism.

Al-Khansa, the first online jihadi magazine targeted specifically at women appeared in 2004. Stormfront's 'Ladies Only' sub-forum was established in 2007 and has 1,156 threads and 48,789 posts at the time of writing. Astoundingly, given their relative visibility and after more than a decade of research, the online activity of jihadi and extreme right females is the subject of just a handful of studies (Castle and Chevalier 2011; Seib and Janbek 2011, ch. 5; Bloom 2013; Boyle et al. 2015; Pere_in 2015; Saltman and Smith 2015). Women featured fairly prominently on the websites of the FARC, New People's Army, and Tamil Tigers in the 1990s and early 2000s; the roles of ethnic-nationalist or nationalist-separatist women online have been the subject of no research at all however. The role and influence of women in violent extremist cyberspaces are therefore largely unknown. A number have clearly played powerful roles online that may not have been afforded them in more conventional settings including, for example, Malika El-Aroud's central role in the establishment of the French-language 'jihadisphere' (Ducol 2012, pp. 54–55). When addressed, it is generally female extremists' power as online motivators of their male counterparts that is highlighted (Sageman 2008b, p. 112) albeit the role of so-called 'jihadi brides' resident in Syria in persuading other young women to follow in their footsteps has received considerable recent global media attention. In terms of widening therefore, an additional step omitted earlier is to include women as a category of violent online extremists.

Study of the gender dimensions of violent extremist and terrorist online activity does not, indeed *should* not, be restricted to female users however. Not all, probably not even most, portrayals of women and their roles in violent extremism and terrorism are by women, but are instead depictions of women's roles as assigned by men. Interesting comparison would be between the depiction of jihadi women and their roles in official online publications, such as *al-Khansa*, *Inspire* and *Dabiq*, versus the desired roles expressed by women in their social media activity and in other online spaces or the portrayal of women in violent jihadi cyberspaces versus in extreme right cyberspaces. How has the portrayal of women changed over time? If we ascertain an increased role for and influence of women in extremist cyberspaces in the last decade, can we link this to changes in the volume and types of depictions of women over the same period or are there other factors at play?

A number of images of violent jihadi women 'training' with guns and posing with weapons around a luxury car have become well-known via social media and their reproduction in the Western press. It is suggested that these images go to distinctions between 'frontstage' and backstage' portrayals of the role of women in violent jihadism alluded to earlier, because they are carefully constructed 'frontstage' portrayals of 'romance' and adventure almost wholly outside of 'normal' female jihadi activity in Syria. The vast majority of violent jihadi videos and other online content are striking, in fact, for their almost complete absence of female bodies. An Arabic-language text that was circulated widely in Arab jihadi online networks, but not available in English until translated by a UK researcher, is probably more indicative of the 'jihadi bride' experience than the 'girls with guns' images. The Arabic document entitled 'Women in the Islamic State' is unequivocal regarding female roles: 'the greatness of her position, the purpose of her existence is the Divine duty of motherhood'. It goes on to extol the virtues of being a dutiful wife – a role that may appropriately be fulfilled from the age of nine – and the necessity of women remaining within the walls of their homes at almost all times.[15] The document is an interesting item of content in itself, but is also a noteworthy instance both of how online audiences may continue to be separated quite effectively by language and, relatedly, an awareness on the part of IS of the desire of some young women to play a more central role than that of simply *muhājirāt* or 'migrants' and thus IS's attempts at constructing a more attractive online narrative for these. The competing online constructions are drawn together in a tweet by one young woman: 'I wonder if I can pull a Mulan and enter the battle field' (Boyle *et al*. 2015, p. 32).

'Pulling a Mulan' refers to the Disney film in which a young woman impersonates a man to join the military. While the likelihood of successfully carrying off such an impersonation in 'real life' is improbable, gender-switching is commonplace online. From its earliest days, the Internet was viewed by some as the ideal realm in which to 'play' with their gender. Online gender-switching has been extensively studied in online gaming (e.g. Bruckman 1996; Roberts and Parks 1999; Herring 2001; Hussain and Griffiths 2008; Martey *et al*. 2014). What is the likelihood of high levels of gender-switching in, say, jihadi online spaces? Early research on radicalisation via YouTube found that the higher one's status within the online group studied, on several different measures, the less likely one was to provide information about one's gender. Of the top ten users who frequently ranked in the top three of various social network measures in the study, five were of unknown gender and five identified themselves as female. It was thus surmised that at least some of the five users of unknown gender were probably in fact female (Bermingham *et al*. 2009, pp. 234–35). This is not without precedent; in the past, jihadi online forums were often segregated on the basis of gender. Anecdotal evidence collected by the author suggests that female researchers accessing extremist forums of various sorts are wont to adopt male personae, including screen names and avatar images, in those settings, but that male researchers retain male identities in the same circumstances. This is a potentially interesting phenomenon facilitated by the Internet that could mean that female users are more influential in extremist cyberspaces than previously thought. (Switching in the other direction is a possibility too, of course, and also has the potential for interesting findings (Martey *et al*. 2014).)

Conclusion

In closing, and by way of full disclosure, I am somebody who believes the Internet is playing significant and diverse roles in contemporary violent extremism and terrorism. Rapoport argues that structural factors are very important in terms of influencing the various waves of terrorism identified by him. Historically, new communication technologies (e.g. mass circulation newspapers, radio, audio cassettes, TV) have been shown to be particularly influential and have a history of transforming terrorism; the Internet is unlikely to be any different. Given the resources, in terms of both time and money, they are inputting to online campaigns, a diversity of contemporary violent extremists certainly thinks it's having an impact too. In addition, some of the anecdotal evidence is compelling. Taking just IS as an example: online outreach to young women has resulted in an influx of 'jihadi brides' to Syria, similar online calls for families to migrate to the 'caliphate' have seen an uptick in family groups departing various countries and a spate of previously uncommon types of terrorist attacks (e.g. running down people with cars, knifings) appear to correlate with online calls for these types of attacks to be undertaken. None of this is sufficient, of course; what needs to be supplied is theoretically sound, empirically verifiable, social science research detailing – I hesitate to use the word 'proving' in a social science context, especially *this* social science context – the role of the Internet in contemporary radicalisation processes.

The earliest piece of analysis on violent extremism and the Internet appeared in 1985 (ADL 1985), but the vast bulk only began to be produced in the 2000s, with a significant uptick since c.2010 and a particular spike from mid-2014. Research in this area is thus not long underway and so, of course, there are many *what* and *why* questions still to be asked and answered. The nature of the Internet means that it changes very fast; it is thus quite difficult to effectively research the Internet and its workings over time. Direct audience research is also problematic because of the nature of violent extremist and terrorist online content, which presents problems for undertaking the kinds of experiments that are standard in other areas of Internet audience research as it would require introducing subjects to online content with allegedly radicalising effects and, in fact, almost certainly necessitate exposing youth and young adults to distressing levels of violence. Progressing research in this area is thus not easy; it is also not impossible however. There are, of course, a whole host of issues that couldn't be addressed in this article (e.g. Internet research ethics, the role of Internet companies as political intermediaries), but what it seeks to do is to make six major practical suggestions for progressing research on the role of the Internet in contemporary violent extremism and terrorism with, perhaps, the side effect of also kick-starting discussion of colleagues' additional or preferred steps in this regard.

Notes

1 It's worth mentioning here too the contestability of 'radicalisation' as a concept as discussed in, for example, Awan *et al.* (2012).
2 See also, on conduits, Kimmage (2008) and Kimmage and Ridolfo (2007).
3 As borne out in, for example, Sreberny and Mohammadi (1994).
4 Sageman argued in his previous work that the Internet was an important facilitator, but unlikely to transcend the necessity for face-to-face connections for development of deep interpersonal ties; see Sageman 2004, p. 157 and 163.
5 Violent online radicalisation is conceived herein as 'a process whereby individuals, through their online interactions and exposure to various types of Internet content, come to view violence as a legitimate method of solving social and political conflicts' per Bermingham *et al.* 2009, p. 1.
6 For example, the Australian government announced the *Combating Terrorist Propaganda in Australia* initiative at the February 2015 White House Summit on Countering Violent Extremism, which commits AUS$17.9 million 'to combat the lies and propaganda terrorist groups are promulgating online'. Media release available at www.attorneygeneral.gov.au/Mediareleases/Pages/2015/FirstQuarter/20-February-2015-Combating-terrorist-propaganda-online.aspx
7 Unpublished research by the author recorded 680,000 threads on Stormfront in August 2012; at the time of writing, in February 2015, Stormfront was showing 861,972 threads. The figure for average new threads monthly reported here were arrived at by calculating the number of threads initiated between August 2012 and February 2015 (i.e. 181,972) and dividing this by the number of months elapsed (i.e. 31).

8 It's worth noting here that Syrian government forces, Free Syrian Army units, the PKK and Kurdish *Peshmerga* forces, and other parties to the Syria conflict also maintain online presences and engage via the Internet, another issue that has not received sufficient scholarly attention to-date.
9 Justpaste.it is a particularly important node in the contemporary violent jihadi online scene; Pastebin and Paste.ee are also used as repositories. In terms of video hosting, Dailymotion, MediaFire, Vid.me, Vimeo and a host of other more obscure sites (e.g. Hugefiles.net, Uploadhero.com, Uptobox.com) are also employed.
10 These include Ask.fm, Diaspora, Flickr, Instagram, SoundCloud, Tumblr, VKontakte and others.
11 See, for example, the University of Amsterdam's Digital Methods Initiative at www.digitalmethods.net, particularly their Summer and Winter Schools.
12 See http://ai.arizona.edu/research/terror (accessed 21 April, 2015).
13 For more information, see www.voxpol.eu (accessed 21 April, 2015).
14 See https://gnip.com and http://datasift.com (accessed 21 April, 2015). Datasift supplied access to the Twitter 'firehose' up until mid-April 2015, when this was retracted by Twitter from all partners excepting GNIP, which Twitter now owns.
15 Charlie Winter's translation of 'Women in the Islamic State' is available online at www.quilliamfoundation.org/wp/wp-content/uploads/publications/free/women-of-the-islamic-state3.pdf; see also Winter 2015.

References

Adams, J and Roscigno, VJ (2005), 'White Supremacists, Oppositional Culture and the World Wide Web', *Social Forces*, vol 84, no 2.

Anti-Defamation League (1985), 'Computerized Networks of Hate: An ADL Fact Finding Report'. Available at https://archive.org/details/ComputerizedNetworksOfHate

Arab Social Media Report (2011), 'Dynamic Dashboard: Facebook Penetration', 31 December 2011. Available at www.arabsocialmediareport.com/Facebook/LineChart.aspx?&PriMenuID=18&CatID=24&mnu=Cat

Archetti, C (2013), *Understanding Terrorism in the Age of Global Media: A Communication Approach*, Basingstoke: Palgrave.

Archetti, C (2015), 'Terrorism, Communication and New Media: Explaining Radicalization in the Digital Age, *Perspectives on Terrorism*, vol 9, no 1.

Awan, A, Hoskins, A and O'Loughlin B (2012), *Radicalisation and Media: Connectivity and Terrorism in the New Media Ecology*, London: Routledge.

Bartlett, J (2015a), 'You Can't Prevent Terrorism by Singling Out Muslims', *The Telegraph*, 19 February 2015.

Bartlett, J (2015b), *The Dark Net*, London: Windmill Books.

BBC Monitoring (2015), 'Is Islamic State Shaping Boko Haram Media?', *BBC Monitoring*, 4 March 2015. Available at www.bbc.com/news/world-africa-31522469

Beirich, H (2014), 'White Homicide Worldwide', *SPLC Intelligence Report*, Summer 2014, pp. 2–6, Available at www.splcenter.org/sites/default/files/downloads/publication/white-homicide-worldwide.pdf

Benson, DC (2014), 'Why the Internet is Not Increasing Terrorism', *Security Studies*, vol 23, no 2.

Berger, JM and Strathearn, B (2013), *Who Matters Online: Measuring Influence, Evaluating Content and Countering Violent Extremism in Online Social Networks*, King's College London: ICSR.

Berger, JM and Morgan, J (2015), *The ISIS Twitter Census: Defining and Describing the Population of ISIS Supporters on Twitter*, Washington, DC: Brookings.

Bermingham, A, Conway, M, McInerney, L, O'Hare, N, and Smeaton, A (2009), 'Combining Social Network Analysis and Sentiment Analysis to Explore the Potential for Online Radicalisation', in *ASONAM 2009: Advances in Social Networks Analysis and Mining*, IEEE Computer Society, Digital Library.

Bertram, S and Ellison, K (2014), 'Sub-Saharan African Terrorist Groups' Use of the Internet', *Journal of Terrorism Research*, vol 5, no 1.

Bloom, M (2013), 'In Defense of Honor: Women and Terrorist Recruitment on the Internet', *Journal of Postcolonial Cultures and Societies*, vol 4, no 1.

Bostdorff, DM (2004), 'The Internet Rhetoric of the Ku Klux Klan: A Case Study in Web Site Community Building Run Amok', *Communication Studies*, vol 55, no 2.

Bouhana, N and Wikström, POH (2011), *Al-Qa'ida-influenced Radicalisation: A Rapid Evidence Assessment Guided by Situational Action Theory*, London: UK Home Office.

Bowen, G and Bowen, R (2015), 'Brand Trust in Offline and Online Environments: Lessons for Social Media', in Bowen G and Ozuem W (eds), *Computer-mediated Marketing Strategies: Social Media and Online Brand Communities*, Hershey, PA: IGI Global.

Bowman-Grieve, L (2009), 'Exploring Stormfront: A Virtual Community of the Radical Right', *Studies in Conflict and Terrorism*, vol 32, no 11.

Bowman-Grieve, L (2010), 'Irish Republicanism and the Internet: Support for New Wave Dissidents', *Perspectives on Terrorism*, vol 4, no 2.

Bowman-Grieve, L and Conway, M (2012), 'Exploring the Form and Function of Dissident Irish Republican Online Discourses', *Media, War and Conflict*, vol 5, no 1.

Boyle, C, Bradford A and Frenett, R (2015), *Becoming Mulan: Female Western Migrants to ISIS*, London, Institute for Strategic Dialogue.

Brennan, JO (2015), 'Remarks at the Council on Foreign Relations', Washington, DC, 13 March 2015, Available at www.cia.gov/news-information/speeches-testimony/2015-speeches-testimony/director-brennan-speaks-at-the-council-on-foreign-relations.html

Bruckman, AS (1996), 'Gender Swapping on the Internet', in Ludlow P (ed.), *High Noon on the Electronic Frontier: Conceptual Issues in Cyberspace*, Cambridge, MA: MIT Press.

Bryce, J and Fraser, J (2014), 'The Role of Disclosure of Personal Information in the Evaluation of Risk and Trust in Young Peoples' Online Interactions', *Computers in Human Behavior*, vol 30, pp. 299–306.

Burke, J (2011), 'Al-Shabab's Tweets Won't Boost Its Cause', *The Guardian*, 16 December 2011.

Burris, V, Smith, E and Strahm, A (2000), 'White Supremacist Networks on the Internet', *Sociological Focus*, vol 33, no 2.

Caiani, M and Parenti, L (2013), *European and American Extreme Right Groups and the Internet*, London: Ashgate.

Caiani, M and Wagemann, C (2009), 'Online Networks of the Italian and German Extreme Right', *Information, Communication and Society*, vol 12, no 1.

Cammaerts, B (2009), 'Radical Pluralism and Free Speech in Online Public Spaces: The Case of North Belgian Extreme Right Discourses', *International Journal of Cultural Studies*, vol 12, no 6.

Campana, A and Ducol, B (2014), 'Voices of the 'Caucasus Emirate': Mapping and Analyzing North Caucasus Insurgency Websites', *Terrorism and Political Violence*, vol 27, no 4.

Carter, JA, Maher S and Neumann, PR (2014), *#Greenbirds: Measuring Importance and Influence in Syrian Foreign Fighter Networks*, King's College London: ICSR.

Castle, T and Chevalier, M (2011), 'The Women of Stormfront: An Examination of White Nationalist Discussion Threads on the Internet', *Internet Journal of Criminology*, Available at www.internetjournalofcriminology.com/Castle_Chevalier_The_Women_of_Stormfront_An_Examination_of_White_Nationalist_Discussion_Threads.pdf

Çelebi, E (2008a), 'Analysis of PKK/KONGRA-GEL Websites to Identify Points of Vulnerability', in NATO Centre of Excellence for Defence Against Terrorism (.s), *Responses to Cyberterrorism*, Amsterdam: IOS Press.

Çelebi, E (2008b), 'Female Separatism: The Role of Women in the PKK/Kongra-Gel Terrorist Organization', in Dienel HL, Sharan Y, Rapp, C and Ahituv, N (eds), *Terrorism and the Internet: Threats, Target Groups, Deradicalisation Strategies* Amsterdam: IOS Press.

Chau, M and Xu, J (2007), 'Mining Communities and Their Relationships in Blogs: A Study of Online Hate Groups', *International Journal of Human-Computer Studies*, vol 65, no 1.

Chroust, P (2000), 'Neo-Nazis and Taliban On-line: Anti-modern Political Movements and Modern Media', *Democratization*, vol 7, no 1.

Conway, M (2005a), 'Cybercortical Warfare: Hizbollah's Internet Strategy', in Oates, S, Owen D and Gibson R (eds), *The Internet and Politics: Citizens, Voters and Activists*, London: Routledge.

Conway, M (2005b), 'Terrorist Web Sites: Their Contents, Functioning, and Effectiveness', in Seib, P (ed), *Media and Conflict in the Twenty-First Century*, New York, NY: Palgrave.

Conway, M (2007), 'Terrorism and the Making of the 'New Middle East': New Media Strategies of Hizbollah and al Qaeda', in Philip Seib (ed.), *New Media in the New Middle East*, London: Palgrave.

Dartnell, M (2001), 'The Electronic Starry Plough: The E-nationalism of the Irish Republican Socialist Movement (IRSM)', *First Monday*, vol 6, no 12.

De Kostera, W and Houtman, D (2008), 'Stormfront is like a Second Home to Me: On Virtual Community Formation by Right-Wing Extremists', *Information, Communication, and Society*, vol 11, no 8.

De Munck, VC (1998), 'Participant Observation: A Thick Explanation of Conflict in a Sri Lankan Village', in De Munck, VC and Sobo, EJ (eds), *Using Methods in the Field: A Practical Introduction and Casebook*, Oxford: Oxford University Press.

De Vaus, DA (2001), *Research Design in Social Research*, London: Sage.

Ducol, B (2012), 'Uncovering the French-speaking Jihadisphere: An Exploratory Analysis', *Media, War and Conflict*, vol 5, no 1.

Duggan, M, Ellison, NB, Lampe, C, Lenhart, A and Madden, M (2015), 'Social Media Update 2014', *Pew Research Centre: Internet Science and Tech Report*, 9 January 2015. Available at www.pewinternet.org/2015/01/09/social-media-update-2014/

Edwards, C and Gribbon, L (2013), 'Pathways to Violent Extremism in the Digital Era', *RUSI Journal*, vol 158, no 5.

EU Ministers of the Interior and/or Justice (2015), Joint Statement condemning the *Charlie Hebdo* attacks, Paris, 11 January 2015. Available at https://eu2015.lv/images/news/2015_01_11_Joint_statement_of_ministers_for_interrior.pdf

Frenett, R and Smith, MLR (2012), 'IRA 2.0: Continuing the Long War – Analyzing the Factors Behind Anti-GFA Violence', *Terrorism and Political Violence*, vol 24, no 3.

Friberg Lyme, R (2009), *Hizb'allah's Communication Strategy: Making Friends and Intimidating Enemies*, Copenhagen, Danish Institute for International Studies.

Gerstenfeld, P, Grant, D and Chiang, CP (2003), 'Hate Online: A Content Analysis of Extremist Internet Sites', *Analyses of Social Issues and Public Policy*, vol 3, no 1.

Githens-Mazer, J (2010), 'Radicalisation Via YouTube? It's Not So Simple', *The Guardian*, 4 November.

Gray, DH, and Head, A (2009), 'The Importance of the Internet to the Post-modern Terrorist and Its Role as a Form of Safe Haven', *European Journal of Scientific Research*, vol 25, no 3.

Greenwood, C, Sinmaz, E, Infante, F, Rahman, K, Spillett, R and Glanfield, E (2015), 'Brainwashed in their Bedrooms: British Schoolgirl 'Jihadi Brides Who Fled to Syria to Join ISIS' were Following SEVENTY Extremists on Twitter Accounts that the Internet Giant had Refused to Axe', *Daily Mail*, 22 February 2015.

Hannigan, R (2014), 'The Web is a Terrorist's Command-and-Control Network of Choice', *Financial Times*, 3 November 2014.

Hegghammer, T (2015), 'Why Terrorists Weep: The Socio-Cultural Practices of Jihadi Militants', *Paul Wilkinson Memorial Lecture, University of St. Andrews*, 16 April 2015. Available online at http://hegghammer.com/_files/Hegghammer_-_Wilkinson_Memorial_Lecture.pdf

Hegghammer, T (2014), 'Interpersonal Trust on Jihadi Internet Forums', in Gambetta, D (ed.), *Fight, Flight, Mimic: Identity Signalling in Armed Conflicts*. Available at http://hegghammer.com/_files/Interpersonal_trust.pdf

Herring, SC (2001), 'Gender and Power in Online Communication', *Center for Social Informatics (CSI) Working Paper No. WP-01–05*. Available online at https://scholarworks.iu.edu/dspace/bitstream/handle/2022/1024/WP01–05B.html

Hine, C (2000), *Virtual Ethnography*, London: Sage.

House of Commons Home Affairs Committee (2014), *Counter-Terrorism: Seventeenth Report of Session 2013–14*, London: The Stationery Office.

Hussain, G and Saltman, EM (2014), *Jihad Trending: A Comprehensive Analysis of Online Extremism and How to Counter It*, London: Quilliam Foundation.

Hussain, Z and Griffiths, MD (2008), 'Gender Swapping and Socializing in Cyberspace: An Exploratory Study', *CyberPsychology and Behavior*, vol 11, no 1.

Ingold, T (2008), 'Anthropology is Not Ethnography', *Proceedings of the British Academy* Vol 154, p. 69.

Intelligence and Security Committee of Parliament (2014), *Report on the Intelligence Relating to the Murder of Fusilier Lee Rigby*, UK: Her Majesty's Stationery Office.

Ishengoma, FR (2013), 'Online Social Networks and Terrorism 2.0 in Developing Countries', *International Journal of Computer Science and Network Solutions*, vol 1, no 4.

Jackson, R (2012), 'Unknown Knowns: The Subjugated Knowledge of Terrorism Studies', *Critical Studies on Terrorism*, vol 5, no 1.

Kanaley, R (1996), 'Hate Groups Tap into the Internet', *The Philadelphia Inquirer*, 4 July 1996.

Kimmage, D and Ridolfo K (2007), *Iraqi Insurgent Media: The War of Images and Ideas*, Washington DC, Radio Free Europe/Radio Liberty.

Kimmage, D (2008), *The Al-Qaeda Media Nexus: The Virtual Network Behind the Global Message*, Washington, DC: Radio Free Europe/Radio Liberty.

Köhler, D (2015), 'The Radical Online: Individual Radicalization Processes and the Role of the Internet', *Journal for Deradicalization*, no 1 (Winter 2014/15).

Kozinets, R (2009), *Netnography: Doing Ethnographic Research Online*, London: Sage.

Laqueur, W (1999), *The New Terrorism: Fanaticism and the Arms of Mass Destruction*, Oxford: Oxford University Press.

Leimeister, JM and Krcmar, H (2005), 'Acceptance and Utility of a Systematically Designed Virtual Community for Cancer Patients', in Van Den Besselaar, P, De Michelis, G, Preece, J and Simone, C (eds), *Communities and Technologies 2005: Proceedings of the Second Communities and Technologies Conference*, Dordrecht: Springer.

McCants, W (2011), 'Testimony, U.S. House of Representatives, Subcommittee on Counterterrorism and Intelligence, Jihadist Use of Social Media: How to Prevent Terrorism and Preserve Innovation', 6 December 2011. Available online at http://homeland.house.gov/sites/homeland.house.gov/files/Testimony%20McCants.pdf

Meddaugh, PM, and Kay, J (2009), 'Hate Speech or 'Reasonable Racism'? The Other in Stormfront', *Journal of Mass Media Ethics*, vol 24, no 4.

Meleagrou-Hitchens, A (2011), *As American as Apple Pie: How Anwar al-Awlaki Became the Face of Western Jihad*, King's College, London: ICSR.

Meleagrou-Hitchens, A, Maher, S and Sheehan, J (2012), *Lights, Camera, Jihad: Al-Shabaab's Western Media Strategy*, King's College, London: ICSR.

Mikeal Martey, R, Stromer-Galley, J, Banks J, Wu J and Consalvo M (2014), 'The Strategic Female: Gender-switching and Player Behavior in Online Games', *Information, Communication and Society*, vol 17, no 3.

Mozes, T and Weimann, G (2010), 'The E-Marketing Strategy of Hamas', *Studies in Conflict and Terrorism*, vol 33, no 3.

Nalton, J, Ramsey, G and Taylor, M (2011), 'Radicalization and Internet Propaganda by Dissident Republican Groups in Northern Ireland Since 2008', in Currie, PM and Taylor M (eds), *Dissident Irish Republicanism*, New York, NY: Continuum.

Naquin, CE, and Paulson, GD (2003), 'Online Bargaining and Interpersonal Trust', *Journal of Applied Psychology*, vol 88, no 1.

Nissenbaum, H (2001), 'Securing Trust Online: Wisdom or Oxymoron', *Boston University Law Review*, vol 81, no 3.

O'Callaghan, D, Greene, D, Conway, M, Carthy, J and Cunningham P (2013), 'An Analysis of Interactions Within and Between Extreme Right Communities in Social Media', *Lecture Notes in Computer Science*, vol 8329.

Oldham, J (1998), 'Web of Hate is Growing on the Net', *The Jerusalem Post*, 25 January 1998.

Pearlman, L (2012), 'Tweeting to Win: Al-Shabaab's Strategic Use of Microblogging', *The Yale Review of International Studies*, November. 2012. Available at http://yris.yira.org/essays/837

Pearson, E (2009), 'All the World Wide Web's a Stage: The Performance of Identity in Online Social Networks', *First Monday*, vol 14, no 3.

Perešin, A (2015), 'Fatal Attraction: Western Muslimas and ISIS', *Perspectives on Terrorism*, vol 9, no 3.

Ramsay, G (2009), 'Relocating the Virtual War', *Defence Against Terrorism Review*, vol 2, no 1.

Rapoport, D (2002), 'The Four Waves of Rebel Terror and September 11', *Anthropoetics*, vol 8, no 1. Available at www.anthropoetics.ucla.edu/ap0801/terror.htm?goback=.gde_3131037_member_5798090843084578819

Rawlinson, K (2015), 'Sanction Tech Firms Over Hate Speech' says Hollande', *BBC News*, 28 January 2015.

Reilly, P (2011), *Framing the Troubles Online: Northern Irish Groups and Website Strategy*, Manchester: Manchester University Press.

Rieger, D, Frischlich, L and Bente, G (2013), *Propaganda 2.0: Psychological Effects of Right-wing and Islamic Extremist Internet Videos*, Cologne, Germany, Wolters Kluwer.

Roberts, LD and Parks, MR (1999), 'The Social Geography of Gender-Switching in Virtual Environments on the Internet', *Information, Communication and Society*, vol 2, no 4.

Rogan, H (2006), *Jihadism Online: A Study of How al-Qaida and Radical Islamist Groups Use the Internet for Terrorist Purposes*, Norway: FFI.

Sageman, M (2004), *Understanding Terror Networks*, Philadelphia: Pennsylvania University Press.

Sageman, M (2008a), 'The Next Generation of Terror', *Foreign Policy*, March/April.

Sageman, M (2008b), *Leaderless Jihad: Terror Networks in the Twenty-First Century*, Philadelphia: University of Pennsylvania Press.

Salmons, JE (2014), *Qualitative Online Interviews: Strategies, Design, and Skills*, London: Sage.

Saltman, EM and Smith, M (2015), *'Till Martyrdom Do Us Part': Gender and the ISIS Phenomenon*, London: Institute for Strategic Dialogue.

Seib, P and Janbek, DM (2011), *Global Terrorism and New Media: The Post-al-Qaeda Generation*, London and New York: Routledge.

Silke, A (2007), 'The Impact of 9/11 on Research on Terrorism', in Ranstorp M (ed.) *Mapping Terrorism Research: State of the Art, Gaps and Future Direction*, London: Routledge.

Silverstone, R (2005), *Media, Technology and Everyday Life in Europe: From Information to Communication*, Aldershot: Ashgate.

Smyth, P (2015), 'The Shiite Jihad in Syria and Its Regional Effects', *Policy Focus* No 138. Available online at www.washingtoninstitute.org/uploads/Documents/pubs/PolicyFocus138_Smyth-2.pdf

Sreberny, A and Mohammadi, A (1994), *Small Media, Big Revolution: Communication, Culture, and the Iranian Revolution*, Minneapolis: University of Minnesota Press.

Stenersen, A (2008), 'The Internet: A Virtual Training Camp?', *Terrorism and Political Violence*, vol 20, no 2.

Stevens, T and Neumann, P (2009), *Countering Online Radicalisation: A Strategy for Action*, King's College, London: ICSR.

Suler, J (2005), 'The Online Disinhibition Effect', *International Journal of Applied Psychoanalytic Studies*, vol 2, no 2.

Sullivan, R (2014), 'Live-tweeting Terror: A Rhetorical Analysis of @HSMPress_ Twitter Updates During the 2013 Nairobi Hostage Crisis', *Critical Studies on Terrorism*, vol 7, no 3.

Tateo, L (2005), 'The Italian Extreme Right On-line Network: An Exploratory Study Using an Integrated Social Network Analysis and Content Analysis Approach', *Journal of Computer-Mediated Communication*, vol 10, no 2.

Tufekci, Z (2014), 'Big Questions for Social Media Big Data: Representativeness, Validity and Other Methodological Pitfalls'. Available online at http://arxiv.org/ftp/arxiv/papers/1403/1403.7400.pdf

United Nations Independent International Commission of Inquiry on the Syrian Arab Republic (2014), *Rule of Terror: Living under ISIS in Syria*, New York: UN.

Von Behr, I, Reding, A, Edwards C and Gribbon, L (2013), *Radicalisation in the Digital Era: The Use of the Internet in 15 Cases of Terrorism and Extremism*, Brussels and Cambridge: RAND Europe.

Wang, YD and Emurian, HH (2005) 'An Overview of Online Trust: Concepts, Elements, and Implications', *Computers in Human Behavior*, vol 21, no 1.

Watt, N and Wintour, P (2015), 'Facebook and Twitter have 'Social Responsibility' to Help Fight Terrorism, says David Cameron', *The Guardian*, 16 January 2015.

Weatherby, G and Scoggins, B (2005), 'A Content Analysis of Persuasion Techniques Used on White Supremacist Websites', *Journal of Hate Studies*, vol 4, no 1.

Winter, C (2015), 'Women of The Islamic State: Beyond the Rumor Mill', *Jihadology.net*, 31 March, 2015. Available online at http://jihadology.net/2015/03/31/guest-post-women-of-the-islamic-state-beyond-the-rumor-mill/

Zelin, A (2013), *The State of Global Jihad Online: A Qualitative, Quantitative, and Cross-Lingual Analysis*, Washington, DC: New America Foundation.

8 Grasping at thin air

Countering terrorist narratives online

Sarah Logan

Introduction

In the months following 9/11, security agencies focused on disrupting core al-Qaeda(AQ) networks and pre-empting threats. Measures such as increased surveillance and increased powers of the police and security services, which continue to define today's counterterrorism environment, were put in place in these early days. This chapter outlines an innovation in counterterrorism that has emerged since 2001, indeed largely since 2005: the promotion of online counternarratives by security agencies, targeted at shaping the way consumers of online content view the world around them in the context of post-9/11 terrorism. This innovation developed in response to the emergence of al-Qaeda-inspired and directed home-grown extremism of the sort exemplified by the 2005 London bombings.

Counternarratives are a mode of counterterrorism that directly target the role of narratives in inspiring terrorism, especially home-grown extremism (Schmid 2014).[1] Briggs and Feve (2013, 14) describe counternarratives as texts that aim to directly deconstruct, discredit and demystify violent extremist messaging through ideology, logic, fact or humour. They situate counternarratives in a range of activities they term the 'counter-messaging spectrum'. This spectrum includes activities ranging from strategic communication by the government, which explains government policy, to the provision of alternative narratives – describing, for example, what a government is for rather than against – to counternarratives, which they describe as texts

> ... aimed at individuals, groups and networks further along the path to radicalisation, whether they be sympathisers, passive supporters or those more active within extremist movements. These more targeted programmes explicitly deconstruct, delegitimise and de-mystify extremist propaganda in order to achieve a number of aims, from de-radicalisation of those already radicalised to sowing the seeds of doubt among 'at risk' audiences potentially being exposed to or seeking out extremist content.
>
> (Briggs and Feve 2013, 49)

Such measures are distinct from 'negative' measures, which target AQ messaging online, such as take-downs or filtering of terrorist material online. Ultimately, these measures sit largely within the broad domain of strategic narratives identified by Miskimmon *et al.* (2012), which stretches from public diplomacy to the cultivation of soft power. However, the counternarrative measures discussed in this chapter are distinguished by the fact that they explicitly target extremist messaging in a post-9/11 counterterrorism context, especially – though not only – in the context of home-grown extremism. In doing so, they respond to a specific threat and a specific narrative-driven tactic employed by terrorist groups.

This chapter begins by briefly tracing the emergence of narratives and the online space underpinning radical Islamist strategy. It goes on to detail the construction of online counternarrative policies in the US and the UK. The US and the UK are not alone in this regard: other countries including Australia, Canada, Denmark and Sweden operate counternarrative programmes online and there is an increase in multilateral and bilateral efforts.[2] However, as arguably the most active Western powers in the post-9/11 environment, operating in close cooperation, the US and the UK offer a useful overview of leading policy responses to the issue. Their experiences also exhibit significant differences. These differences suggest that online counternarrative work is not clear-cut. As Briggs and Feve (2013, 1–5) point out, narratives are a diffuse tool, difficult to measure and implement. There is as yet no consensus on what works in the counternarrative realm, or indeed on what should be done.

As argued below, experiences of the US and the UK confirm that there is no clear policy template for online counternarrative work. In addition, the differences in their approaches – despite close cooperation between the two countries on almost every aspect of counterterrorism policy – suggest that domestic political considerations can influence online counternarrative policies in particular ways that move beyond simple decisions about efficacy (Rees and Aldrich 2005).

A shifting threat

Initial responses to the online environment after 9/11 did not focus on counternarrative work, focusing instead on surveillance. In the US, the Uniting and Strengthening America by Providing Appropriate Tools Required to Intercept and Obstruct Terrorism (PATRIOT) Act of 2001 facilitated widespread surveillance of US citizens' online activity, while in the UK such surveillance had already been made possible by the Regulation of Investigatory Powers Act (RIPA) of 2000, although surveillance powers were updated by the Anti-Terrorism, Crime and Security Act of 2001.

However, by 2005, this focus had shifted somewhat, as security agencies began to confront the role of the Internet as a highly effective vector of narratives as well as an efficient organising tool.[3] Security agencies were responding in this instance to a shift in AQ-core tactics to include a distinct focus on the creation and distribution of online narrative content as a mode of inspiration for home-grown extremism. AQ had engaged in relatively sophisticated media strategies from its earliest days – its media wing, al-Sahab, began releasing material even before 2001. These media strategies involved the dissemination of propagandistic material that drew on an overarching master narrative. This narrative is a unifying framework of explanations that provides terrorist actors with a cohesive and satisfying portrayal of the world in which they live and their role therein, offering a sense of identity and meaning. Drawing on analyses of primary AQ texts and materials, Schmid (2014, 6) summarises the content of AQ's master narrative as follows:

1   There is a basic grievance – the Muslim world is in chaos and a Zionist-Christian alliance is held responsible for most, if not all, that is wrong in Muslim countries and the way Muslims are humiliated, discriminated and/or (mis-) treated in the world. The collusion of corrupt Muslim rulers with the West keeps Muslims impotent; these rulers and those who follow them have turned away from True Islam by allowing Western ways in Muslim lands.
2   There is a vision of the good society: a single political entity – the Caliphate – that replaces corrupt, apostate rulers under Western influence, by rule under Sharia (Islamic Law) wherever there are Muslims so that Allah's will be done and order is restored; and
3   There is a path from the grievance to the realisation of the vision: the eradication, in a violent jihad, led by a heroic vanguard (Al Qaeda) to get rid of Western influence in the Muslim world. However, great sacrifices are needed to turn the tables. Every true Muslim has to engage in a holy jihad against the invading Crusaders to defend the faith and the Muslim lands from enemies near and far in order to achieve victory and humiliate the oppressors.

In the years following 2001, the dissemination of media products that drew on this master narrative increased substantially and grew in sophistication. Lynch (2006, 1) argues that AQ underwent a 'constructivist turn', employing not only violence but also an 'array of persuasive rhetoric and public spectacle' towards the end of strategic social construction.[4] This shift intensified around 2005, as AQ strategists sought to utilise the promulgation of narratives, especially online, as a recruitment tool for home-grown extremists. At this time, noting the impossibility of defeating US-associated forces in a land war in Afghanistan, key AQ strategists such as al-Qurashi, Naji and al-Suri, as well as master propagandists such as Anwar al-Awlaki, highlighted the importance of the creation and dissemination of online narratives to inspire acts of home-grown extremism in the West as legitimate acts of global jihadism in themselves (Brachman and McCants 2006; Lia 2008; Ryan 2013).

This meant that the 'master narrative' described above began to be disseminated by actors associated with AQ, in forms that directly targeted potential home-grown extremists, especially in the West. These efforts involved, for example, YouTube videos featuring American or European citizens, speaking in English and urging their fellow citizens to commit acts of home-grown extremism. Also prominent were English-language magazines – most notably, *Inspire* – targeted especially at Western citizens and offering instructions for committing terrorist acts as well as inspiration to do so.[5] Although debate rages about the actual radicalising effect of these efforts, they are important examples of concerted attempts by AQ-core to foster a sense of shared identity coalescing around a master narrative, particularly in the context of home-grown extremism.

This shift in strategy energised security agencies' attention to counternarrative work, especially in the West, and to online counternarratives in particular. Today, policymakers grapple with the Internet and the different discursive structures it enables compared to relevant precedents. Technology plays an important role in an emerging 'leaderless jihad', which has resulted from AQ's tactical shift providing a 'tolerant, virtual environment' and facilitating a 'sense of unity and purpose' progressed via shared narratives despite geographic dispersal (see also Hoffman 2008; Sageman, 2008b, 2).

This 'constructivist turn' (Lynch 2006) is now progressed by more diffuse actors than simply AQ-core. In particular, social media has played an important role in recruitment of foreign fighters and the dissemination of narratives in recent conflicts led by Islamic State of Iraq and al-Sham (ISIS) or Islamic State of Iraq and the Levant (ISIL) in Syria and Iraq (Berger 2015). These individuals now have the option to create their own personalised narratives of the battlefield, meaning the more centralised model of narrative dissemination initially highlighted by AQ-core has become even more diffuse. Referring to the role of the Internet and social media, a respected terrorism expert recently testified that Syria was the 'most socially mediated conflict in history'. He noted that not even insurgent leaders are able to control the online narrative under current circumstances (see also Farrell 2014; Hegghammer 2014).

A shift in policy: countering online narratives in the UK

In response to the shift in tactics outlined above, the UK government was the first major Western government to explicitly employ online counternarratives in its counterterrorism policy. This shift took place largely in response to the 7/7 bombings of 2005. The bombings killed 52 and wounded over 700, and were committed by British citizens (and one permanent resident) who had been largely organised online and trained abroad. The men had been avid consumers of online narrative material in the form of lectures by radical preachers and footage of atrocities committed in Afghanistan and Iraq, allegedly by coalition troops (HoC 2006). This material was packaged and consumed in the context of AQ's master narrative; the radicalisation of the bombers, therefore, sitting within the shift in AQ-core tactics outlined in the previous section.

In response to the bombings, the UK government introduced a ground-breaking and controversial counter-radicalisation programme known as 'Prevent' (Jackson *et al.* 2009; Heath-Kelly 2013). This programme was contained within a larger counterterrorism strategy known as CONTEST, and focused on countering practices and identities that the government saw as fostering extremism and leading to radicalisation of British citizens on a path towards home-grown extremism.

Initially, 'Prevent' was largely concerned with initiatives that focused on fostering a shared British identity and on local community policing initiatives that built on lessons learned from the Northern Ireland conflict. These included, for example, citizenship classes in schools, theatre productions and community outreach forums (see HoC 2010, 2012, for an overview of programmes).

As Nouri and Whiting (2015, 85–86) argue, the bulk of British activity targeting the role of Internet-born narratives in this context has focused on the removal of content rather than the active design of counternarratives. For example, The Counter Terrorism Internet Referral Unit (CTIRU), first piloted in 2010, seeks to remove extremist material from UK-hosted websites, recognising its persuasive potential. The unit removes online content referred by the public, which it assesses against the Terrorism Act 2006. Under the terms of the Act, such material includes not only content that contains instructions for violent material, but also content that incites or glorifies terrorism. From 2010 to 2013, over 5,000 websites had reportedly been taken down (Wintour and Jones 2013). The unit works closely with international agencies but has been hamstrung by the problem of international hosting by companies such as YouTube and Facebook (HMG 2009, 94; HoC 2012a, 24). In light of the 2015 Charlie Hebdo attacks, the government's focus on the role of such companies has increased, with Prime Minister David Cameron calling for social media companies to take more responsibility for content (Watt *et al.* 2015). Similarly, as well as expanding CTIRU, the 2011 iteration of 'Prevent' called for limiting access to harmful online content in public buildings (HMG 2011a, 77).

While policy documents have highlighted the problem of Internet-born narratives, they have been less successful in outlining concrete solutions to them. The 2006 iteration of 'Prevent' highlighted the Internet as a factor facilitating the spread of extremist ideas (HMG 2006, 10), and later versions of 'Prevent' highlighted the increasing danger from Internet radicalisation (Stevens and Neumann 2009). The 2009 version of CONTEST, the government's overarching counter-terrorism strategy, listed the Internet and its capacity to foster extremism as a problem in the context of radicalisation in a special section on the Internet and 'Prevent' (HMG 2009, 90, 43), while the 2011 version of CONTEST also had its own section dealing with the Internet under 'Prevent' (HMG 2011a, 64). Indeed, the 2011 version of the policy listed 'the Internet' as a sector for action equivalent to education, faith and health (2011a, 77). The updated 'Prevent' policy released under the new Cameron government in 2011 pledged to increase the confidence of civil society activists to 'challenge online extremist content effectively and to provide credible alternatives' (HMG 2011a, 52), and to work with social media enterprises like Facebook in this endeavour. By 2012, fifteen civil society groups had been funded in this manner (HMG 2013, 22).

These documents suggest that the online environment has become increasingly important for counternarrative work that progresses broader British policy goals concerning home-grown extremism. However, as the following paragraphs show, the UK government remains highly secretive about its online counternarrative work. This makes understanding the details of its exact tools difficult, although we can be certain about a shift in emphasis towards countering narratives in the online as well as the offline world.

The most prominent of the government's attempts to engage in online counternarrative work is housed within a broader attempt at countering narratives in the media at large. In mid-2007, the Home Office established the Research, Information and Communications Unit (RICU) within the Home Office. RICU was designed to assist the government in understanding and countering the 'communications challenge' across all communications media, including the Internet. The unit was staffed across three departments: the Department of Communities and Local Government (DCLG), the Foreign and Commonwealth Office (FCO) and the Home Office, emphasising the transnational nature of the online communications problem. Most of RICU's work appears to focus on British audiences, although in 2010, reports indicated that existing or projected activities within RICU included the development and dissemination of documentary materials on British Islam to overseas audiences (Briggs and Feve 2013).

RICU's work is highly classified, and focuses on understanding target audiences for government messaging, analysing terrorist propaganda and dissemination, and providing advice on effective communications both online and offline. RICU has a Domestic and International Campaigns Team that implements strategic communications activities, including digital campaigns aimed at vulnerable communities; and an Insight and Analysis Team, which conducts research on target audiences on and offline. Its early work included the design of key messages to be used in government communication including advice on specific language – for example, advice to avoid using 'war on terror' in government communications. It also trained local practitioners on communication skills and strategies, researched the effectiveness of various channels of communication and provided advice on the best way to manage government responses to specific events such as a Dutch anti-Islam video released online in 2006, for example (Corera 2007; RICU 2007; State 2007, 2009). In the online sphere, RICU provided advice on government messaging and also sponsored research on online terrorist activity, as with a controversial exercise seeking to identify the most 'influential radical Islamic blogs' (Stevens 2010).

The government has also sponsored online counternarrative activities outside RICU's remit. The Radical Middle Way website, for example, has been funded under 'Prevent' since 2008 via DCLG to 'promote debate within UK Muslim communities, using the internet to reach audiences in the UK and overseas' (HMG 2009, 95). This extended even to theological advice, as the FCO partnered with RICU to ensure that such advice was available on the Internet in a variety of languages (HMG 2009, 95). Similar projects were delivered not only at the international but also at the local level – one civil society organisation received y60,000 to produce online counternarratives relevant to their local area (Kundnani 2009, fn 206).

In recent years, RICU has engaged in more targeted work on the direct challenge of extremist narratives online through 'road-testing ... innovative approaches to counter-ideological messages' (HoC 2012b) although again, details are scarce

(HoC 2012b). The unit's work has also recently focused on countering narratives that draw British citizens to Syria as foreign fighters (Milmo 2014a, b). For example, via RICU, the Foreign Office reportedly spent nearly n200,000 in 2014 on 'social media activity' to deter Britons from going to fight in Syria. Refusing to elaborate on the content of this activity, RICU has only confirmed that it was 'emphasising the genuine risks of travel and the reality of the dangerous situation on the ground' (Milmo 2014b). The department's goal in this case seems to be shared by several civil society campaigns that have sprung up online (Milmo 2014a), to highlight the dangers and hardships faced by young Britons who leave to fight in Syria. A similar programme funded by RICU focuses on creating documentaries around this subject for online and offline use (Milmo 2014a).[6]

Countering online narratives in the US

Unlike the UK, the US is relatively open about its online counternarrative work. The Obama administration established the most obvious manifestation of this in May 2010 with the opening of the Center for Strategic Counterterrorism Communication, an interagency unit housed in the State Department.[7] The Centre built on a small Digital Outreach Team in the State Department, comprising just ten people, which had been in existence since 2006. Executive Order 13584 of September 2011 increased the prominence of the Center's work and established a separate budget. The Executive Order states that the initial remit should expand so that the Center shall coordinate, orient, and inform Government-wide public communications activities directed at audiences abroad and targeted against violent extremists and terrorist organizations, especially al-Qa'ida and its affiliates and adherents, with the goal of using communication tools to reduce radicalisation by terrorists and extremist violence and terrorism that threaten the interests and national security of the United States, including:

i monitoring and evaluating narratives (overarching communication themes that reflect a community's identity, experiences, aspirations, and concerns) and events abroad that are relevant to the development of a U.S. strategic counter-terrorism narrative designed to counter violent extremism and terrorism that threaten the interests and national security of the United States;
ii developing and promulgating for use throughout the executive branch U.S. strategic counterterrorism narratives and public communications strategies to counter the messaging of violent extremists and terrorist organizations, especially al-Qa'ida and its affiliates and adherents;and
iii identifying current and emerging trends in extremist communications and communications by al-Qa'ida and its affiliates and adherents in order to coordinate and provide thematic guidance to U.S. Government communicators on how best to proactively promote the U.S. strategic counterterrorism narrative and policies and to respond to and rebut extremist messaging and narratives when communicating to audiences outside the United States,

as informed by a wide variety of Government and non-government sources, including nongovernmental organizations, academic sources, and finished intelligence created by the intelligence community' (White House 2011c).

As of mid-2014, the Center consisted of a team of about fifty analysts working in various languages to counter extremist propaganda on Internet forums and chat rooms. The Center is physically located within the State department and has access to intelligence feeds. Its work is dominated by two activities: creating and sharing communications material, such as videos, which counter Islamist themes; and reaching out to multilingual audiences online via social media and in Islamist fora to engage in debate and correct misinformation, performed by a group that builds on the original Digital Outreach Team.

The first of these activities is a reactive process, in that videos are created and released as events occur. For example, in 2012, the CSCTC responded to photos posted online by AQ'Q affiliate in Yemen. The photos showed coffins draped in American flags, celebrating American deaths in Yemen. In response, the Center produced a video that replaced the flags with the Yemeni flag, conveying the message that most victims of attacks in the conflict of Yemen had been locals, not American soldiers. Similarly, the Center released a video immediately following the destruction of Islamic shrines in Northern Mali by al-Qaeda in the Islamic Maghreb (AQIM) as part of an uprising in 2012. Captioned in Arabic and released on YouTube, the video highlighted the importance of these ancient shrines – which had been destroyed under AQIM's direction – to the Islamic faith. The video was likely based on intelligence gleaned from documents found soon after the raid, which suggested that the issue was problematic within AQIM (Siegel 2013).

In relation to the second activity noted above, the Center staff have active Twitter identities and a strong presence on social media outlets as well as within Islamic fora. Interestingly, and in stark contrast to the highly secretive UK model, even within radical Islamist fora, CSCTC staff post using their individual identities, clearly badged as State Department employees. This is characterised by CSCTC management as an attempt to clearly 'engage' with users who are hostile – a process made more credible by those marked clearly as State Department employees. Such credible engagement is judged by the Center's leadership to make the delivery of counternarratives more effective, although no metrics exist (Silverman 2014).

A 2012 study found that the range of topics discussed by the Digital Outreach Team was surprisingly diverse, ranging from messaging that stressed US support for a Palestinian state and religious tolerance, to messages that ridiculed conspiracy theorists (Khatib et al. 2012, 359). In a December 2013 speech, the Center's head suggested that its output had amounted to '18,000 engagements' (Silverman 2014). However, the Center had until recently limited its English-language engagement, for reasons outlined below. This began to change at the end of 2013, as the Center began a pilot programme to address the recruitment of Westerners to the conflict in Syria (Schmitt 2013). The programme uses a hashtag, #thinkagainturnaway, to mark material that shows participation in the Syrian conflict as dangerous and unjust. The Center's English-language staff had doubled by 2014, and in mid-2014 the State Department engaged a private contractor to expand its English-language offering further (Silverman 2014).

Unlike the UK, US online counternarrative work has not explicitly focused on the domestic environment and has limited its work in English until recently, for a number of reasons. This is at least in part due to differences in threat perception. US policymakers did not register the threat from home-grown extremism as a priority in the same way as policymakers in the UK. In the years following 2001, US policymakers and commentators saw the risk of such attacks in the US as far lower than in Europe or the UK, and attributed this to clear differences in integration, wealth and education between Muslim minorities in the US and in the UK and Europe (Vidino 2009). Despite several early plots in America and the London bombings of 2005, even by 2007 the National Intelligence Estimate persisted in describing the threat from home-grown extremism as not 'likely to be as severe as Europe', and downplayed it in response to the threat from AQ-core (NIC 2007, 7).

However, the Senate Committee on Homeland Security and Governmental Affairs began hearings on the issue in 2007, and by 2010 the Obama administration had taken it up as a policy problem. The 2007 hearings focused on the problem of Internet radicalisation, with senior committee members focusing on it in their introductory remarks and questioning. Importantly, several respondents noted the first amendment problems of action to combat online radicalisation (Gersten 2007, 57; Lungren 2007, 55–56). Broader civil society responses focused on the constitutional issues at play in domestic counter-radicalisation, including online counternarrative, work. Drawing comparisons to the McCarthy era, such opposition focused on the argument that by acting to change and/or stigmatise political and ideological beliefs, the Act undermined first amendment rights, including rights to free speech online, tagging legislation that resulted from the hearings a 'thought crimes bill' (ACLU 2007; Giraldi 2007; Lithwick 2007; CCR 2012). Because it seeks to influence the way citizens think and feel about political issues, the very concept of counternarrative work is problematic in a constitutional sense in the US, then, in a way it is not in the UK.[8]

By 2008, a spike in home-grown threats,[9] especially 'lone wolf' threats, had begun to concern policymakers, with the Internet featuring strongly in these concerns (Bjelopera and Randol 2010, 34). In Senate testimony in September 2011, the Chief of the National Counterterrorism Coordinating Center (NCTC) (the government's key counterterrorism coordinating agency), Mathew G Olsen, emphasised this aspect of the threat, marking it as a 'key element of the evolution and diversification of the threat since 9/11'. He noted in particular the growth of online English-language violent extremist content over the past three years, stating that it had fostered greater 'cohesion, but not necessarily collaboration' among home-grown extremists. He went on to note the importance of a US-specific narrative promulgated over the Internet, and encouraged, if not directed, by AQ core (2011, 5–6).

US counter-radicalisation policy was formalised in 2011 with the release of two high-level policy documents by the White House. The more comprehensive of these, the Strategic Implementation Plan (SIP), links attention to the Internet specifically to its third key goal: 'countering violent extremist propaganda whilst promoting our ideals'. It states: 'We will work to empower families and communities to counter online violent extremist propaganda, which is increasingly in English and targeted at American audiences' (White House 2011a, 6). The strategic implementation plan goes on to identify 'addressing technology and virtual space' as one of four 'crosscutting and supportive activities', noting:

> The Internet has facilitated violent extremist recruitment and radicalisation and, in some instances, attack planning, requiring that we consider programs and initiatives that are mindful of the online nature of the threat. At the same time, the Federal Government can leverage and support the use of new technologies to engage communities, build and mobilize networks against violent extremism, and undercut terrorist narratives.
> (White House 2011b, 5)

The SIP foreshadows a separate federal-level strategy focusing on countering violent extremism online that will be developed 'in the near future' –nyet to emerge in full –eand details several measures that this strategy will address, namely: 1) the latest assessment of the role of the Internet, 2) the absence of clear national boundaries in online space and the relationship between international and domestic radicalisation to violence, 3) relevant legal issues and 4) the differing authorities and capabilities of departments and agencies (White House 2011b, 20). Despite these policy statements, a strategy focused solely or primarily on the domestic threat is yet to emerge or be detailed in full. As described above, the State Department has taken up the mantle of online counternarrative work in the US context, but does not focus explicitly on home-grown extremism. Instead, it addresses online counternarrative work on a broader, global scale, which includes the domestic by definition.

Importantly, despite aforementioned constitutional constraints concerning the targeting of American citizens, legislative measures introduced in 2013 theoretically facilitated the State Department's online counternarrative work, particularly work directed at home-grown extremists who were also American citizens. The National Defense Authorization Act (NDAA) 2013 contained measures that changed the State Department's ability to communicate with American citizens in the pursuit of foreign policy goals. This change was the result not only of essential bureaucratic reorganisation to take account of developments in the communications environment wrought by the Internet, but also of the effect of Cold War era legislation known as the Smith–Mundt Act[10] on the government's ability to effect counter-extremism measures (Thornberry 2012). Section 208(B) of the 2013 NDAA Act amended the Smith–Mundt Act and the Foreign Relations Authorization Act of 1987, allowing for materials produced by the State Department to be released within US borders and striking down a long-standing ban on the dissemination of such material in the US.

This change was directly related to the policymakers' desires to engage in counternarrative work, including online. In fact, a former Under-Secretary for Public Diplomacy described domestic counter-extremism as the 'main driver' of the legislative changes, noting that it

> came out of the House Armed Services Committee interest in combating violent extremism. They were concerned that the US was becoming a source for bad guys and the US media is simply not doing its job on reporting what is going on abroad.
>
> (Armstrong 2013)

One of the bill's sponsors explained in a press release that:

> Smith-Mundt restrictions are incredibly problematic when trying to combat the spread of violent extremist ideologies and extremist recruitment efforts. ... Smith-Mundt's restrictions on domestic distribution of material for foreign audiences through new technologies directly interferes with our efforts to get factual information out in a timely manner to counter the misinformation spread by violent extremists.
>
> (Smith 2012a)

As an example, he referred directly to key clusters of AQ-inspired home-grown extremism in the Somali population in Minnesota, noting that:

> the bar on the US government doing domestic propaganda remains in place. What we amended was the ability of them, if asked, to provide that same content domestically. So one of the examples was that Voice of America had been providing, in Somalia and in those areas, sort of a counter-radicalisation method. And in Minnesota, where they have a substantial Somali population, they had asked, you know, well, can we have that information. Smith-Mundt barred them from providing it. So we amended it to say if somebody asks and if it's information that has already been created for an international audience, then yes, you can provide it. The government still cannot provide purely for domestic consumption any sort of information campaigns, so it was a very limited exception.
>
> (Smith 2012b)

Conclusion

This chapter has outlined the context of online counternarrative work by showing that online narratives have emerged as an important component of the radical Islamist toolbox. It has shown that both the US and the UK have responded to online narratives with dedicated counternarrative policies and bureaucratic reorganisations. It has shown that their responses are arguably constrained by domestic circumstances, including political and social structures (Foley 2013). For example, as a result of constitutional constraints as well as threat perceptions, the

US has perhaps focused less clearly on the domestic arena than the UK, blurring the lines between international and domestic counternarrative work. However, recent indications outlined above suggest that, despite constitutional sensitivities, the country is moving towards measures that may by default target American consumers of online information. In addition, the overt and clearly badged efforts of the US State Department are in stark contrast to covert UK policies. Although the US undoubtedly engages in covert and overt activity, the difference in the CSCTC's approach arguably rests on the way each views its place in the world: the US as a source of credibility, the UK less so.

Despite these differences, all online counternarrative work suffers from similar difficulties.[11] The most important of these is credibility: to work, counternarratives must be persuasive without being bombastic, targeted without being obvious, and responsive in a highly fragmented and volatile consumer market. Any successes are also difficult to identify: how can one measure the success of counternarratives, or indeed any intervention, dissuading a potential terrorist from a certain path? Finally, despite the metrics on shares, likes and engagement readily available for social media activity, what do they actually mean in terms of effectiveness? The area is a developing policy focus in counterterrorism, and one that is unlikely to diminish. As this chapter's overview of US and UK counternarrative work has shown, the US and the UK are equally engaged in online counternarrative as a policy endeavour in the post-9/11 environment: the question remains rather not whether they will engage, but how policies will develop as policymakers learn more from their mistakes, their successes and the violence they seek to prevent.

Notes

1 This chapter uses military theorist David Kilcullen's definition of 'narrative' as a 'simple unifying, easily-expressed story or explanation that organises people's experience and provides a framework for understanding events' (Kilcullen 2006, 33). On the relationship between narratives and real-world activity, Miskimmon *et al.* situate such narratives within the broader ambit of strategic narratives in international politics, which includes such diverse endeavours as public diplomacy and psychological warfare. They argue that (strategic) 'narratives are a means for political actors to construct a shared meaning of. . . . politics, and to shape the perceptions, beliefs, and behaviour of . . . actors'. They further contend that such narratives offer 'a particular structure through which shared sense is achieved, representing a past, present and future, an obstacle and a desired end-point' (2012, 1).
2 For example, Google runs a Network Against Violent Extremism program, while the Counterterrorism Implementation Task Force, situated within the UN system, has had a working group on countering the use of the Internet for terrorist purposes since 2008. Both of these endeavours feature counternarrative initiatives. Similarly, the thirty-member Global Counterterrorism Forum, launched by the US and Turkey and incorporating a multitude of multilateral for a, held a symposium in 2014 on countering terrorists' use of the Internet, which included a focus on counternarratives.
3 Note that the period 2004–2006 saw the launching of Facebook, YouTube and Twitter, successively. In concert with websites that are dedicated to hosting extremist material, these social platforms are important to the creation and spread of counter-narratives online.

4 See Ciovacco (2009) and Soriano (2010) for a further overview of AQ-core's media strategies, and Lia (2008) and Hegghammer, T and S Lacroix (2007) for an overview of radical Islamist thought in this regard.
5 See Meleagrou-Hitchens (2011), Hussain and Salmon (2014), Stenersen (2008, 2013) for an overview of these efforts.
6 The government has also engaged in attempts to limit the reach of websites that it sees as a source of the damaging narratives. In effect, this means that although the activity in which the CTIRU engages is ostensibly nothing more than filtering, its effect is to shape an online narrative by default given that it removes certain narrative-driven material relating to glorification.
7 See LeBaron (2012) for a useful overview.
8 Note that calculating the number of attacks/plots is notoriously difficult because of the need to rely on often emotive press reporting, and because of controversies surrounding issues of entrapment. These numbers come from a Congressional Research Report (Bjelopera 2013) and focus on arrests as an indicator of the (at least partial) verification of plots. See Sageman (2014) for a discussion of problems in data collection.
9 Note that as in the UK, debates continue about the severity of the threat posed by home-grown extremism. See especially Brooks (2011).
10 The original Smith–Mundt Act was passed in 1948 in an environment of virulent anticommunism where Congress was suspicious of the State Department as a hotbed of leftist activism. It prohibited the State Department from disseminating inside the US its own information products designed for audiences abroad. US public diplomacy had undergone a reinvigoration in the years following 11 September 2001, and changes to Smith–Mundt can be directly related to these efforts.
11 See Hussain and Salmon (2014) and Briggs and Feve (2013) for a useful overview of these difficulties.

References

ACLU (American Civil Liberties Union). (2007), 'ACLU Statement on the Violent Radicalization and Homegrown Terrorism Act of 2007', 28 November 2007, www.aclu.org/national-security/aclu-statement-violent-radicalization-and-homegrown-terrorism-prevention-act-2007 Accessed 1 January 2015.

ACPO (Association of Chief Police Officers). (2013), 'Prevent Delivery Unit Update Issue', 24 January 2013, www.acpo.police.uk/documents/TAM/2013/201301TAMPreventBulletinIssue24.pdf Accessed 1 February 2015.

Armstrong, M. (2013), Governor on the Broadcasting Board of Governors, Former Executive Director of the United States Advisory Commission on Public Diplomacy 2011. (Phone interview, 24 October 2013).

Bartlett, J., Birdwell, J. and King, M. (2010), *The Edge of Violence: A Radical Approach to Extremism*, London: Demos.

Berger, J.M. (2015), *The Evolution of Terrorist Propaganda: The Paris Attack and Social Media* Presented to the House of Representatives Committee on Foreign Affairs, Washington, DC, 27 January 2015.

Bjelopera, J. (2013), *American Jihadist Terrorism: Combating a Complex Threat*, Washington, DC: Congressional Research Service.

Bjelopera, J. and Randol, M. (2010), *American Jihadist Terrorism: Combating a Complex Threat*, Washington, DC: Congressional Research Service, no. R41416.

Brachman, J. and McCants, W. (2006), 'Stealing Al Qaeda's Playbook', *Studies in Conflict and Terrorism*, vol 29, no 4, pp. 309–21.

Brachman, J. and Levine, A. (2011), 'You Too Can Be Awlaki', *Fletcher Forum of World Affairs*, vol 35, no 25.

Briggs, R. and Feve, S. (2013), *Countering the Appeal of Extremism Online Institute for Strategic Dialogue*, London.

Brooks, R. (2011), 'Muslim "Homegrown" Terrorism in the United States: How Serious Is the Threat?' *International Security*, vol 36, no 2, pp. 7–47.

Bunzel, C. (2015), *From Paper State to Caliphate: The Ideology of Islamic State Brookings Institute*, Washington, DC.

CCR (Center for Constitutional Rights). (2007), 'Factsheet: The Violent Radicalization and Homegrown Terrorism Prevention Act', http://ccrjustice.org/learn-more/faqs/factsheet%3A-violent-radicalization-and-homegrown-terrorism-prevention-act-2007 Accessed 1 January 2015.

Corera, G. (2007), 'Don't Look Now, Britain's Real Spooks Are Right Behind You', *The Sunday Times*, 2 December 2007. http://cma.thesundaytimes.co.uk/sto/news/uk_news/article76296.ece Accessed 1 January 2015.

Ciovacco, C. (2009), 'The Contours of Al Qaeda's Media Strategy', *Studies in Conflict and Terrorism*, vol 32, no 10, pp. 853–75.

Farrell, J. (2014), 'How ISIS Uses Social Media', *Politics and Strategy*, www.iiss.org/en/politics%20and%20strategy/blogsections/2014-d2de/october-931b/isis-media-9d28 Accessed 10 October 2014.

Foley, F. (2013), *Countering Terrorism in Britain and France: Institutions, Norms and the Shadow of the Past*, Cambridge: Cambridge University Press.

Gersten, D. (2007), *Testimony, Hearing into Radicalization, Information Sharing and Community Outreach: Protecting the Homeland from Homegrown Terror 5/04/2007*, US House of Representatives Committee on Homeland Security Subcommittee on Intelligence Information Sharing and Terrorism Risk Assessment.

Giraldi, P. (2007), 'The Violent Radicalization and Homegrown Terrorism Prevention Act', www.huffingtonpost.com/philip-giraldi/the-violent-radicalizatio_b_74091.html Accessed 1 January 2015.

Heath-Kelly, C. (2013), 'Counter-Terrorism and the Counterfactual: Producing the "Radicalisation" Discourse and the UK PREVENT Strategy', *The British Journal of Politics and International Relations*, vol 15, no 3, pp. 394–455.

Hegghammer, T. and Lacroix, S. (2007), 'Rejectionist Islamism in Saudi Arabia: The Story of Juhayman Al-Qutaybi Revisited', *International Journal of Middle East Studies*, vol 39, no 1, pp. 103–22.

Hegghammer, T. (2014), *Testimony to Hearing of the House of Commons*, London: Home Affairs Committee, 11 February 2014.

HMG (Her Majesty's Government). (2006), *Countering International Terrorism: The United Kingdom's Strategy*, The Home Office. London: The Stationery Office Cm 6888.

HMG (Her Majesty's Government). (2009), *Pursue, Prevent, Protect, Prepare: The United Kingdom's Strategy for Countering International Terrorism*, The Home Office. London: The Stationery Office Cm 7547.

HMG (Her Majesty's Government). (2011a), *Prevent Strategy*, The Home Office. London: The Stationery Office Cm 8092.

HMG (Her Majesty's Government). (2011b), *Contest: The United Kingdom's Strategy for Countering Terrorism*, The Home Office. London: The Stationery Office Cm 8123.

HMG (Her Majesty's Government). (2013), *CONTEST: The UK's Strategy for Countering International Terrorism*, London: The Stationery Office Cm 8583.

HoC (House of Commons). (2006), *Report into the London Terrorist Attacks on 7 July 2005*, Intelligence and Security Committee, London: The Stationery Office CM 6785.
HoC (House of Commons Communities and Local Government Committee). (2010), *Preventing Violent Extremism*, London: The Stationery Office HC 65.
HoC (House of Commons Home Affairs Committee) (2012a), *The Roots of Violent Radicalisation*, London: The Stationery Office HC 1446.
HoC (House of Commons Intelligence and Security Committee) (2012b), *Annual Report 2011–2012*, London: Intelligence and Security Committee HC1447.
Hoffman, B. (2008), 'Does Osama Still Call the Shots? Debating the Containment of Al Qaeda's Leadership', *Foreign Affairs* July/August.
Hussain, G. and Salmon E. (2014), *Jihad Trending: A Comprehensive Analysis of Online Extremism and How to Counter It*, London: Quilliam Foundation.
Jackson, R., Smyth, M.B. and Gunning J. (2009), 'The Case for Critical Terrorism Studies', in Jackson, R., Smyth, M.B. and Gunning, J. (eds) *Critical Terrorism Studies: A New Research Agenda*, Oxford: Routledge, pp. 1–9.
Khatib, L., Dutton, W. and Thelwall, M. (2012), 'Public Diplomacy 2.0: An Exploratory Case Study of the Digital Outreach Team', *The Middle East Journal*, vol 66, no 3, pp. 453–72.
Kilcullen, D. (2006), 'Twenty-Eight Articles: Fundamentals of Company-level Insurgency', *Military Review*, May-June 2006, pp. 103–08.
Kundnani, A. (2009), *Spooked! How Not to Prevent Violent Extremism*, London: The Institute of Race Relations.
LeBaron, R. (2012), '*Public Diplomacy as an Instrument of Counterterrorism. A Progress Report*'. Remarks by Ambassador (retired) Richard LeBaron at The President's Round Table, Washington, DC: Diplomatic and Consular Officers Retired (DACOR).
Lia, B. (2008), 'Doctrines for Jihadi Terrorist Training'. *Terrorism and Political Violence*, vol 20, no 4, pp. 518–42.
Lockwood, M., Mulley, S., Jones, E., Glennie, A., Paintin, K., and Pendleton, A. (2010), *Policy Coherence and the Future of the UK's International Development Agenda*, London: Institute for Public Policy Research.
Lithwick, D. (2007), 'Bad Ideas: The Law Promoting Outstanding Excellence in Fighting Terrorism – and Why You Never heard About It', *Slate.com*, 27 November 2007, www.slate.com/articles/news_and_politics/jurisprudence/2007/11/bad_ideas.single.html Accessed 1 January 2015.
Lungren, D. (2007), *Testimony, Radicalization, Information Sharing and Community Outreach: Protecting the Homeland from Homegrown Terror*. US House of Representatives Committee on Homeland Security Subcommittee on Intelligence Information Sharing and Terrorism Risk Assessment.
Lynch, M. (2006), 'Al-Qaeda's Constructivist Turn', *Praeger Security International*, www.marclynch.com/wp-content/uploads/2011/03/Al-Qaedas-Constructivism.pdf Accessed 01/01/2015.
McCants, W. and Watts, C. (2013), 'US Strategy for Countering Violent Extremism: An Assessment Foreign Policy Research Institute', www.fpri.org/articles/2012/12/us-strategy-countering-violent extremism-assessment Accessed 1 January 2013.
Malet, D. (2013), *Foreign Fighters: Transnational Identity in Civil Conflicts*, Oxford: Oxford University Press.
Meleagrou-Hitchens, A. (2011), *As American as Apple Pie: How Anwar al-Awlaki Became the Face of Western Jihad*, London: International Centre for the Study of Radicalisation.

Milmo, C. (2014a), 'Government Aims to Win Hearths and Tackle Extremism in Documentary on Families of Dead Jihadists' *The Independent*, 27 June 2014, www.independent.co.uk/news/uk/politics/government-aims-to-win-hearts-and-minds-with-documentary-on-families-of-dead-jihadists-9569288.html Accessed 1 January 2015.

Milmo, C. (2014b), 'Social Media is the New Weapon in War on British Jihadis', *The Independent*, 9 March 2014, www.independent.co.uk/news/uk/politics/social-media-is-new-weapon-in-war-on-british-jihadis-9179099.html Accessed 1 January 2015.

Miskimmon, A., O'Loughlin, B. and Roselle, L. (2012), *Forging the World: Strategic Narratives and International Relations Working Paper*, Centre for European Politics, Royal Holloway University of London, London: New Political Communication Unit.

NIC (National Intelligence Council). (2007), *National Intelligence Estimate: The Terrorist Threat to the US Homeland Office of the Director of National Intelligence*, Washington, DC.

Nouri, L. and Whiting, A. (2015), 'Prevent and the Internet', in Baker-Beall, C., Heath-Kelly, C. and Jarvis, L. (eds) *Counter-Radicalisation: Critical Perspectives*, Oxford: Routledge, pp. 175–90.

Olsen, M. (2011), *Testimony, '10 years after 9/11: Are We safer?'* 13 November 2011, Washington, DC: US Senate Committee on Homeland Security and Governmental Affairs.

Patel, F. (2011), *Rethinking Radicalization*, New York, NY: Brennan Center for Justice at New York University Law School.

PCC (Strategic Communication and Public Diplomacy Coordinating Committee) (2007), United States National Strategy for Public Diplomacy and Strategic Communication GPO, www.au.af.mil/au/awc/awcgate/state/natstrat_strat_comm.pdf

Rees, W.Y.N. and Aldrich R.J. (2005), 'Contending Cultures of Counterterrorism: Transatlantic Divergence or Convergence?' *International Affairs*, vol 81, no 5, pp. 905–23.

RICU. (2007), *Counterterrorism Communications Guidance: Communicating Effectively with Community Audiences*, London: The Home Office.

Ryan, M. (2013), *Decoding Al-Qaeda's Strategy: The Deep Battle Against America*, New York, NY: Columbia University Press.

Roy, O. (2006), *Globalized Islam: The Search for a New Ummah*, New York, NY: Columbia University Press.

Sageman, M. (2008a), *Leaderless Jihad: Terror Networks in the 21st Century*, Philadelphia: University of Pennsylvania Press.

Sageman, M. (2008b), 'Does Osama Still Call the Shots? Debating the Containment of Al Qaeda's Leadership, *Foreign Affairs* July/August.

Sageman, M. (2014), 'The Stagnation in Terrorism Research', *Terrorism and Political Violence*, vol 26, no 4, pp. 565–80.

Schmid, A. (2014), *Al-Qaeda's 'Single Narrative' and Attempts to Develop Counter-narratives: The State of Knowledge International Centre for Counter-Terrorism*, Amsterdam: The Hague.

Schmitt, E. (2013), 'A US Reply, in English, to Terrorists' Online Lure', *The New York Times*, 4 December 2013, www.nytimes.com/2013/12/05/world/middleeast/us-aims-to-blunt-terrorist-recruiting-of-english-speakers.html?_r=0 Accessed 1 January 2015.

Siegel, P. (2013), *'AQIM's Playbook in Mali' CTC Sentinel*, Combating Terrorism Centre, Washington, DC, www.ctc.usma.edu/posts/aqims-playbook-in-mali Accessed 1January 2015.

Silverman, J. (2014), 'The State Department's Twitter Jihad', *Politico*, 22 July 2014, www.politico.com/magazine/story/2014/07/the-state-departments-twitter-jihad-109234_Page2.html#ixzz3PtDY7edI Accessed 1 January 2015.
Stenersen, A. (2008), 'The Internet: A Virtual Training Camp?' *Terrorism and Political Violence*, vol 20, no 2, pp. 215–33.
Stenersen, A. (2013), 'Bomb-Making for Beginners': Inside al Al-Qaeda E-Learning Course', *Perspectives on Terrorism*, vol 7, no 1, pp. 25–37.
Stevens, T. and Neumann, P. (2009), *Countering Online Radicalisation: A Strategy for Action*, London: International Centre for the Study of Radicalisation and Political Violence.
Stevens, T. and Neumann, P. (2009), *Countering Online Radicalisation: A Strategy for Action*, London: International Centre for the Study of Radicalisation.
Smith, A. (2012a), 'Rep. Smith Clarifies the Intent and Impact of the Thornberry-Smith Amendment' *US Congressman Adam Smith: Representing Washington's 9th District*, 23 April 2012. http://adamsmith.house.gov/blog/?postid=296708 Accessed 1 January 2013.
Smith, A. (2012b), 'American Propaganda Allowed Stateside, Transcript', *Onthemedia*, www.onthemedia.org/story/307767-american-propaganda-allowed-stateside/transcript/ Accessed 01/09/2013 2013.
Soriano, M. (2010), 'Jihadist Propaganda and Its Audiences: A Change of Course?' *Perspectives on Terrorism*, vol 1, no 2, www.terrorismanalysts.com/pt/index.php/pot/article/view/9/21 Accessed 1 January 2015.
State (Department of State). (2007), *EUR Senior Adviser Pandith and S/P Adviser Cohen's Visit to the UK, 9–14 October 2007*. Confidential. Department of State. WikiLeaks 07LONDON4045_a.
State (Department of State). (2009), Cable: US Government Seeks Deeper Counter-Radicalization Coordination (Confidential) Department of State. WikiLeaks 09LONDON 1933_a
Stevens, D. (2010), *Estimating Network Size and Tracking Information Dissemination Amongst Islamic Blogs RICU*, London.
Thornberry, M. (2012), 'Thornberry and Smith Introduce Bill to Help Counter Threats in the Information Age', *US Congressman Mac Thornberry, Serving the People of the 13th District of Texas*, http://thornberry.house.gov/news/documentsingle.aspx?DocumentID=296108 Accessed 1 January 2015.
Vidino, L. (2009), 'Homegrown Terrorism in the United States: A New and Occasional Phenomenon?' *Studies in Terrorism and Political* Violence, vol 72, no 1, pp. 1–17.
Watt, N. Mason, R. and Traynor, I. (2015), 'David Cameron Pledges a New Terror Law for Internet After Paris Attacks', *The Guardian*, 12 January 2015, www.theguardian.com/uk-news/2015/jan/12/david-cameron-pledges-anti-terror-law-internet-paris-attacks-nick-clegg Accessed 20 January 2015.
White House. (2011a), National Strategy for Counterterrorism.
White House. (2011b), Strategic Implementation Plan for Empowering Local Partners to Prevent Violent Extremism in the United States.
White House. (2011c), Executive Order 13584 Developing an Integrated Strategic Counterterrorism Communications Initiative.
Wiktorowicz, Q. (2005), *Radical Islam Rising: Muslim Extremism in the West*, London: Rowman & Littlefield.
Wiktorowicz, Q. (2006), 'Anatomy of the Salafi Movement', *Studies in Conflict and Terrorism*, vol 29, no 3, pp. 207–39.

Wintour, P. and Jones, S. (2013), 'Theresa May's Measures to Tackle Radicalisation Come Under Fire', *The Guardian*, 27 May 2013, www.theguardian.com/uk/2013/may/27/theresa-may-woolwich-radicalisation Accessed 1 September 2015.

9 Narratives and counter-narratives of Islamist extremism

Halim Rane

Introduction

Since the turn of the century, combatting Islamist extremism has become a major concern of Western governments. As argued in various chapters of this book, Internet-based communications technology has enabled Islamist extremist groups to deliver their message to global audiences on an unprecedented scale. Islamist extremism is a political ideology that has developed and is maintained based on a series of narratives derived from the Quran, prophetic traditions (*hadith*) as well as early, classical and modern Muslim history. The narratives utilised by Islamist extremists are well known to Muslims globally and generally have political connotations. A key element in the narratives of Islamist extremists is an assumed relationship between Islam and politics, which has profoundly altered the meaning and function of Islam in the modern world and has significant implications for Muslim thought and actions concerning the organisation and administration of Muslim states and societies.

This chapter argues that the most effective response to Islamist extremism is to depoliticise Islam through a metanarrative of political secularism. It discusses the ideology of Islamist extremism and then explains the concepts of narratives and master narratives as they relate to this phenomenon. Of particular focus is the politicisation of Islam by which ideas about Islamic law and polity have become central not only to Islamist extremism but to Muslim thought more generally. This chapter then discusses counter-narratives as part of an overall communications strategy in response to Islamist extremism and radicalisation. The central argument presented is that in order to most effectively undermine Islamist extremism and the radicalisation of young Muslims, the counter-narratives used as part of this communication strategy must support the separation of politics from Islam. While the central medium for the dissemination of these ideas will be Internet-based communications technology, this chapter will focus on the message rather than the process of transmission.

Islamist extremism

It is important to begin this chapter by defining some key terms. Islamist extremism refers to a stage of radicalisation in the progression towards terrorism in the name of, and usually informed by, an interpretation of Islam. While radicalisation refers to the process of adopting extreme ideas, terrorism refers to acts of violence with political, religious and/or ideological intent for the purpose intimidating a government and/or civilian population. What are considered radical or extreme ideas, however, will differ according to different social, cultural, religious and political contexts. Within the Western context, radicalisation involves the rejection of key democratic values including human rights, gender equality, civil liberties, pluralism, non-sectarian sources of law and non-violent transitions of political power. Ideas commonly found among radicalised Muslims in the West include justification of jihadist violence, support for the implementation of punitive *shariah* laws, intolerance of other social groups and support for the establishment of a caliphate (Rabasa and Benard 2015).

Islamist extremism in the modern world is represented by jihadist and Salafist groups who seek to use violence and terrorism to establish so-called Islamic states based on the implementation of *shariah* and the restoration of an idealised version of the caliphate, which is understood by its proponents to be the 'Islamic' form of government. While Salafists generally adhere to more literalist, conservative and often puritanical approaches to Islam based on an interpretation of what they perceive to be the religion's original beliefs and practices, they may be political or apolitical, violent or non-violent. The major antagonists for this vision include 'Western' values and institutions, particularly secularism and democracy. While the contents of this chapter relate generally to Islamist extremism, special attention will be given to the growing phenomenon of radical Islamists among Muslim minority communities in the West. Radical Islamism in the West may be more difficult to eradicate than its counterpart in Muslim-majority countries, as the latter can often be overcome by political solutions that include bringing them into the political process. The former, however, act in response to feelings of alienation, discrimination and grievances that arise in relation to global and local political contexts, including the foreign policies towards Muslim countries and anti-terror laws of Western governments.

In the Muslim world

The idea of an Islamic state characterised by the implementation of *shariah* is a modern phenomenon developed by Abul A'la Maududi (d. 1979), in the context of British colonial rule and the identity politics of the Indian subcontinent in the years preceding partition, and Sayyid Qutb (d. 1966), in the context of authoritarian rule in Egypt. In response to the Muslim League's call for a Muslim state of Pakistan, Hindu calls for a secular India, and communist calls for a socialist state, Maududi perceived a threat to Islamic identity and called for the establishment of 'Allah's government', *hukumat-e-ilahiya* or an Islamic state (Ahmad 2009). Although the concept became a central pillar of Islamism across the Muslim world by the latter half of the twentieth century, so without foundation in Islamic thought was his idea of an Islamic state that Maududi initially struggled to convince the Indian *ulema* (Islamic religious scholars) and those in his own party of its legitimacy. He was forced to engage in an elaborate reconceptualising of the concepts of God, lordship, worship and religion in relation to politics in order to lay the theological foundations for his case (Ahmad 2009).

Central to Maududi's advocacy of what he called theo-democracy and his opposition to democracy was his conception of *tawhid* (Islamic monotheism). Maududi interpreted sovereignty as belonging exclusively to God, precluding the legitimacy of any legislation other than what he considered to be of divine origin (Maududi 1976). This perspective denies that *shariah* is a human interpretation of the Quran and the prophetic traditions compiled hundreds of years after the death of the Prophet Muhammad (Rane 2010). Maududi (1976) considered Islam to be 'the very antithesis of secular Western democracy' as 'the philosophical foundation of Western democracy is the sovereignty of the people' (p. 264). Bernard Lewis (1993) explains that according to this interpretation of Islam, 'in principle the state was God's state, ruling over God's people; the law was God's law; the army was God's army; and the enemy, of course, was God's enemy' (p. 95). A very limited role was left for the people beyond a prescribed elaboration and curtailed interpretation of the Quran. Maududi's concept of an Islamic state found support among other influential Islamic thinkers and leaders including Qutb in Egypt and Ayatollah Ruhollah Khomeini (d. 1989) in Iran who helped to popularise the vision of an Islamic state among Muslim masses globally and make it a central pillar of Islamism from the late twentieth century (Hassan 2003).

To understand Islamism as a social and political force that swept across the Muslim world in the second half of the twentieth century, one must appreciate the psychological, social, economic and political impact of European colonial occupation on most Muslim-majority countries. European colonial rule left a legacy of anti-Western sentiments, fragmentation of legal codes, inter-religious and inter-ethnic conflict, poverty and underdevelopment, and unrepresentative authoritarian rule. The struggle to reassert an Islamic identity in the sociopolitical context that ensued gave rise to political Islam and the concept of the Islamic state based on implementation of the *shariah*. An enduring perception among many Muslims until today is that European colonial rule attempted to weaken Islam by replacing Islamic identity with Western cultural norms and values (Rane 2010).

Islamists continue to fixate on asserting an Islamic identity and pursuing moralistic policies in order for society to retain or regain its lost glory (Rane 2010). In the latter part of the twentieth century, Islamists formed political parties and attempted to use the democratic process, where possible, to realise their goal of establishing an Islamic state. The rise and success of these parties are seen by many Muslims as completing the process of independence from European colonial rule as those at the forefront of achieving independence and who came to power in the aftermath were largely seen, in a cultural sense, as an extension of the former colonial rulers. For many Muslims, the process of independence would not be complete until the election of Islamic parties that reflect the identity and values of the people (Juergensmeyer 2009). However, with few exceptions, such as Turkey's Justice and Development Party, Islam and democracy have not successfully coexisted. Islamic political parties have been suppressed by the authoritarian regimes they sought to replace or were otherwise unsuccessful in their appeal to a sufficiently broad electorate for them to be a viable alternative (Rane 2010). Moreover, democracy continued to be opposed by many Islamists, particularly those at the more extreme end of the political spectrum.

For those who adopt violent extremist interpretations of Islam, democracy is viewed as a form of *shirkh* (idolatry). For instance, al-Qaeda leader Ayman al-Zawahiri considers democracy a false religion that must be destroyed because God is the only source of legislation, not human beings. From his perspective, democracy allows human beings to legislate and thereby set themselves in the place of God. Emerging from prison in 1984, al-Zawahiri condemned the Egyptian Muslim Brotherhood as *kuffar* (infidels) for their attempts to participate in the political process of the country, an act he regarded as 'sacrificing Allah's authority by accepting the notion that the people are the ultimate source of authority' (Rabasa and Benard 2015, p. 27). More recently, Jürgen Todenhöfer, the first Western journalist to be allowed extensive access to Islamic State in Iraq and Syria (ISIS) within territories they control in Iraq and Syria, reported upon his return that ISIS fighters believe that 'all religions who agree with democracy have to die' (Withnall 2014).

In the West

Islamist extremism is supported by a small minority of Muslims residing in Muslim-majority countries and even fewer among Muslims in the West. However, a growing concern in Western countries is the radicalisation of young Muslims. According to Rabasa and Benard (2015), feelings of disaffection and a search for identity create an opening for radical ideas. Often answers are found within radical Salafism, which offers an alternative identity based on the idea of a global Muslim identity in which the disaffected Muslim finds a new identity and sense of belonging in 'an imagined worldwide Muslim community' (p. 192). Central to the appeal of the Salafist ideology is the sense of grievance that is evoked in relation to the suffering of Muslims around the world directly due to the policies of Western governments or indirectly due to un-Islamic Muslim rulers who they support. This sense of grievance is generally not a consequence of personal experience but 'fostered by the narratives of Muslim oppression' (p. 192).

Only a very small minority of Muslims in the West could be classified as violent extremists. Within Europe, for instance, the subgroups in which most radicalisation occurs are second- and third-generation British Muslims of Pakistani ancestry, first- or second-generation North African Muslims on continental Europe and converts to Islam. Converts to Islam seem to be vulnerable to radicalisation as they are often from lower socioeconomic backgrounds and not well educated. Their conversion experience, particularly the ideological groups through which conversion occurs, seems to be an important factor. However, other factors – namely, a record of criminality – tend to be much stronger predictors of radicalisation (Rabasa and Benard 2015).

Many Muslims in the West may be functionally integrated in terms of language proficiency; primary, secondary and even tertiary education; obedience to the law;

and political participation, while many are not well integrated in a sociocultural sense in terms of their dress; social networks; participation in mainstream cultural events; and identification with mainstream norms and values. However, this integration deficit correlates weakly with the risk of radicalisation (Rabasa and Benard 2015). A lack of integration refers to inadequate levels of social, economic and political participation, unemployment, criminality and various other social issues. Among Muslims in the West, it is largely a separate problem that does not generally correlate or has only an indirect relationship with radicalisation. However, to the extent that narratives associated with radicalisation are imbedded within particular Muslim communities, the relevance of integration deficits to the phenomenon of radicalisation increases. Rabasa and Benard (2015) identify three separate phenomena among European Muslim communities and radicalisation: 1) integration of Muslim communities into European societies; 2) radicalisation of sectors within these communities and 3) the recruitment of radicalised Muslims into extremist and terrorist groups.

Those Muslims in the West who come to engage in jihadist violence tend to be those who on the surface appear to be functionally, and to a fair extent culturally, integrated. They are often Western-born and educated or spent their formative years growing up in a Western country, they fluently speak the language of their country and are generally consumers of Western cultural commodities. However, there is a strong tendency among radicalised Western Muslims to be unskilled, unemployed or underemployed (Rabasa and Benard 2015). Studies that profile dozens of Muslim terrorism suspects in Europe (Rabasa and Benard 2015) and Australia (Bergin *et al.* 2015) show that while some commence a college or university diploma or degree, many drop out and do not obtain post-secondary school qualifications. Moreover, it is noteworthy that none of the suspects listed possess a humanities or social science degree. Those with tertiary qualifications tend to be trained in information technology, business, finance, engineering and science. Islamist extremists are most often socially integrated according to socio-economic indicators but psychologically alienated to the point of being hostile towards the country in which they live and its people. A humanities or social science education may allow young Muslims to better understand history, society, religion and international relations, which may enable them to not only resist and reject Islamist ideology and narratives but to develop counter-narratives and a Western Muslim identity for the benefit of their community and relations with the wider society. Undertaking tertiary education in the humanities and social sciences may enable Western Muslims to find solutions to problems within their own communities. Herein may be an important, yet currently unexplored, topic of research.

It should be acknowledged, however, that most 'education' about Islam currently occurs outside of formal institutions such as schools, universities and even mosques. Social media and other forms of Internet-based communication have been embraced by Muslims globally and used widely for exchanging social, political and religious ideas (Rane and Salem 2012). As such, social media and the Internet in general are playing a central role in the manifestation of Islam and Muslim identities in the twenty-first century. Islamist extremists have been particularly astute in their use of such technologies as tools for the dissemination of information, communication with supporters and opposition, and the recruitment of new members. Rabasa and Benard (2015, p. 193) observe that

> although there is no question that the Internet plays an increasingly important role in disseminating radical Islamist narratives, the transition from radicalisation to terrorism almost always takes place in face-to-face encounters and very seldom on the Internet, although first contact may be online.

Ostensibly non-violent groups, such as the Tablighi Jamaat, often act as a gateway to extremist violence due to the ideas that such groups propagate, including disrespect of non-Muslims and Western society, emphasis on proselytising and zeal for martyrdom. Other ostensibly non-violent Islamist groups like Hizbut Tahrir potentially act as a conveyer belt to extremist violence through their rejection of Western systems and institutions, opposition to integration and advocacy for a caliphate. The appeal and importance of groups with more conservative interpretations of Islam is their perceived credibility among Muslims. Western governments have tended to view such groups as appropriate representatives and spokespeople for Muslim communities (Rabasa and Benard 2015). However, such groups share the narratives and propagate the ideas of Islamist extremists. Understanding the pervasiveness of these narratives and the prominence of conservative, albeit non-violent, groups in their propagation is a crucial element in the communications strategy for combatting Islamist extremism. It is first necessary to examine the narratives used by Islamist extremists.

Islamist narratives

The term narrative is often used interchangeably with story. A story is 'a particular sequence of related events that are situated in the past and recounted for rhetorical/ideological purposes' (Halverson *et al.* 2011, p. 13). A narrative is

> a coherent system of interrelated and sequentially organised stories that share a common rhetorical desire to resolve a conflict by establishing audience expectations according to the known trajectories of its literary and rhetorical form.
>
> (Halverson *et al.* 2011, p. 14)

Narratives are utilised by both violent jihadists such as al-Qaeda as well as non-violent Islamist groups like the Tablighi Jamaat. They are compelling for many Muslims because

> they possess an internal coherence for the audiences that connects them to grand, deeply culturally embedded, views of history – to master narratives – that Muslim audiences, in broad terms, readily understand, identity with, or feel little need to question.
>
> (Halverson *et al.* 2011, p. 13)

A master narrative is 'a transhistorical narrative that is deeply embedded in a particular culture' (Halverson *et al.* 2011, p. 14).

Halverson *et al.* (2011) identify several master narratives derived from the Quran that exist within Muslim cultures and are utilised by Islamist extremists in direct relation to their political goals. These master narratives include 1) the pharaoh, an arrogant tyrant who refuses to submit to the will of God; 2) *jahiliyya*, a reference to a society or state characterised by ignorance of God's will, injustice and vice; 3) the battle of Badr, a military victory of a smaller, poorly equipped Muslim force over a larger, military-superior infidel force; 4) hypocrites, those who outwardly profess to be Muslims but secretly seek to undermine the Islamic state; 5) the battle of Khaybar, which relates to non-Muslim religious minorities who commit treachery against the Islamic state through violation of their covenant; 6) the battle of Karbala, which highlights the wickedness of corrupt regimes and the honour of dying rather than living under them; 7) the Mahdi, the foretold great leader of true Muslims who will appear at the end of time to bring an era of justice; 8) Crusaders, infidel invaders who occupy Muslim lands and must be repelled; 9) the year 1924 when the Ottoman caliphate was abolished and replaced with a secular republic, thereby undermining Islam; 10) *Nakba* or catastrophe for Palestinians and the Muslim world as the state of Israel was imposed over the lands of Palestine, which must ultimately be rectified by the defeat of the Jews and 11) seventy-two virgins, the reward of those who sacrifice themselves through militant jihad.

These master narratives assist Muslims in making sense of events, connecting new to existing information, justifying actions and orienting action towards future goals (Halverson *et al.* 2011). For example, the crusader master narrative 'explains' the presence of US forces in Iraq or Afghanistan in terms of an invasion that is part of a war on Islam that must be resisted. The death and destruction rained down by US forces is to conquer Muslims and undermine Islam with the imposition of Western ideas, institutions and infrastructure. The invaders must be repelled by any means and an 'Islamic' order must be upheld. Those who oppose this vision are collaborators or hypocrites and should be targeted with violence. By extension, the citizens of the invading countries are seen as complicit and also legitimate targets.

It should be noted that ideology rather than religion *per se* is central to jihadist and radical Islamist movements. While Islam is concerned with matters of life and afterlife in relation to an almighty deity, Islamist ideology is much more a system of ideas concerning the propagation of a particular political vision. Master narratives serve important ideological functions, which 'exist in Muslim societies and cultures' but have been 'exploited and employed specifically by Islamic extremists' (Halverson *et al.* 2011, p. 1). As such, to the extent that the Islamist extremist ideology can be countered and discredited, jihadist movements can be undermined by an inability to recruit and maintain bases of support. Two core elements of this ideology are 1) the authority of the Quran and Sunnah (way of the Prophet Muhammad) over all other sources of Islam as perceived to be practiced by the Prophet Muhammad and his companions and 2) a view of *tawhid* (Islamic monotheism) in political terms whereby the legitimacy of state and society rests on the implementation of *shariah*, which is perceived to be a divine law. From these ideas develop a view of ideal Muslims as members of a global community or *ummah* and a global polity called the caliphate (Rabasa and Benard 2015). In this way, Islamists in general and Salafists in particular are able to construct a theoretical alternative to a modernity based on Western values and institutions.

Counter-narratives

Halverson *et al.* (2011) propose five strategic principles for countering the narratives of Islamist extremism:

1 *Avoiding reinforcement*, which is largely a matter for Western governments involving prevention of mistakes that provide Islamist extremists with 'proof' that affirms their narratives. For instance, the crusader narrative was significantly reinforced when the United States' response to 9/11 was referred to as a 'crusade' by George Bush in 2001, when Western soldiers were identified wearing patches that read 'pork eating crusaders', and when Biblical reference were found on gun sights used by Western forces (Halverson *et al.* 2011, p. 196–97).
2 *Contesting analogies* that are made between historical and contemporary events by either invalidating the analogy or replacing it with a new one. For instance, the analogy drawn between the eleventh century crusades and the twenty-first century US invasion of Afghanistan and Iraq could be invalidated by noting that the latter cannot be a holy war against Islam given that the Muslim world overwhelmingly rejected the Taliban's extremist interpretation of Islam and opposed the tyrannical rule of Saddam Hussain.
3 *Decompressing time* involves disrupting the links that Islamist extremists attempt to construct with an idealised past. An effective response in the case of Salafists, for instance, who claim to practice Islam according to the authentic teachings of the Prophet and his companions, is to point out the similarities between Salafism and the Kharajites, a sect that literally invented violent Islamist extremism and assassinated the fourth Rashidun Caliph Ali bin Abi Talib in 661.
4 *Deconstructing binaries* involves countering perceptions of 'us and them' and 'good versus evil'. One response might be to highlight that tens of millions of Muslims are now citizens of various Western countries where their right to freely practice Islam is respected and that a majority of non-Muslim citizens in Western countries opposed the invasions of Afghanistan and Iraq and continue to support Palestinian human rights and statehood (Han and Rane 2013).
5 *Recasting archetypes* involves putting a spotlight on the credentials, actions and consequences of Islamist extremist leaders. This involves questioning

whether such leaders are qualified to make religious declarations and whether the outcomes are actually consistent with Islam's higher objectives (Rane 2009).

Essentially, the ideology of Islamist extremism and the narratives that support it are political. It is necessary to construct an overarching counter-narrative or, rather, a metanarrative of political secularism in Islam according to which Islam is separated from politics. It is difficult to overstate the complexity of this challenge. Many Muslims hear anti-religion or anti-Islam when the word secularism is mentioned and shun the concept. For instance, following the fall of Hosni Mubarak in 2011, Turkey's then Prime Minister Recep Tayyip Erdogan visited Egypt and received a hero's welcome from its people. However, members of the Egyptian Muslim Brotherhood rejected Erodgan's suggestion to consider secularism as part of an inclusive political system. Representatives of the Muslim Brotherhood stated, 'we welcome Turkey and we welcome Erdogan as a prominent leader, but we do not think he or his country alone should be leading the region or drawing up its future' (Yezdani 2011). Erdogan's explanation that 'secularism doesn't mean a lack of religion but creating respect for all religions and religious freedoms for all people' was not acceptable to Egypt's Islamists. Former deputy leader of the Freedom and Justice Party Essam El-Erian stated in response that secularism has 'a very bad perception among Egyptians' and 'we have no need for this term' (Champion and Bradley 2011). Although various Tunisian political leaders also endorsed the so-called Turkish model of balancing Islam and democracy (Rane and Minogue 2013), they too find Turkey's secularism a bridge too far. Former Tunisian Foreign Minister Rafik Abdessalem Bouchlaka acknowledged the Turkish model's appeal insofar as it demonstrates that Islam and democracy can coexist, but he conceded that a different interpretation of secularism from Turkey's would be needed in Tunisia as his country strongly values its Arab, Muslim identity (No author 2012).

The case for secularism in Islam

There is a sound case for secularism in Islam based on both historical and scriptural sources. Ira Lapidus (1975) explains that in the Muslim world, 'religious and political life developed distinct spheres of experience, with independent values, leaders, and organisations' (p. 364). The end of the *Rashidun* period in 661 effectively marked the collapse of unified political and religious leadership in the Muslim world. The *Rashidun* caliphs were replaced by the Umayyads who ruled in a largely secular capacity from Damascus, relatively far from the religious centres of Mecca and Medina. Moreover, within these holy cities developed a new elite of religious scholars who formed an alternative leadership and a check on the political power of the caliph (Feldman 2008). As Lapidus writes, the 'religious communities developed independently of the states or empires that ruled them', and the people looked to the religious scholars or *ulema* 'for guidance on how to live a proper Muslim life' (p. 364).

The religious schools that produced the *ulema*

> gave advice in matters of family law – marriage, divorces, inheritance, and so on. They regulated certain aspects of commercial life, administered educational institutions and the properties endowed for their support, distributed charitable funds, provided legal services, and settled disputes.
>
> (Lapidus 1975, p. 364)

In short, the Islamic religious schools performed many of the same functions as their Christian counterparts in Europe and elsewhere although they were organised differently. The key factor, however, in the context of this discussion, is that these 'religious organisations, institutions, personnel and activities were clearly separate from the ruling regimes' (p. 365).

Since the eleventh century until today, however, Islamist political thought has declared the caliphate to be the 'Islamic' system of government. In the modern era, this notion acquired further credibility with the Ottoman sultan Abdul Hamid II (d. 1909) declaring himself caliph and universal leader of all Muslims (Ali 2009). The system of caliphate was defended by religious scholars such as Rashid Rida (d. 1935), who in 1923 wrote *al-Khilafah al-Uzhmah* (*The Grand Caliphate*) claiming that the Quran and Sunnah affirm the caliphate as an obligatory system for Muslims (Ali 2009). In spite of the abolition of the Ottoman caliphate in 1924 by the Republic of Turkey, the caliphate has continued to be an aspiration for Muslims across the globe. In fact, a poll conducted in 2007 by World Public Opinion found that 65 per cent of Muslims globally support the goal 'to unify all Islamic countries into a single Islamic state or caliphate' (Kull 2007). Muslim groups including Hizbut Tahrir, al-Qaeda and ISIS have made the establishment of a caliphate their expressed aim. However, when ISIS leader Abu Bakr al-Baghdadi declared himself caliph in mid-2014, his caliphate was met with rebuke from other Muslim leaders and Islamic scholars who considered it deviant and invalid (Mandhai 2014). It should be noted that this opposition was directed at al-Baghdadi and his group and not the institution of the caliphate.

The most distinguished voice of opposition to the caliphate is the seminal work of Ali Abd al-Raziq (d. 1966), *Al-Islam wa Usul al-Hukm: Bahth fi al-Khalifah wa al- Hukumah fi al-Islam* (*Islam and the Foundations of Rule: Research on the Caliphate and Government in Islam*), written in 1925. Al-Raziq presents a compelling argument that the caliphate is a human innovation rather than a religious imperative. His work is particularly important due to his education and position at the time of his writing as well as the methodology he employed. Al-Raziq was a student of the renowned Islamic scholar Muhammad Abduh (d. 1905) and a graduate of Egypt's prestigious Al-Azhar University. He held the rank of *alim* (Islamic scholar) and was a member of the institution's Supreme Council of Ulama (Islamic scholars). Al-Raziq constructed his case for political secularism in Islam based on in-depth analysis of Islamic sources, including the Quran, Hadith, sira (biography of Prophet Muhammad), classical works of Islamic political thought and Islamic history.

Al-Raziq determined that neither the Quran nor the Prophet Muhammad articulated a specific form of government, which is reinforced by the fact that Muslims have adopted various approaches to leadership and succession and various forms of government over the centuries. He observes that the Quranic verses and prophetic traditions that are quoted in support of the caliphate institution, such as 4:59, are ambiguous, imprecise, taken out of context and do not qualify as evidence from a scholarly standpoint. He explains that this particular verse, although extensively quoted by classical scholars in support of the caliphate, has 'a much wider and general meaning than the caliphate in the context these scholars mention, and that such a meaning is quite contrary to the other and has almost no relation to it' (Ali 2009, p. 34). In respect to his claim that the Quran and the Prophetic traditions offer no support or evidence for an 'Islamic' political institution called a caliphate, al-Raziq states the following:

> If there were one single evidence in the Quran, these scholars would have never hesitated to refer to it and praise it. Or even if there were in the Noble Book what resembled an evidence for *wujub al-Imamah*, someone among the supporters of *Khilafah* would have tried to turn any such resemblance into evidence. However, the fair scholars failed to find *hujah* or evidence in favour of their opinion in God's Book. Thus they left the Book and went to find evidence in the claim of *Ijma'* [consensus among legal scholars or jurists] at times, and *Qiyas* (reasoning by way of analogy), at other times.
> (cited in Ali 2009, p. 73)

Moreover, as far as Sunni Islam is concerned, 'there was no universally accepted doctrine of the caliphate – evidenced by the fact that such an assumption finds little support in the writings of Muslim jurists and scholars on the subject' (Ali 2009, p. 22).

Al-Raziq's argument for the separation of Islam and politics directly contradicts the concept of *al-Hakimiyyah li Allah* (sovereignty belongs to God) popularised by Maududi and Qutb, which is central to Islamist political thought. The central point of al-Raziq's findings is that Islam is a religion concerned with spiritual matters and not with politics and government; the Prophet Muhammad was a religious not a political leader. The Prophet's roles as arbiter of disputes, military commander and community leader were incidental to his role as God's messenger. His mission was 'to found a religion, not a state' (Ali 2009, p. 8). Al-Raziq's repeated assertion is that 'Islam is a religion, not a state; a message, not a government' (Ali 2009, p. 70). Although the Prophet led armies and appointed military commanders, al-Raziq explains that jihad during Muhammad's time was for the protection of the Muslim community and expansion of the Islamic religion, not to establish a state. In support of this point, al-Raziq quotes extensively from the Quran verses in which God informs Muhammad 'we have not sent thee to watch over them' (4:80), 'say: "not mine is the responsibility for arranging your affairs"' (6:66–67), 'say ... "I am not sent over you to arrange your affairs"' (10:108), 'nor art thou set a custodian over them' (39:41) and 'We have not sent thee as a guard over them; thy duty is but to convey' (42:48). Al-Raziq argues that these and other similar verses 'makes it crystal clear that the Prophet Muhammad did not have any rights over his *ummah*, apart from the right to proclaim the spiritual message' (Ali 2009, p. 78).

Al-Raziq further claims that 'the caliphate was a disaster for Islam and Muslims, a source of tyranny and corruption which the religion of Islam and our world are better off without' (Ali 2009, p. 71). Although Muslims past and present look to the *Rashidun* era (632–61) with nostalgia as the ideal model for the institution of caliphate, al-Raziq contends that not only was their caliphate without religious legitimacy as it was not endorsed by the Quran and the Prophet did not appoint a successor, it was a political institution 'which laypeople assumed [incorrectly] was religious' (Ali 2009, p. 82). In contrast to the Prophet Muhammad whose mission was to convey a religious message, the caliphate – which began with Abu Bakr (d. 634) – was a political enterprise that established 'an Arab state based on a religious call, a state that had a marked, undeniable influence in the transformation and development of Islam' (Ali 2009, p. 80).

Abu Bakr's caliphate was marked by the so-called 'wars of apostasy' (*ridda*) against those who were supposedly *murtaddun* (apostates) for not accepting his political authority, which was construed as a renouncement of Islam (Ali 2009, p. 81). Al-Raziq explains that as Abu Bakr assumed the title of *Khalifat Rasul Allah* (successor to God's messenger), subsequent generations of Muslims would 'erroneously believe that the *khilafah* [caliphate] was a religious seat, and whoever was in charge of Muslims affairs necessarily occupied the same seat of power as the prophet, who received his revelation from God' (Ali 2009, p. 83). Furthermore, 'this attitude was deliberately used to make people believe that obedience to caliphs, imams, and sultans is part of obedience to God and, by implication, disobedience to them is disobedience to God' (Ali 2009, p. 83).

Unfortunately, such thinking has had a detrimental impact on the Muslim world. The modern conventional interpretation of Islam as all-encompassing dulled the mental faculties of Muslims, resulting in them becoming 'unable to see beyond religion in what should be matters of pure administration and politics' (Ali 2009, p. 83). Moreover, their understanding of religion became limited and devoid of appreciation for the essence of Islam, contends al-Raziq. In sum, 'Islam is a code of disciplinary and religious precepts binding upon the individual conscience without any relation to power or politics' (Ali 2009, p. 86). Al-Raziq argues that Islam neither endorsed nor denied the various political institutions that humans have developed; rather 'it has been left for people to decide how to use their minds, other nations' experiences, and the principles and fundamentals of politics in organising their governments' (Ali 2009, p. 84).

Contemporary studies of the Muslim world have found no positive correlation between a more full or comprehensive implementation of *shariah* and progress towards a more just and equitable social order in terms of human, gender and minority rights; political participation and stability; good governance and government accountability and transparency; economic advancement; equitable distribution of wealth; educational attainment; and national power (Fuller 2004).

This point has been reaffirmed by Scheherazade and Askari (2010). Applying an Islamicity Index, which measures a country's adherence to Islamic principles using four sub-indices related to economic, legal and governance, human and political rights and international relations, the authors found so-called Islamic countries to rate poorly against all measures. Given these findings, it is unsurprising that Muslims vote for Islamist parties to a much lesser extent than most observers would expect. Research by Kurzman and Naqvi (2010) finds that over the past generation, Islamist political parties have attracted a median of less than 8 per cent of the vote when they have participated in elections. Most notably, they tended to do better in the Arab countries and under conditions where the political environment is less free. Under such conditions, Islamist political parties have won a median of 15 per cent of the vote. However, the authors contend that in those Muslim-majority countries where elections were freest, Islamist parties performed worse (Kurzman and Naqvi 2010).

Over time, Islamist political parties have been less successful and consequently have had to evolve from ideologically oriented to policy oriented parties in order to survive. They have had to abandon slogans calling for *shariah* and an Islamic state, and develop policies concerning economic growth and development, employment, education, housing and social services (Rane 2010). Moreover, a number of experienced Islamic political leaders have gone further and constructed Islamic discourses in support of secularism. Malaysia's Anwar Ibrahim, for instance, draws on the concept of *maqasid al-shariah* (higher objectives of the *shariah*) to articulate his vision as follows:

> [T]he *maqasid al-shariah* (higher objectives of the *shariah*) sanctify the preservation of religion, life, intellect, family, and wealth, objectives that bear striking resemblance to Lockean ideals that would be expounded centuries later. Many scholars have further explained that laws which contravene the *maqasid* must be revised or amended to bring them into line with the higher objectives and to ensure that they contribute to the safety and development of the individual and society. Notwithstanding the current malaise of authoritarianism plaguing the Muslim world, there can be no question that several crucial elements of constitutional democracy and civil society are also moral imperatives in Islam – freedom of conscience, freedom of expression, and the sanctity of life and property – as demonstrated very clearly by the Koran, as well as by the teachings of the Prophet Muhammad.
>
> (Ibrahim 2006, p. 7)

In the aftermath of the uprisings in Tunisia, the leader of the En-Nahda Party, Rachid Ghanouchi (2012), delivered a speech at a forum hosted by the Centre for the Study of Islam and Democracy (CSID), in which he made a case for the place of secularism within an Islamic worldview:

> The greater part of the debate taking place nowadays in our country is a misunderstanding of such concepts as secularism and Islam. . . . secularism

is not an atheist philosophy but merely a set of procedural arrangements designed to safeguard the freedom of belief and thought.

Ghanouchi explained that within the legal tradition of Islam, there is acknowledgement of the distinctions between or separation of the civil (*mu'amalat*) and the religious (*ibadat*) in terms of human action and interaction. He added to this point that:

> It is not the duty of religion to teach us agricultural, industrial or even governing techniques, because reason is qualified to reach these truths through the accumulation of experiences. The role of religion, however, is to answer the big question for us, those relating to our existence, origins, destiny, and the purpose for which we were created, and to provide us with a system of values and principles that would guide our thinking, behaviour, and the regulations of the state to which we aspire.

In reconciling Islam and secularism, Ghanouchi draws on the *maqasid* (higher objectives of Islam), referring specifically to its historical and contemporary founders:

> This distinction between the religious and the political is also clear in the thought of Islamic scholars/jurists. They have distinguished between the system of transactions/dealings (*mu'amalat*) and that of worship (*ibadat*). Whereas the latter is the domain of constancy and observance i.e. reason cannot reach the truth, the former is the domain of searching for the general interest, for Islam came to realize people's interests as confirmed by such great jurists as Al-Shatibi and Ibn Ashur. These scholars have agreed that the highest objective of all divine messages is to establish justice and realize people's interests, and this is done through the use of reason in light of the guidelines, objectives, values, and principles provided by religion. Thus, there is a domain of transactions/dealings which is constantly evolving and represents the sphere of variables, and there is the domain of creed, values, and virtues which represents the sphere of constants.

At the time of writing, two trends at opposite ends of the Muslim world's political spectrum can be observed. At one end, jihadist groups in the MENA region, East Africa and South Asia, including ISIS, al-Shabaab and the Taliban are implementing punitive *shariah* laws, declaring Islamic states and a return of the caliphate. At the other end are Islamic political leaders and intellectuals, including those discussed above, who are attempting to disentangle Islam from politics and present a case for political secularism as part of the process of establishing genuine democracies in the Muslim world. The importance of these efforts should not be understated. As Olivier Roy (2004) explains, such endeavours in the Muslim world to separate religion from politics are 'to save Islam from politics' rather than in the case of Western secularisation where the process was to 'save politics from religion' (p. 91). Political secularism in Islam will have to compete directly with the prevailing ideas and narratives of Islamist extremism within the arena of Internet-based communications technology. Convincing the Muslim masses will depend on an effective communications strategy, which this chapter will now discuss.

Strategic Communication

Strategic communication intends 'to persuade an audience to support one or more specific goals' (Halverson *et al.* 2011, p. 179). Its effectiveness requires that those on the receiving end are the main focus. Message recipients are not passive and will not necessarily interpret a message in the same way the sender of the message intended. A range of human factors, including gender, age, culture, identity, religion, education, socio-economic conditions and life experiences in general, make reception of a message an active process. Contemporary scholars of communication understand the communication process to be 'audience based, culturally dependent, and meaning-centred' as well as being constantly connected to 'the ongoing narrative stream that informs, surrounds and constitutes' messages (Goodall *et al.* 2008, p. 6). As it is the receiver of a message who is ultimately the one who makes sense of it, effective human communication depends on a deep understanding of the recipient's culture and how facts will be interpreted based on cultural narratives (Goodall *et al.* 2008).

Corman and Schiefelbein (2008) identify three key goals of Islamist extremists: legitimation, propagation and intimidation. Because Islamist extremists engage in actions such as terrorism, which the overwhelming population of Muslims as well as Islamic scholars regard as un-Islamic, there is an ongoing need for them to legitimise their movement. Causing harm to innocent people harms their legitimacy. Their communication strategies must, therefore, be directed towards emphasising the ends over the means, portraying the enemy's violence to be more unjustified, and reclassifying victims to deprive them of their innocence. As the legitimacy they require is not only social but also religious, Islamist extremists must resort to reinterpretation of religious texts as well as historical and contemporary events in order to sustain their cause.

Islamist extremist movements are expansionist in nature and seek dominance. As such, they require a base of social and community support and must propagate their message among people who reside in places into which they want to expand. In response to opponents both outside of and from within their own faith group, they use intimidation as a means by which to bolster their position and inhibit dissention. A complementary perspective is proposed by Halverson *et al.* (2011), who identify that the main strategic goals of Islamist extremists are to: 1) resist by fighting foreign invaders and those who seek to undermine Islam from without and within; 2) rebuke so-called apostate Muslim rulers who are complicit in the policies and actions of perceived enemies of Islam and 3) renew Islamic civilisation by reversing the decline through the reestablishment of the caliphate and reconstitution of *shariah*.

With these strategic communication goals of Islamists in mind, an effective counter strategy can be devised. This entails effectively communicating information that undermines the legitimacy that Islamist extremists seek to establish and maintain. In respect to the use of violence against innocent civilians, this should begin with a contextualised and objective-oriented methodology and involve reiteration of Quranic verses that prohibit unlawful killing, emphasise peaceful relations between people and speak to the harmony that characterised early Muslim engagement with non-Muslims. In my earlier work, *Reconstructing Jihad amid Competing International Norms*, I present a detailed account and analysis of the Quranic verses pertaining to war and peace (Rane 2009). Similarly, in response to proclamations of an Islamic state or caliphate, it should be emphasised that the Quran and the prophetic traditions contain no prescription for a particular political model or form of government. Numerous Quranic verses make clear that Muhammad was a prophet whose mission was to deliver a religious message and not a political ruler tasked with establishing a government or state. Moreover, it should be highlighted that the early Muslims who established the caliphate did so not in reference to the Quran or prophetic traditions but on an ad hoc basis according to their particular circumstances, prevailing norms and political aspirations.

A critical aspect of strategic communication concerns the legitimacy of those individuals and groups who advocate particular narratives and those who present counter-narratives. Various communities, groups, stakeholders and entities may have the capacity to confer legitimacy. The government is one such entity. Certain Western governments have taken the view that more conservative groups and individuals are likely to have more credibility with vulnerable Muslim youth than more liberal Muslims in respect to preventing them from engaging in extremist violence. However, because there is a relatively thin line between the ideology of conservative groups such as violent Salafists and the ostensibly non-violent Tablighi Jamaat, for instance, and that the ideas of such groups provide fertile ground from which radicalism often grows, there are rising concerns over working with such groups. Rabasa and Benard (2015) explain that

> although working with Islamist organisations might produce results in the short run, over the long term, it legitimises Islamists as spokesmen for the European Muslim communities and abets their efforts to create parallel societies separate from the broader national community. (p. 180)

The authors add that 'the British government, for instance, has now refused to work with organisations that oppose values of universal human rights, equality before the law, democracy, and full participation in society' (p. 173).

Rather, the preference is to work with Muslim organisations that support 'Western values and institutions and believe that Muslims need to become full members of European societies and of Western modernity' (p. 180). This strategic shift has been informed by research showing that the threat posed by radical Islam to the stability of Western societies is greater than that of terrorism itself (Rabasa and Benard 2015). As such, radical ideologies must be addressed in the first

Conclusion

Islamist extremism is an ideology that relies on a number of master narratives that not only transcend time and place but connect highly diverse, global Muslim populations. Their potency must be understood within the context of a modern world in which Muslims are acutely aware of the dominance of Western civilisation as well as the social, economic and political failings of most Muslim-majority countries. The master narratives utilised by Islamist extremists serve their political goals and because they assist Muslims in making sense of complex, often tragic events and provide them with an outlook for the future in which Muslims are ultimately victorious. They are central to the legitimacy and credibility of such groups. Countering such narratives is key to combatting Islamist extremism. Constructing an effective counter-narrative requires strategic communication. This must be oriented towards Muslim communities on which Islamist extremists rely for support and from which they derive their legitimacy. Taking all of these factors into account, the most effective response to Islamist extremism is to depoliticise Islam. This chapter has shown that based on religious and historical sources, a metanarrative of political secularism in Islam is not only possible but has been credibly argued by eminent Islamic scholars and leaders past and present. Freedom from politics would not only deprive Islamist extremists of their *raison d'etre* but would allow Muslims to rediscover the true essence of their faith. Such a development would have profoundly positive implications for Islam–West relations.

References

Ahmad, I (2009). *Islamism and Democracy in India: The Transformation of Jamaat-e-Islami*. Princeton, NJ: Princeton University Press.
Ali, S (2009). *A Religion Not a State: Ali Abd al-Raziq's Islamic Justification of Political Secularism*. Salt Lake City, UT: University of Utah Press.
Bergin, A, Clifford, M, Connery, D, Feakin, T, Gleiman, K, Huang, S, Huschison, G, Jennings, P, Lang, D, Long, A, Murphy, C, Roworth, S, Turner, R and Yasmeen, S (2015). Gen Y Jihadists: Preventing Radicalisation in Australia, Australian Strategic Policy Institute. Accessed from: www.aspi.org.au/publications/gen-y-jihadists-preventing-radicalisation-in-australia
Champion, M and Bradley, M (2011). Islamists Criticize Turkish Premier's Secular Remarks. *The Wall Street Journal*, September 15. Accessed from: http://online.wsj.com/article/SB10001424053111904491704576570670264116178.html
Corman, S, Trethewey, A and Goodall, HL (2008). *Weapons of Mass Persuasion: Strategic Communication to Combat Violent Extremism*. New York, NY: Peter Lang.
Corman, S and Schiefelbein, J (2008). Communication and Media Strategy in the Islamist War of Ideas. In Corman, S, Trethewey, A and Goodall, HL (eds), *Weapons of Mass*

Persuasion: Strategic Communication to Combat Violent Extremism. New York, NY: Peter Lang, 69–95.

Feldman, N (2008). *The Fall and Rise of the Islamic State*. Princeton, NJ: Princeton University Press.

Fuller, G (2004). *The Future of Political Islam*. New York, NY: Palgrave Macmillan.

Ghanouchi, R (2012). Secularism and Relation Between Religion and the State from the Perspective of the Nahdha Party. *Lecture at CSID-Tunisia*. 2 March. Accessed from: http://imbdblog.com/?p=1742

Goodall, HL, Trethewey, A and Corman, S (2008). Strategy: Missed Opportunities and the Consequences of Obsolete Strategic Communication Theory. In Corman, S, Trethewey, A and Goodall, HL (eds), *Weapons of Mass Persuasion: Strategic Communication to Combat Violent Extremism*. New York, NY: Peter Lang.

Halverson, J, Goodall, HL and Corman, S (2011). *Master Narratives of Islamist Extremism*. New York, NY: Palgrave Macmillan.

Han, E and Rane, H (2013). *Making Australian Foreign Policy on Israel-Palestine: Media Coverage, Public Opinion and Interest Groups*. Carlton: Melbourne University Press.

Hassan, K (2003). The Influence of Mawdudi's Thought on Muslims in Southeast Asia: A Brief Survey. *The Muslim World*, 93(3–4): 429–64.

Ibrahim, A (2006). Universal Values and Muslim Democracy. *Journal of Democracy*, 17(3): 5–12.

Juergensmeyer, M (2009). *Global rebellion: Religious Challenges to the Secular State, from Christian Militias to Al Qaeda*. Berkeley, CA: University of California Press.

Kurzman, C and Naqvi, I (2010). Do Muslims Vote Islamic? *Journal of Democracy*, 21(2): 50–63.

Lapidus, I (1975). The Separation of State and Religion in the Development of Early Islamic Society. *International Journal of Middle East Studies*, 6(4): 363–85.

Lewis, B (1993). Islam and Liberal Democracy. *The Atlantic*. Accessed from: www.theatlantic.com/magazine/archive/1993/02/islam-and-liberal-democracy/308509/

Maududi, A (1976). The Political Theory of Islam. In Donohue, J and Esposito, J (eds) (2007). *Islam in Transition: Muslim Perspectives*. (2nd edn). New York, NY: Oxford University Press.

Mandhai, S (2014). Muslim Leaders Reject Baghdadi's Caliphate. *Aljazeera Online*, July 7. Accessed from: www.aljazeera.com/news/middleeast/2014/07/muslim-leaders-reject-baghdadi-caliphate-20147744058773906.html

No author (2012). Turkish Democracy Model for Tunisia. *Hurriyet Daily News*, January 12. Accessed from: www.hurriyetdailynews.com/turkish-democracy-model%20fortunisia.aspx?pageID=238&nID=11283&NewsCatID=357

Rabasa, A and Benard, C (2015). *Eurojihad: Patterns of Islamist Radicalisation and Terrorism in Europe*. Cambridge: Cambridge University Press.

Rane, H (2009). *Reconstructing Jihad amid Competing International Norms*. New York, NY: Palgrave Macmillan.

Rane, H (2010). *Islam and Contemporary Civilisation: Evolving Ideas, Transforming Relations*. Carlton: Melbourne University Press.

Rane, H and Minogue, B (2013). Turkey's Role in the Diffusion of Democracy in the MENA Region. *NCEIS Research Papers*, 5(8): 1–28. Accessed from: http://nceis.unimelb.edu.au/__data/assets/pdf_file/0004/718060/Rane_Minogue_Turkish_Model_Paper_1.pdf

Rane, H and Salem, S (2012). Social Media, Social Movements and the Diffusion of Ideas in the Arab Uprisings. *Journal of International Communication*, 18(1): 97–111.

Roy, O (2004). *Globalised Islam: The Search for a New Ummah*. London: Hurst & Co.
Scheherazade, R and Askari, H (2010). How Islamic Are Islamic Countries? *Global Economy Journal*, 10(2): 1–40.
Withnall, A (2014). Inside ISIS: The First Western Journalist Ever Given Access to the 'Islamic State' Has Just Returned – and this Is What He Discovered. *The Independent*, 21 December. Accessed from: www.independent.co.uk/news/world/middle-east/inside-isis-the-first-western-journalist-ever-given-access-to-the-islamic-state-has-just-returned–and-this-is-what-he-discovered-9938438.html
Yezdani, I (2011). Muslim Brotherhood Debates Turkey Model. *Hürriyet Daily News*, September 14. Accessed from: www.hurriyetdailynews.com/default.aspx?pageid=438&n=muslim-brotherhood-debates-turkey-model-2011-09-14

Index

Abduh, M. 176
Abdul Hamid II 176
Abdullah, A. 52
Abrahms, M. 84
Abu Bakr 178
activation 57
Adebolajo, M. 76, 82
Adebowale, M. 76
Afghanistan 2, 14, 151, 174
Africa 65, 82
African Mission to Somalia (AMISOM) 70, 80
agency 110, 120
al-'Adnani, A.M. 50, 57
al-Amriki, A.M. 54, 65, 79
Alawites 50
al-Awlaki, A. 151; charisma 25–6, 28–9, 32, 36–40; electronic jihad 9, 11
al-Baghdadi, A.B. 28, 39, 52, 176
al-Britani, A.A. 54–5
al-Faloja 48
al-Faranci, A.M. 59
al-Furqan 51
al-Golani, A.M. 50
al-Hayat Media 50, 52, 58
alienation 40, 57, 171
Al-Islam wa Usul al-Hukm 176
al-Kata'ib Foundation 54
Al-Khansa 138–9
al-Khilafah al-Uzhmah 176
Allah 29
Al-Lami, M. 118
#AllEyesOnIsis 50
al-Maqdisi, A.M. 30–1
al-Nusra Front 15, 50
Alplatformmedia.com 52

al-Qaeda 2, 49, 81; charismatic preachers 28, 39; counternarratives 149–52, 155, 157; electronic jihad 8–12, 14
al-Qaeda in the Arabian Peninsula (AQAP) 39
al-Qaeda in the Islamic Maghreb (AQIM) 51, 156
al-Qaradawi, Y. 30, 35
al-Qassam brigades 51
al-Raziq, A.A. 176–8
al-Sahab 49, 151
al-Shabaab 15, 54, 65–84, 131
al-Shishani, A.H. 57
al-Shumukh al-Islam 130
al-Somood 49
al-Suri, A-M. 28
al-Tawhid 17
al'Uyayree, Y. 36–7
Aly, A. 5, 106–20
al-Zarqawi, A-M. 28
al-Zawahiri, A. 17–18, 54, 170
al-Zubeir, M.A. 54
analogies 174
Ansar al-Mujahideen 38, 53
Ansaruddin Movement 53
apostasy 178
appeals 91, 93, 96, 100
apps 47, 49, 108
AQ Chef 58
Arabic 36, 132
Archetti, C. 137
archetypes 174
Arizona University 135
Askari, H. 179
Ask.fm 54–5
Asrar Al-Mujahideen 54

Index

Assad, B. 50
Association of Chief of Police Officers (ACPO) 128
audience 69, 71–2, 107–9, 120; as mass/outcome/agent 109–10; research frameworks 111–19
Australia 2–3, 88–9, 96–9, 101–2, 118
authority 29, 36, 108–9
Azawad 53
Azzam, A. 37

backstage 134–5, 139
Bali bombing 49
Bargh, J.A. 112
Begin, A. 52
Benard, C. 170–2, 182
Benbrika trial 88–96, 101–3
Berger, J.M. 138
Bertram, S. 65, 73
Bettison, N. 128
Bilardi, J. 2–3
bin Laden, O. 36
binaries 174
Bipartisan Policy Center 60
Birmingham 116
Black, D. 130
blogs 46, 154
Boko Haram 131
Boston Marathon 56
Bouamama, S.O. 53
Bouchlaka, R.A. 175
Bowie, N. 82
Briggs, R. 149
British Empire 168
Brookings Institution 13
Burke, J. 126
Bush, G. 174

Caliphate 12, 151, 175–8
Call in Iraq and Syria to Global Islamic Resistance 28
camera phones 2
Cameron, D. 74, 153
Canada 9, 15, 28, 79
Capitol building 58
Captivation Phase 116
cell phones 2, 47
Center for Naval Analysis 59

Center for Strategic Counterterrorism Communication (CSCTC) 155–7, 160
Centola, D. 112
Centre for Contemporary Cultural Studies 116
Centre for Social Cohesion 11, 36
Centre for the Study of Islam and Democracy (CSID) 179
Cerantonio, M. 120
Channel 34
charisma 29, 36; *see also* preachers
charity 16
Charlie Hebdo 58, 153
Chechnya 49, 56–7
children 73
civil society 153–5, 179–80
coding 69
Cohen, K. 119
colonialism 168–9
Colorado 45
command and control 79
communication 27–8, 113, 116–17, 154–5, 181–3
communication studies 137–8
comparative research 130–3
composition 68, 72–8
computer science 135, 137–8
Conroy, M. 107
conservatives 182
conspiracy 96–9
constructivist turn 151–2
content 68–9, 78–83, 113; control/deletion 129
CONTEST 152
converts 170
Conway, M. 5–6, 123–41
Cordes, B. 110
Corman, S. 181
Cornell, C.L. 58
Counter Narratives to Interrupt Online Radicalisation (CNOIR) 118–19
Counter Terrorism Internet Referral Unit (CTIRU) 153
Countering Online Radicalization in America 60
Countering online Violent Extremism Research (CoVER) 118
countering violent extremism (CVE) 129

counternarratives 70, 107–8, 149–50, 152, 159–60; legitimacy 182; principles 174–5; UK 152–5; US 155–9
counterterrorism 1, 83–4, 97, 149; social media 59–61; UK 152–3; US 155, 157
Course in the Art of Recruiting 39
Court of Criminal Appeal (CCA) 100
credibility 70, 84, 183
Criminal Code [Australia] 89–90, 96
criminal trials 87–8, 102–4; Benbrika case 88–96; Elomar trial 96–101
crusaders 173–4
culture 134
cyberterrorism 18, 76
Cyberterrorism Project 3
Cyrus, M. 120

Dabiq 39, 54, 139
Dalgaard-Nielsen, A. 25
Dark Web 135–6
data 124, 135–6, 138
DataSift 136
Dauoud, A. 52–3
dawa 34–5
Dawn of Glad Tidings 47, 108
de Goede, M. 101
de Graaf, B. 101
de Poot, C.J. 33
Dearlove, R. 120
decentralisation 108
decodings 116–17
Deep Web 55
deepening research 133–5
democracy 169–70, 175, 179
Denver 45
descriptive research 8, 124
Dhere, S.A. 73
diaspora 115
digital natives 123
Digital Outreach Team [US] 155–6
digitized ummah 10, 37
dis-inhibition effect 127
Dutch National Coordinator for Counterterrorism 26
Duyvesteyn, I. 84

education 170–1, 176
Egypt 168, 170, 175
El-Aroud, M. 139

elections 179
electronic jihad 4, 8–12, 14, 38, 51
El-Erian, E. 175
Ellison, K. 65, 74
Elomar trial 88, 96–103
En-Nahda Party 179
encoding/decoding model 116–17, 120
encryption 54
English 71
entertainment 114
Erdogan, T.R. 175
ethereal audience 111
ethnic-separatism 131, 138
ethnography 134
Europe 157, 169–70
European Union (EU) 131–2, 136
evidence 87–8, 90–4, 98, 100–3
explanatory research 124
extremism: Islamist 167–72, 181–3; right-wing 130

Facebook 1, 46–51
Facebook Invasion 48, 53
FARC 130, 138
fatwas 109
FBI 58
Feve, S. 149
financing 16–17, 93
Fisher, A. 72
flagging 60
Flickr 47, 50
Foreign and Commonwealth Office (FCO) 154
Foreign Relations Authorization Act 158
forums 11, 13–14, 37–8; progressing research 130, 137, 140
France 52–3, 57–8
Frank, M. 119
Frankfurt 45
Freedom and Justice Party 175
French 50, 132, 139
frontstage 135, 139
function 78–9
funding 16–17, 93
funnel 57

Gadahn, A. 49
GCHQ 127
gender 14, 51, 73, 138–40; -switching 140

Gendron, A. 4, 25–41
geography 132
Germany 17, 45, 53, 131
Ghanouchi, R. 179–80
Global Islamic Information Forum 17
Global Islamic Media Front (GIMF) 9–10, 17, 54
GNIP 136
God 169–70
Goffman, I. 135
Google Play 47
governments 182; *see also* states
grassroots activism 126
gratifications 114–16, 118, 120
Gressang, D. 111
gulfup.com 73

Hadfi, B. 1
Hall, S. 111, 116–17
Halverson, J. 173–4, 181
Hamas 130
Hammami, O. 54, 65, 79
Harakat al-Shabaab al-Mujahideen 54
Hardy, K. 5, 87–104
Harman, J. 61
hawalas 16
Hegghammer, T. 134, 137
Hizbollah 130
Hizbut Tahrir 172, 176
Hoffman, B. 13, 29
Hofmann, D. 26, 31
Hofstad 17
Hollande, F. 53
Home Affairs Select Committee 13, 126
Home Office [UK] 154
Homeland Security Project 60
Horn of Africa 83
Hoskins, A. 2
hostage-taking 110
House of Commons [UK] 13, 126
House of Representatives [US] 79
@HSMPress 67
@HSM_Press 68, 70, 72
@HSM_SUPERSTARS 82
humanities 171
Hussain, S. 174

Ibn Tamiyyah 35, 40
Ibrahim, A. 179

idealists 33
identity 114
ideology 80, 173
images 76–7, 95, 98, 100–1
inchoate liability 97
incitement 13–14
India 168
infection 57
infidels 170
influence 112, 120
information 114
Inspire 39, 76, 151; electronic jihad 14–17; progressing research 127–8, 139; social media 49, 54, 56, 58
Instagram 47
integration 114, 171
intelligence 59, 156
interactivity 53–5
interdisciplinary research 136–8
International Centre for the Study of Radicalisation and Political Violence (ICSR) 112, 114
Internet Live Stats 71
Internet penetration 128
Internet Studies 137–8
interpersonal relations 113
interviewing 133
intimidation 181
IRA 130
Iran 125, 169
Iraq 2, 50, 52, 89, 174
Ireland 130–1
ISIS 87, 108, 152; charismatic preachers 28, 35, 39–40; counternarratives 170, 176; electronic jihad 12, 15; lone wolves 57–8; progressing research 123, 131, 134, 136, 138–40; social media 45, 47, 50, 52–5, 60
ISIS Twitter Census 138
Islam: secularism 175–81; tradition 108–9
Islamic Emirate of the Caucasus (IEC) 49
Islamic State (IS) *see* ISIS
Islamicity Index 179
Islamists 167–72, 183; counternarratives 174–5; narratives 172–4; strategic communication 181–3
isolation 32
Israel–Palestine 6, 156, 173–4

Jabhat-al-Nusra 72
Jackson, R. 137
jahiliyya 32, 173
jema'ah 90, 93
Jenkins, B. 69
jihad 35; *see also* electronic jihad
Jihad in Europe 16
Jihad Jane 17
Jihad Umma 51
'jihadi brides' 139, 141
journalists 75, 81
juries 91, 93, 96, 100–1, 103

Karbala 173
Katz, E. 113
Katz, R. 61
Kavkaz Center 49
Kenya 65, 69, 71–4, 77, 79
Keppel, G. 26, 31
Kharajites 174
Khaybar 173
Khomeini, R. 125, 169
Khosrokhavar, F. 33
Kohlmann, E. 45
kuffar 170
Kurdistan Workers' Party (PKK) 130
Kurzman, C. 179

language 36, 71, 132
Lapidus, I. 175
Laqueur, W. 125–6
Latvia 54
law 179; *see also* criminal trials
Lazarsfeld, P.F. 113
leaderless jihad 16, 28, 152
leadership 26–7, 29
legitimacy 70, 181–3
Leung, L. 115
Lewis, B. 27, 169
liability 97
libraries, online 11, 37
limited effects perspective 110
LinkedIn 47
Logan, S. 6, 149–61
logistics 68
London bombings 2, 152
lone wolves 15–16, 55–9, 157
Los Angeles Times 61
Lynch, M. 151

McCants, W. 59, 124
McCarthy era 157
Macdonald, S. 68
McKenna, K.Y. 112
McLuhan, M. 2
Madrid 17
magazines 10, 39, 151
Mahdi 173
Mair, D. 5, 65–84
Maiwandi, A.S. 49
Malaysia 179
Mali 53, 156
maqasid 179–80
marketing 51–2, 109
master narrative 151, 173, 183
Matsumoto, D. 119
Maududi, A.A. 168–9, 177
meanings 114, 116–17, 120
media ecology 2, 118
media needs 115–16
media studies 137
media theory 108–10, 113–14, 120
Melbourne 2, 88, 96
Merah, M. 57
message 107–14, 116–20, 181
methodology 8–9, 66–8; *see also* research
Metro 73
MI5 11, 127
MI6 120
Middle East Research Institute (MEMRI) 54–5, 60
migration 140
Military Studies in the Jihad Against the Tyrants 8
Minnesota 159
Miskimmon, A. 150
MIT 56
mobile phones 2, 47
money laundering 16–17
Morgan, J. 138
Morley, D. 117
Mosul 66
motivations 82–3
Mubarak, H. 175
Muhammad, Prophet 29, 173, 177–8, 182
Mumbai 66
murtaddun 178
Muslim Brotherhood 175
Muslim League 168

Nairobi 65, 79
nakba 173
Naqvi, I. 179
narratives 151, 167, 172–4, 183; *see also* counternarratives
narrowcasting 51–3
National Counterterrorism Coordinating Center (NCTC) 157
National Defense Authorization Act (NDAA) 158
National Intelligence Estimate 157
nationalist-separatism 131, 138
needs 115–16
Netherlands 17
netnography 134
netting 56–7
New People's Army 138
New South Wales Court of Criminal Appeal 100
New South Wales Supreme Court 96, 103
New Terrorism thesis 82, 84
news 2, 80, 83
Northern Ireland 130–1, 153
Norwegian Defence Research Establishment 16
Nouri, L. 153

Obama, B. 155, 157
objectives 69–70, 79–80
Ohio 58
Olsen, M.G. 157
online libraries 11, 37
online materials 95–6, 98–103
Ontario 28
Open Source Jihad 15, 56, 58
Operation Pendennis 88, 90
operations 17
Operative Phase 116
organisation 89–90, 92
Ottomans 176
Oxford University 18

Pakistan 168
Palestine 6, 156, 173–4
Pantucci, R. 79
Paris 1, 17, 58
participant observation 134–5
parties, political 169–70, 179
Patek, U. 49

PATRIOT Act 150
Pauwels, L. 107
Pearlman, L. 65–6, 74, 78
personal identity 114
Pew Internet Project 47
Pew Research Centre 132
phases 116
Pinterest 47
PKK 130
politics 82–4, 167–70, 175–7, 179–82
Post, J. 33
pre-crime 97, 102–3
preachers 4, 11, 25–32, 40–1; demand/supply 32–6; importance of ICT 36–7
Precht, T. 26, 31
prejudice 91, 100, 103
preparation 93–9, 101–2
Prevent 128, 152–4
Price, H.E. 110
propaganda 78, 106
propagation 181
Prophet Muhammad 29, 173, 177–8, 182
proscription 89–90
prosumers 133
Prucha, N. 72
psychological warfare 79, 84
public-private partnerships (PPPs) 61

Quilliam Foundation 34
Quran 169, 173, 176–7, 182
Qutb, S. 168, 177

Rabasa, A. 170–2, 182
Radical Middle Way 154
radicalisation 1, 4–7, 13, 79; audience 106–7, 118–19; charismatic preachers 25–6, 30–6, 39–41; counternarratives 157–8, 167–8, 170–1; progressing research 123, 125–8
radio 71, 111–12
Ragi, A.M. 54
RAND Corporation 33, 83, 106
Rane, H. 6, 167–83
Rapoport, D. 126, 140
Rashidun 175, 178
Reconstructing Jihad amid Competing International Norms 182
recruitment 14–15, 39–41, 79

Regulation of Investigatory Powers Act (RIPA) 150
religion 69, 82–4, 90, 95; politics and 175–8, 180–1
research 124–5; frameworks 111–19; methodology 8–9, 66–8; suggestions for progress 128–40
Research, Information and Communications Unit (RICU) 154–5
Revolutionary Armed Forces of Colombia (FARC) 130, 138
Rida, R. 176
Rigby, L. 76
right, extreme 130
Roy, O. 180
Rudner, M. 4, 8–18
Russia 56

Sageman, M. 16, 106–7, 109, 128
Salafism 34, 40, 168, 170, 174
Saudi Arabia 14
Sayyid, A.R. 79
sceptical views 125–7
Scheherazade, R. 179
Schiefelbein, J. 181
Schils, N. 107
Schmid, A. 82, 151
Scolari, C. 118
Searching Phase 116
secularism 175–81, 183
Seduction Phase 116
self-disclosure 114
Senate [US] 157
shariah 151, 168–9, 174, 178–80
Shi'a 131
shirkh 170
Shumoukh al-Islam 54
Shumukh al-Islam 14
silver bullet theory 106, 113
Smith–Mundt Act 158–9
social integration 114, 171
social isolation 32
social media 4–5, 12, 39, 45–51, 171; audience 108, 112, 114–15; counterterrorism 59–61; interactivity 53–5; lone wolves 55–9; narrowcasting 51–3; progressing research 126, 129, 132–3, 136; *see also* Facebook; Twitter
social science 135, 138, 141, 171

software 135
Somalia 15, 54, 159; Westgate attack 65, 71, 77, 79
Sonnenschein, A. 33
Soufan Group 53
SoundCloud 73
Southern Poverty Law Center (SPLC) 130
Spain 17
State Department [US] 155–8, 160
states 6, 168–9, 177
Stern, J. 106
Stormfront 130, 138
story *see* narratives
Strategic Implementation Plan (SIP) 158
strategy 8, 28, 181–3
suicide missions 111
Sullivan, R. 66
Sunnah 173, 176
Sunnis 177
surveillance 90, 150
susceptibility 34
Swahili 73
Swansea University 3
Sydney 88, 96, 101
Syria 112; counternarratives 152, 155–7; research 139–40; social media 45, 50, 52–5

Tablighi Jamaat 172, 182
Taliban 2–3, 49
Tamil Tigers 138
tawhid 169, 173–4
Tchernev, J.M. 114
television 111–12
terrorism, definitions 89
Terrorism Act [UK] 153
terrorism studies 137–8
Terrorists' Use of the Internet Symposium 3
tertiary education 171
theo-democracy 169
Think Again Turn Away 61, 156
threats 77–8, 80
Todenhöfer, J. 170
Toronto 28
Toulouse 57
training 15–16, 94
translation 36, 132

trials *see* criminal trials
triggers 31
trolling 127
Tsarnaev, D. & T. 56
Tunisia 175, 179
Turkey 169, 175–6
Twenty-Year Strategic Plan 8, 28
Twitter 4–5, 13, 46–7, 49–50, 54–5, 60; audience 112, 120; conversations within 74–6; counternarratives 156; progressing research 126, 133, 136, 138; Westgate attack 65–74, 76–84
two-step model 113

Ubaydah, R.M. 58
UK 13, 34, 88, 150; counternarratives 152–5, 157, 159–60; research 126–8, 133
Uka, A. 45
ulema 29, 168, 175–6
Umayyads 175
ummah 10, 27, 37
Understanding Terrorism in the Age of Global Media 137
upscaling research 135–6
US 1, 39, 79; counternarratives 150–1, 155–60, 173–4; social media 47, 55, 58–61
US Institute of Peace 12
uses and gratifications model 114–16, 118, 120

victimization 30
Victorian Supreme Court 91–2, 103

videos 91, 93, 95, 100, 103
Vimeo 46
Von Behr, I. 133
von Knop, K. 115–16, 118
VOX-Pol 136

Wadoud, A. 52–3
Wang, Z. 114–15
war on terror 1–2, 154
wars of apostasy 178
wave theory 126
Weber, M. 26, 29
Weimann, G. 4–5, 12, 45–61, 109, 115–16, 118
West 151; al-Shabaab 72, 81–2; charismatic preachers 27, 30; counternarratives 168, 170–2, 182–3
Westgate attack 5, 65–6, 83–4; intended audience 71–2; research methodology 66–71; tweet composition 72–8; tweet content 78–83
WhatsApp 54
Whealy J. 97, 99–100
white supremacists 112
Whiting, A. 153
widening research 129–31, 139
Wilson Center 61
women 14, 51, 73, 138–40

Yemen 156
YouTube 30, 39, 45, 140, 151

Zakat 16
Zelin, A. 125

Printed in Great Britain
by Amazon